CAMBRIDGE LIBRARY COLLECTION

Books of enduring scholarly value

British and Irish History, Seventeenth and Eighteenth Centuries

The books in this series focus on the British Isles in the early modern period, as interpreted by eighteenth- and nineteenth-century historians, and show the shift to 'scientific' historiography. Several of them are devoted exclusively to the history of Ireland, while others cover topics including economic history, foreign and colonial policy, agriculture and the industrial revolution. There are also works in political thought and social theory, which address subjects such as human rights, the role of women, and criminal justice.

Two Yorkshire Diaries

These diaries by Ralph Ward (*fl.* 1754–6) and Arthur Jessop (1682–1751) were first published in 1952 and paint a valuable portrait of the trials, tribulations and pleasures of everyday life for the middle classes in rural Yorkshire in the mid-eighteenth century. A transcription of Jessop's diary from 1861 was first discovered in a Huddersfield bookshop in 1927. A local apothecary and pious community man, Jessop depicts the cycles of life in West Yorkshire, displaying a very British preoccupation with the weather. His diary, which covers the period 1730–46, notably discusses the impact of the Jacobite uprising of 1745. Ralph Ward was a fairly wealthy cattle trader, farmer and businessman in North Yorkshire. He was involved in local government, which he describes factually and clearly. His diary, covering the period 1754–6, also discusses business transactions, farming methods and, of course, the weather.

Cambridge University Press has long been a pioneer in the reissuing of out-of-print titles from its own backlist, producing digital reprints of books that are still sought after by scholars and students but could not be reprinted economically using traditional technology. The Cambridge Library Collection extends this activity to a wider range of books which are still of importance to researchers and professionals, either for the source material they contain, or as landmarks in the history of their academic discipline.

Drawing from the world-renowned collections in the Cambridge University Library and other partner libraries, and guided by the advice of experts in each subject area, Cambridge University Press is using state-of-the-art scanning machines in its own Printing House to capture the content of each book selected for inclusion. The files are processed to give a consistently clear, crisp image, and the books finished to the high quality standard for which the Press is recognised around the world. The latest print-on-demand technology ensures that the books will remain available indefinitely, and that orders for single or multiple copies can quickly be supplied.

The Cambridge Library Collection brings back to life books of enduring scholarly value (including out-of-copyright works originally issued by other publishers) across a wide range of disciplines in the humanities and social sciences and in science and technology.

Two Yorkshire Diaries

The Diary of Arthur Jessop
and Ralph Ward's Journal

Edited by C.E. Whiting

CAMBRIDGE
UNIVERSITY PRESS

CAMBRIDGE UNIVERSITY PRESS

Cambridge, New York, Melbourne, Madrid, Cape Town,
Singapore, São Paolo, Delhi, Mexico City

Published in the United States of America by Cambridge University Press, New York

www.cambridge.org
Information on this title: www.cambridge.org/9781108058391

© in this compilation Cambridge University Press 2013

This edition first published 1952
This digitally printed version 2013

ISBN 978-1-108-05839-1 Paperback

The Anniversary Reissue of Volumes from the Record Series of the Yorkshire Archaeological Society

To celebrate the 150th anniversary of the foundation of the leading society for the study of the archaeology and history of England's largest historic county, Cambridge University Press has reissued a selection of the most notable of the publications in the Record Series of the Yorkshire Archaeological Society. Founded in 1863, the Society soon established itself as the major publisher in its field, and has remained so ever since. The *Yorkshire Archaeological Journal* has been published annually since 1869, and in 1885 the Society launched the Record Series, a succession of volumes containing transcriptions of diverse original records relating to the history of Yorkshire, edited by numerous distinguished scholars. In 1932 a special division of the Record Series was created which, up to 1965, published a considerable number of early medieval charters relating to Yorkshire. The vast majority of these publications have never been superseded, remaining an important primary source for historical scholarship.

Current volumes in the Record Series are published for the Society by Boydell and Brewer. The Society also publishes parish register transcripts; since 1897, over 180 volumes have appeared in print. In 1974, the Society established a programme to publish calendars of over 650 court rolls of the manor of Wakefield, the originals of which, dating from 1274 to 1925, have been in the safekeeping of the Society's archives since 1943; by the end of 2012, fifteen volumes had appeared. In 2011, the importance of the Wakefield court rolls was formally acknowledged by the UK committee of UNESCO, which entered them on its National Register of the Memory of the World.

The Society possesses a library and archives which constitute a major resource for the study of the county; they are housed in its headquarters, a Georgian villa in Leeds. These facilities, initially provided solely for members, are now available to all researchers. Lists of the full range of the Society's scholarly resources and publications can be found on its website, www.yas.org.uk.

Two Yorkshire Diaries
(Record Series volume 117)

The editor of this volume, the Rev. Professor C.E. Whiting (1871–1953), taught at the University of Durham from 1918 until his retirement in 1939, and he became the first holder of the chair of modern history there in 1931. He was also the editor of the *Durham University Journal*. For the last five years of his life he was president of the Yorkshire Archaeological Society. An obituary and partial bibliography can be found in the *Yorkshire Archaeological Journal*, 38 (1951–5), 419–20. The current location of the original of the diary of Arthur Jessop is unknown, but the journal of Ralph Ward is held by Durham University Library, where it has the reference Additional Manuscripts 1.

TWO YORKSHIRE DIARIES

THE YORKSHIRE ARCHÆOLOGICAL SOCIETY

FOUNDED 1863   INCORPORATED 1893

RECORD SERIES

VOL. CXVII

BEING THE FIRST VOLUME FOR 1951

TWO YORKSHIRE DIARIES

The Diary of Arthur Jessop

and

Ralph Ward's Journal

EDITED BY

C. E. WHITING, D.D., F.S.A.

PRINTED FOR THE SOCIETY

1952

*Made and Printed in Great Britain
by Northumberland Press Limited
Gateshead on Tyne*

INTRODUCTION

THIS volume contains what remains of two Yorkshire diaries. The first is incomplete: the second may be complete, but if there was another volume it does not seem to have come to light. They are both concerned with Yorkshire affairs in the middle part of the eighteenth century.

ARTHUR JESSOP was the elder of the two sons of Arthur Jessop, who was born on May 3rd, 1639, and died in February 1727, in the eighty-eighth year of his age. This elder Arthur lived for many years on a small farm at Mytham Bridge in the township of Honley, in the parish of Almondbury. As well as the two sons, Arthur and Joshua, he had three daughters, all older than their brothers.

Arthur Jessop, the younger, was the writer of the diary and was born on July 24th, 1682. According to Dr. Henry James Morehouse, the historian of Kirkburton, there is reason to think that he received his training as an apothecary from Mr. Elihu Jackson,[1] a well-known medical man at Doncaster at that period. A Presbyterian by religion, Jessop was a member of the dissenting congregation at Lydgate and a trustee of the chapel there.

What is left to us of the diary illustrates life in West Yorkshire in the middle of the eighteenth century. We have, amongst other things, a vivid picture of the excitement caused by the Jacobite rising in 1745. As the hills round Holmfirth vary in height from 600 to 1,600 feet, the inhabitants of the scattered homes thereabouts were sometimes spoken of as "the mountaineers". Under Mr. Eden, the Presbyterian minister, the men of the "mountains" bound themselves to defend their homes against the rebels, as they insisted on calling the Scottish army, but, perhaps fortunately, "Captain" Eden's regiment never came in contact with the foe. We have evidence of much wishful thinking on the part of the populace at the time, and many wild rumours went abroad, such as we have experienced on a larger scale in the twentieth century, when if we lost men, the enemy lost many more, and when we won or lost fights which never took place. Happily for them the Holmfirth people in 1745-6 were hardly affected by the warfare.

Arthur Jessop lived a busy life as an apothecary at New-mill. He had occasional troubles with patients or their relatives, like Mr. and

---

[1] Elihu Jackson, born 27 Dec., 1669; built Wooldale Hall in 1714. See *The Genealogist*, N.S., Vol. XXXVII.

Mrs. Kaye. He was kindly disposed towards his neighbours and frequently lent money on business terms. He farmed his own land. He took a great interest in a practical way in the local book club which he helped to found, and he seems to have been a well-read man with tastes for classical writers and for theological works. He noted particulars about the parliamentary election of 1741, and such matters as the trouble about the churchyard at Kirkburton. He frequently refers to the happenings at funerals, gives details about the weather and the frequent floods, and on Sundays he sets down the name of the preacher and his text. We gather from him that if his fees were low, prices were low also, and we to-day can feel little sympathy when he complains that he had to pay fourpence a pound for mutton and threepence half-penny for veal, ''the dearest meat we have ever bought''

He was a pious soul, and composed prayers for special occasions, like New Year and his birthdays. Some of these the transcriber has omitted. He refers to Easter, but not once to Christmas. He lived at the time when our extracts begin at Totties and removed to Underbank on May 5th, 1742. He became heir to a small estate at New Laith and therewith he held five closes of land which he had purchased, the Croft, the Great Close, the Round Close, the Hey and Luke Ing. For many years he was busy in his medical work, riding many long journeys to visit his patients in his scattered practice. During the last twenty years of his life he wrote a diary, in which he entered all things, small and great, which interested him. He died April 2nd, 1751, aged sixty-eight years, and was buried at Lydgate. Neither he nor his brother nor his sisters had ever married. On his death, Joshua, the brother, came into the estate of New Laith. He, however, died in September that same year, and bequeathed his property to his executor, George Morehouse, who was to enter into possession on the death of the last surviving sister. This George Morehouse gave the land to Lydgate Chapel by indenture in 1789. He was the grandfather of Henry Morehouse, M.D., F.S.A., who lived at Stoney Bank, New Mill, Huddersfield, and wrote a *History of Kirkburton and the Graveship of Holme*, in which there are references to Arthur Jessop and his diary. He was one of the founders of the Yorkshire Archæological Society, and died in 1890.

In May 1927 a MS. volume of extracts from the diary was found amongst the remaining stock of Mr. Robert Blackman, a bookseller, of Wood Street, Huddersfield, who had died in the September of the previous year. The original diary, now lost, was written for the most part in shorthand, and this volume was a transcript made by Dr. Morehouse not later than 1861. It is bound in leather and contains about 190 pages measuring 7½ by 5 inches, and is written in Morehouse's small, neat hand. Some portions of the original he was unable to read and therefore omitted, and here and there, especially in the case of names of books of the Bible, he just copies Jessop's hieroglyphic when he is at a loss for its meaning. The text, as we have it, extends from January 1st, 1730, to June 1746, and would appear to be fairly complete as far as it goes, but the entries for the year 1734 are missing, having been lost from the original. The diary had been continued from 1746 until within three days of Jessop's death, but for some reason or other these years do not appear in our copy.

The little book was bought in 1927 by the Rev. C. H. Dennis from the shop above mentioned, and I take this opportunity of thanking his son, the Rev. Dr. C. P. L. Dennis, for the loan of the MS. for a very long time. Amongst many to whom I am indebted are Mr. E. W. Aubrook of the Tolson Museum, Mr. Wilfred Robertshaw, M.A., the Cartwright Memorial Hall, Bradford, and Mr. J. W. Houseman, M.A., of the Grammar School, Hipperholme, for help in topographical matters, Mr. A. Hunter of the Royal Observatory, Greenwich, and Mr. B. Colgrave of the University of Durham.

The Journal of RALPH WARD here published is of foolscap size, with stiff covers and a morocco strip down the spine. It is in the library of the University of Durham. Of the writer we know nothing, except what he tells us incidentally in this manuscript which is concerned with his affairs in north-east Yorkshire from 1754-6. Whether there ever was another volume or volumes is uncertain; the present writer has so far failed to find any. Pasted in the MS. is an omitted entry in the same hand as the rest, and there is also an address in another hand written to Ralph Ward, Esq., "at Gisborough, by North Allerton". We gather that he had various pieces of property round about; a farm at Boulby, which he let for £145 a year, another farm and some houses at Aislaby, a third farm called Stoddo, also let to a tenant, a fourth at Long Hall, a little house at Pinchinthorp, and a stable at Sands End. It is to be noticed that he is called esquire, and that was in the days when the term was generally applied accurately, and certainly not indiscriminately as to-day. He had a sister who had married a man named Jackson, and amongst his relatives were the Peases of Darlington.

His principal occupation appears to have been that of a cattle dealer. He bought and sold cattle, sheep and hides, attended fairs and markets for the purpose, and bought steers for "wintering", that is, taking charge of them and their winter feeding. He does also a great deal of money lending, sometimes, indeed, he lends very large sums. In a book written in the early part of the present century, the writer noted that the successful cattle dealers of the district in his day had money to lend and help one another, though he also added the comment that this prosperity frequently did not

last.[2]   Ward lent on strictly businesslike terms, but there is no
evidence that he was exorbitant or even a hard-dealing man, in
fact quite the reverse.

Our friend was evidently very comfortably off.   He had a fair
amount of silver plate and was by no means overjoyed when he
heard it was to be taxed.   He attended church fairly regularly, and
had a pew in the gallery there.   He occupied himself fully in local
affairs; he was a Justice of the Peace, an Officer of Highways, and
a Commissioner of Land Tax.   He subscribed liberally towards the
building of two bridges at Skelton Ellers, and he was a Commissioner
appointed for the division of some lands between Redcar and
Marske.

[2] R. W. S. Bishop, *My Moorland Patients*, 1922, pp. 162-3.

THE DIARY OF ARTHUR JESSOP

1729-30

Jan^{ry} 1st.

4th. S. Misty morning: cold. No service at the Chapel.

8. very cold & frosty morning a close dark day.

9. Mr Elston was here this night & stayd half an hour.

10. Frost broke & came down drisling Rain in the morning & cold dark day.

11th. S. No service at the Chapel.

14th. Yesternight I received 5 Books[1] the Whole concern of man at 2/6 a book in all 12/6.

18th. S. Windy with some little rain. I was at the Chapel. Mr Denton preached from Isaiah 26.4.

19th. We had service yesterday, we had been 12 Sundays without service.

24. I hear James Booth the Clark of Kirk Burton was buried on thursday the 22^d inst.

25. S. I was at Huroyd[2] to visit Mrs Armitage Had no Services at the Chapel.

30. Frost & wind very cold.

Feb^{ry} 1st. S. Frosty & cold. Mr John Smith preached from Eccles. 11.8.

5. The Schoolmaster of Holm married Wid^w Green or Grin on sunday last. Mr Dobson was here and I lent him £7.

6th. A prodigious strong wind last night.[3]

8. S. Cold rainy day. No Service at the Chapel.

10. very great wind last night with rain & sleet. I was at Huflats[4] to visit Benj^m Ramsden.

Feb^{ry} 11th. Cold some hail and sleet. Mr Jackson of Sowerby[5] buried this day.

13. A rainy tempestuous afternoon a great flood.

15th. A very boisterous day. Sleet, hail & Snow, very cold. Mr

---

[1] *The Whole Concern of Man* or what he ought to know and do in order to eternal Salvation laid down in a plain and familiar method for the use of all, but especially the meanest reader: divided into 17 chapters. Necessary for all families, with Devotions for several occasions, ordinary and extraordinary. Printed for J. Lawrence at the Angel and T. Cockerill at the Three Legs and Bible in the Poultry, 1701.

[2] Highroyd.

[3] The transcriber writes at end of this entry, "Something more here cannot make out".

[4] Hu Flatts, High Flatts in Denby.

[5] He was curate of Sowerby.

3

Dobson was here having received a letter this day from Mr John Hotham.

22. Had no service at the Chapel, very Stormy & windy.

23. I hear Abraham Beaumont of Netherthong died yesterday.

26. The great Fair at Penistone.[6] Hail & Snow.

27. Snowed all day, a very great snow, windy, and very great drifts.

March 1. We had no service. Mr Smith should have preached but did not come, prevented by the snow.

5. rain last night, a rainy day, the Snow goes faster, there are some great drifts. It is very bad travelling.

8. A very cold rainy tempestuous day. We had no Service at the Chapel. The assizes at York this week. Received a prescription from Dr Nettleton for medicine for Joel Morehouse of Thurstonland. Mr Smith called yesterday, but he had no service for he had no auditory & he did not preach.

17th. rain. I was at Halifax & got home at 9 o'clock. Dr Nettleton was extraordinaryly kind to me and promises me freely to write to London to enquire if it be possible to obtain a Licence from the College of Physicians. I expect to make application to York. In the event both fail I shall write to North Britain & do not doubt of succeeding there.[7]

22. No Service at the Chapel. Showers.

Mar. 29. We had no Service.

31. Fine Spring weather.

April 5th. I was not at chapel in the afternoon. Mr Smith preached in the forenoon from 2 . . . 5.30[8] afternoon text from Matt[w]. 5.4.

[6] Penistone Fair held on Thursday before Feb. 28: the last Thursday in March before old May-day and the Thursday after old Michaelmas day, for horned cattle and horses (Owen's *Book of Fairs*, 1770).

[7] Medical men practising in towns took care to become members of the College of Physicians or College of Surgeons or the Society of Apothecaries. Membership in the first was largely restricted to graduates of the old universities; membership of the other two was obtained by apprenticeship and examinations. There was much competition from Scottish graduates. A qualified person obtained a licence from the bishop or, as here, the Archbishop of York. This gave him certain privileges. The number of Scottish graduates who practised in England made the competition keener (Traill & Mann, *Social England*, v. 758). In Aberdeen the M.D. was given until 1817 merely on the recommendation of doctors of note (Rait, *Univ. of Aberdeen*, 1895, p. 206; R. G. Cant, *Short Hist. Univ. St. Andrews*, pp. 86, 108). Smollet, the novelist, was apprenticed to a medical man in Glasgow, and during his apprenticeship attended classes at the University. He makes his character, Roderick Randon, an assistant at the house of two apothecaries successively, without much teaching from either. He passed the Navy Board's oral examination in surgery and became a surgeon's mate. Apothecaries charged for medicine supplied and not for advice.

[8] He seems to have forgotten the book and only supplies an empty bracket, or, more probably, the transcriber did not understand his shorthand. The same occurs frequently.

8th. I called at Blackhouse[9] to visit Mr Lockwood.

10th. Mr Dobson was here this afternoon. Cold, some little rain.

12th. We had no Service. Rain & wind.

13. Visited Mr Armitage of Huroyd.

19. Mr Elston preached from Hebr. 3.15.

24. Called at John Thurles who would promise to contribute nothing towards the maintenance of a Minister and hath given nothing for many years and at last I told him he was not worth talking to but if he would do nothing to encourage the cause they deserved no Minister at all.

25. Holmfirth fair this day.

26. We had no service. I was at Bullhouse[10] in the morning to visit Mr Dobsons Maid. I did not stay service.

May 3. very cold wind. Had no Service.

6th. I was at the chapel in the afternoon and met Mr Ab^m Lockwood, Thomas Moorhouse, Ab^m Heeley and Thomas Hobson to consult about raising a maintenance for a minister.

10. Mr Smith preached at Lydgate[11] from Philip. 2.12-13.

11. Mr Elihu Jackson sent for me to Joseph Woodheads and I walked with him to the Spring and newwoods and back with him to Jos' Turner's.

12. I was with Mr Elihu Jackson in Wooldale and went with him to the Spring and came back He told me that Dr Winteringham[12] of York was 3 years at the University of Cambridge run by . . . a course of Philosophy and Mathematics and a course of Chemistry under Vigane[13] Professor . . . and his standing being low he took no degree at all not so much as Batchelor of Physic. His name is Clifton Winteringham. He went up to Cambridge with Nich: Sanderson.[14] His father was Vicar of Redford.

May 17. Had no Service. It is a year since my Sister Rachel died & was buried on the 19th.

31th. Mr Staniforth a young man from Sheffield preached at

---

[9] Black House, a corruption of Blake House, in Thurstonland.

[10] Bullhouse, a new meeting house at Bullhouse in Penistone was recorded under the Toleration Act in April 1692.

[11] Lydgate. Here there was the Presbyterian chapel referred to (Morehouse, *Hist. of Kirkburton*).

[12] Dr. Clifton Wintringham, M.D., of York. Son of William Wintringham, vicar of East Retford, 1674-1701. He wrote a treatise (in Latin) of the diseases especially prevalent at York. If he did not get a degree at Cambridge he probably obtained his M.D. from one of the Scottish universities.

[13] John Francis Vigani, a chemist, born at Verona. Wrote *Medulla Chymae*, at Dantzig. In 1682 he was made Teacher of Chemistry in Cambridge. He was professor there from 1703-12, and died in 1712.

[14] Nicholas Sanderson was a teacher of Mathematics at Cambridge, who had been blind from the age of two years. He was M.A., 1711, LL.D., 1728, F.R.S., 1719. He became Professor of Mathematics at Cambridge, and died in 1739. His published writings only appeared after his death. In spite of his infirmity he had a great reputation as a mathematician.

Lydgate in the forenoon from Revel. 2.2. I was not at chapel in the afternoon. I went to Shipley to visit Josʰ Hepworth & Joseph Wortley.

June 2. I was at Kirk Burton to visit Mary Morehouse at John Booth's.

7. S. Was at Thurstonland, called at Joel Morehouse who is ill of the Gout in both feet. Had no sermon at chapel.

14. S. Mr Smith preached from Exod: 10.27.

15. I went to Halifax and was at Dr Nettleton's[15] & got home about 8 or 9 o'clock.

23. I was with Mr George Morehouse & he tells me Mr Elston[16] . . . purposeth to come and serve us here but cannot make an . . . promise.

28. Mr Staniforth preached in the forenoon Psalm 27.4. In the afternoon from Canticles 5.16.

July 5. Mr Dobson[17] preached from Luke 18/12. I was at Stony Bank at night with Mr Dobson.

24. Mr Elihu Jackson sent for me to bring a horse and call on him at Totties.[18] I was with Mr Jackson at Totties, in the afternoon. Mr Wharam Lᵈ Malton's[19] Steward & Dr Goodwins[20] a clergyman and . . . had been with him in the forenoon to view his Lands and was with him at Totties. Extraordinarily hot, rain, thunder and lightning at night.

July 26. Mr Dobson preached from . . .

27. I was at Mr Ludlam's of Blackhouse for a book which he had promised me. I staid a good while and got my dinner with him.

Augᵗ 2. Drisling rain. Had no Service at the Chapel. We expected Mr Smith but were disappointed.

8. I went to Joseph Beevers and paid him 8/- for making coat & waistcoat & 2/- for black cloth for facings and sleives in all 10/-

9ᵗʰ. S. Rainy. Mr Smith preached from John 6.44.

14. I was at Stony Bank at night with Mr Wadsworth & got

---

[15] Dr. Nettleton, "a very eminent and useful physician" (Heywood & Dickinson, N. C. Register). Practised in Halifax and died in 1742. Author of a *Treatise concerning Virtue and Happiness.*

[16] Mr. Elston, the Rev. Hananiah Elston, M.A., who was admitted to the Presbyterian ministry in 1738 and served the chapel here for two years after which he moved to Elland.

[17] There was a Mr. Joshua Dobson, described as "a preacher", near Rhodes Hall, who married Elizabeth Smith of Mixenden in 1723.

[18] Totties, also spelt Tottyes. Totties Hall in Wooldale was built by Henry Jackson in 1684 in the hamlet of Totties.

[19] Lord Malton. Thomas Watson Wentworth of Wentworth Woodhouse. M.P. for York 1727, and created Baron Malton in the following year. Later he became Marquess of Rockingham.

[20] Richard Goodwin, S.T.P., Rector of Tankersley (1715-52). He died Sept. 28th, 1753. He was also Rector of Prestwich.

home a little before 12.0'clock. I lent him Dr Nettleton's book[21] and he says he shall read some to my Lord Gallway.[22]

15. I am at Stony Bank this morning to speak to Mr Wadsworth.

16th. S. we had no Service. Windy.

23th. S. Showers. Windy. Mr Smith preached in the forenoon from Luke 8.27 and in the afternoon from Isaiah 57.21. There is no peace, saith my God . . . to the wicked.

30. S. Mr Aldred[23] preached from Psalms 32.10. I called at Stony Bank as I went to the chapel in the afternoon to speak with him.

31. Easterly winds all last week & still continue but good harvest weather.

1730. Sept. 2nd. Good harvest weather.

5. Thunder Lightening & rain last night.

6. S. Mr Dobson preached from Titus 2.11-12. I was with him at Stony Bank at night.

8. Showers. I was at Halifax and I went to see Mr Ellson who lives low in the Town. I left him a paper which we had drawn up and signed with respect to his ordination. I got home at night 9 o'clock.

9. Mr Elston is to be ordained at Halifax this day, my Brother is gone to the ordination. I bought a Perewig yesterday at Halifax of one Jackson. Price 6/- and a box to bring it in.

Sep[t] 11th. Frosty morning very cold, a very rainy day.

13th. S. had no Service at the chapel, some rain Great showers in the night.

17. Windy, I was with Mr Elihu Jackson at Totties & Scholes I went with him as far as Jackson Bridge.

20. S. A thick close mist, Mr Elston preached from I Thess. 5.2. I was at chapel in the forenoon.

27th. S. No Service in the Chapel.

Oct. 4. S. No Service.

Oct. 9 & 19. Very rainy days.

11. Rainy. Mr Elston preached from Eccles 12 last. He is now to supply us constantly and is to settle with us.

[21] Dr. Nettleton's book, *Concerning Virtue and Happiness*.

[22] John Monckton, created a peer of Ireland in 1727 as Baron of Killard and Viscount Galway. He was M.P. for Clitheroe and afterwards for Ponte-fract, and Commissioner for H.M. Revenue (Ireland), 1734. Took his seat in Irish House of Lords 1737; Surveyor of Woods and Forests, England and Wales.

[23] Mr. Aldred. There were two ministers of this name (a) Timothy Aldred, who from Morley Old Chapel transferred to Batley. It is recorded of him that he was only once absent from his pulpit in fifty-four years. He resigned in 1763. (b) John Aldred of Wakefield, educated at Franklands' Academy. He ministered for many years at a chapel at Westgate End, known as the Bell Chapel, because it was one of the few dissenting chapels which had a bell.

13. My head ached all last night, a rainy day. Mr Thompson was here.

14. I went to visit Mr Kenworthy's daughter.

17. Holmfirth Fair.

18. S. Mr Elston preached from John 10.28. misty and close, some drisling rain.

21. Mr Goddard who preached here several years ago is disordered in his head. He was not fit for his work when here.

25. S. Mr Elston preached from Rom: 6.21. Mr Jno Lockwood was at chapel in the forenoon.

Nov. 1. S. Windy & turbulent. Some rain very great wind in the night & heavy showers. Mr Elston preached from Matt^w 4.11.

2. Rainy turbulent weather a very extraordinarily high wind.

5th. A fair day. Mr Elston preached from Psalm 64.9.10.

8. Rain. Mr Elston preached from Matt^w 5.29. Search the Scriptures.

15. Cloudy some little rain. Mr Elston preached from . . . 15.10.

17. Great wind in the night. A very great wind this day. A very rainy day.

20. Exceedingly great wind, a great flood.

22. Mr Elston preached in the forenoon from . . . 4.8, afternoon from 37 Psalm 3 "Trust in the Lord".

27 Nov. I was at Thickhollins^{24} to meet Mr Armitage's daughter Mary who married Frin Dison's son.

29. Frost, wind & sleet. Mr Elston preached in the forenoon from 4 . . . 3. In the afternoon from Colossians 3.17, and whatsoever ye do in word or deed do all in the name of the Lord Jesus.

30. A Hat was brought for me out of Lancashire which cost me 5/6.

Dec. 3. exceedingly sharp frost. I was at Ranaw^{25} at Mr Joseph Greaves's Daughter.

6. Frost fair. Mr Elston preached from John 1.12.

13. Fair sunny windy forenoon. Mr Elston preached from John 8.32. "And the truth shall make you free."

16. I hear Mr Elihu Jackson is dead. He despatched this life on thursday the 10 of this month & was buried on the 13th. The last time he was here in Sept. last on the 14th of that month I went to see him at Totties and we went to Scholes and when he set out for Doncaster I set him as far as Jackson Bridge. This was the last time I saw him. He was aged about 62 years.

17. Sharp frost some snow last night. I was at Stony Bank.

---

^{24} Between Meltham and Holmfirth.
^{25} Ranaw or Ranah or Renhag, in Thurlstone. The name of a farm.

Ann Beaumont, Thomas Hobson's wives mother aged 88 buried this day.

20^{day}. Sharp frost & close. Mr Elston preached from . . . 1.24.

27. S. Mr Elston preached from Matt^w 1.21 "for he shall save his people from their sins".

Dec. 31. Frosty morning.

hath brought one to the conclusion of another year and many hath been taken away which I have been spared and if the Lord continues me I will not consent[26] . . . comp . . . full not but be it for peace and plenty preserved . . . be . . . men in . . . provided for the poor that they may eat and be satisfied. May they be (filled) with (thy) goodness and not forget to pr(aise) . . . pray . . . reduced to great straits were forced to live upon coarse mean fare such as is not usual for man to eat but life was preserved to turn our scarcity into plenty and a plentiful crop the last year and continued (his) goodness to us in sending another plentiful crop this year. So may here the price of corn is as low as it was high the year before last. But God who provided for us in dear years . . . had good bread enough and did not feel any of the (effects) of the scarcity. My . . . without a 4 our lord to praise . . . for goodness to my & my & express my gratd, for comes I my lord two . . . commands much to . . . come small drops towards night scarce felt.

1730-1

Jany 1. Morning fair but cloudy. I praised the Lord who hath spared my life and hath brought me to the conclusion of another year and to the beginning of a new year and having blessed and provided for me during the last year and of my whole life give me a new (heart?) this new year.

Mr Elston preached in the afternoon from I. Corinth 11.28.

3rd. very cold. Sleet and Snow. Mr Elston preached in the forenoon from I Tim 2.5. For there is one God and one Mediator between God & man, the man Christ Jesus & in the afternoon from Coloss: 3.17.

10th. S. morning Mr Crowder[1] preached from Proverbs 3.17..

[26] Parts of the original must have been quite unintelligible to the transcriber.

[1] Mr. Crowder (Crowther) afterwards conformed and was made Vicar of Otley. He was Mr. Elston's intimate friend and was born at Elland.

17th. Frost broke. Mr Elston preached from I Peter 2.2.

24. Snow all forenoon. Sleet afternoon. No Service at the chapel. Mr Elston preached at York this day.

31. Exceedingly cold. Snow, wind, stormy. I was at Chapel in the forenoon Mr Elston preached from Psalm 4.1; Hear me when I call O God of my righteousness; in the afternoon from 2 Peter 3.14.

Feb^{ry} 1th. Snowing all morning a very great snow.

2. Sharp frost. There is a very great snow. I hear Mr John Lockwood of Blackhouse departed this life about 8 this morning. He was at Chapel on the 25th of October which was 14 weeks since last Sunday and had not been. . . . .
he was seized suddenly with a palsy on Sunday morning the 10th of March 1727-8. Hath been at the Bath in Somersetshire twice since was better sometimes but never recovered the use of one side He hath also suffered from the Stone & Gout. The last time I saw him at Blackhouse was Friday the 19th June 1730. He was aged as he told me formerly about 52.

3. Frost broke some rain a great wind and the snow goes apace.

6th. I was invited to the funeral of Mr Jn° Lockwood of Blackhouse who was buried this day by candlelight we put up 9 horses at Jn° Booths and stay'd at . . . I got home about 10 o'clock. I came home with Mr Elston & Mr Th° Moorhouse.

7th. Mr Elston preached from Matt^w 7.21. latter part.

9. I was at Halifax. I visited Mr Elston & I got home about 8. very stormy turbulent wind.

14. Rainy morning with sleet. Mr Elston preached in the forenoon from Job 14.14. 'All the days of my appointed time will I wait till my change come.' Mr Lockwood's Funeral Sermon. He gave him just character as an honest and a good friend a religious (man) who . . . was good and discharged anything that was . . . and a good . . . and is . . . . . . attending him in his tedious illness.

16. It is four years since my father died.

18. I was at Shelley I called at Cliff Top at Mr Matthewman's for a book which Mr E. J. . . . . . . translated & published but he was not at home.

20. Mr Matthewman called here with the Book which I called for on thursday.

21. Frosty & Cold. Mr Elston preached from I . . . 5.3.

28. S. Fair. cold. Mr. Elston preached in the forenoon from Psalm 11.6. afternoon Psalm 11.7.

Mar: 7. Fair. windy. Mr Elston preached from 2. Tim: 2.10, latter part. I was at Bullhouse in the afternoon to visit Mr Dobson.

14. Mr Elston preached.

21. Mr Elston preached morning from Job 28.28. afternoon from Num: 23.10.

23^d. I called at Mr Kenworthy's at Carrell. Mr Thompson called upon me.

28. Sharp frost. Mr Elston preached from Num: 23.10. I was at John Horsfalls of Carlcoats.

30. I was at Shipley lane head at Joseph Firth's.

31. Cold east wind. the wind hath been in the east a long time.

April 2. Mr Elston preached Psalm 26.6.

4. Mr Elston preached from . . . 15.15

8. Frosty morning. Cold. Mr Horsfall[2] of Storth's Hall was buried this day.

Ap^l 11. Frost. Mr Elston preached from Luke 12.15. Wind northwest which had been east so long.

12. I was at Stackwood Hill at William Newton's the wind wheels about sometimes west and sometimes east. fair showers.

14. Marsden fair this day; the first that hath been there.[3]

18. Rainy. Mr Elston preached from Acts 10.42.

24. Holmfirth Fair much rain last night or during the day.

25. Mr Elston preached afternoon from . . . 3.36.

27. Thunder very great claps, lightning rain and Hail very terrible.

May 2. fair. Mr Elston preached from Psalm 119.71.

4. I went to Blackhouse to Mr Lockwood to view the house which Mr Elston should have.

8. I was at Blackhouse to visit Jno Charlesworth's son.

9. I went to Bullhouse this morning to visit Mr Dobson's son aged 2 years. Mr Elston preached at Lydgate in the forenoon from Titus 2.6 afternoon from Matt^w 5.17.

10. Showers. I was at Thurstonland to visit Joel Morehouse to meet Dr Nettleton who had been sent for.

11. Afternoon went to Bullhouse to visit Mr Dobson's son and went to Blackhouse to visit Jno Charlesworth's son. Came back to Bullhouse Hall to speak with Mr Rich.

16. Mr Beal or Neal[4] minister at Idle preached from I . . . 3.8.

17. I was at Indfield Lane in Peniston parish to visit Jn° Condill who is dangerously ill. A very strong wind. It is 2 years this day since Sister Rachel died.

18. Mrs Kay of Netherthong was here this afternoon and was very importunate with me to take her son apprentice, but I advised

[2] The Horsfalls lived at Staithes Hall in Thurstonland.

[3] It does not seem to have continued long. It is not mentioned in Owen's *Book of Fairs*, sixth ed., 1770.

[4] Mr. Nicholas Beal, minister at Idle New Chapel, died at Idle in 1734.

& told her that it would be more convenient for her to put him apprentice to an Apothecary in a Town, but if she had a mind to live at Netherthong (which I found to be resolved upon) it would not be worth his while to practice physic but he had better be put to some other business, say to a Tanner.

19.   Mr Dobson was here and paid me for physic & the interest for £20 on a note this day.

21.   I was at Thurstonland to to visit Joel Morehouse, called at Mr Lockwood's of Blackhouse.   Mr L spoke to me about Mrs Kays son, and with what I said he appeared satisfied.   I wrote a letter to Dr Nettleton at Thurstonland to acquaint him with Joel Morehouses case.

23.   Extraordinary hot, a shower in the forenoon.   Mr Dobson preached from Acts 13.43.

24.   Extraordinarily hot, very much rain and a very great flood.

28.   I was at the funeral of Joel Morehouse.   Mr Thompson preached from Job 3.17.

30.   Mr Buck preached from . . . 1.47.

June 6.   Mr. Elston preached from Luke 16.31.

9.   May 24 when it thundered, lightened & rained so exceedingly hard, there was a very great flood.   A Boy and 2 Girls at Woodhead were hurt by the lightning when the Boy recovered himself the water was coming up where the girls lay for dead he took them & hurried them out of the water & made a shift to get home & told what had happened & they fetched the Girls home: one of the Girls had her stays split in pieces and they are both scorched, burnt and blistered, and recover but slowly.

10.   I was at Hogley to visit Joshua Charlesworth's wife I called at Burnley at Thomas Morton's to look at a wild dog which was some time about Wooldale and which they took for a Martin (?) and hunted it often before they could take it.   It is a little black bitch with a white streak down its face & a white breast.

12.   Mr Buck preached from Mark 11.25.26.

15.   Morning hot. Mr Buck was here this afternoon and staid till almost 8 o'clock.

20.   Had some rain. Mr Elston preached from H. 12.2.

22.   I was at Stony Bank for a Book a very strong wind.

24.   I was at Holme to visit Mr Crosland's child the School Master I called at Mr Thompson's for a Book.

27.   Mr Elston preached H. 12.13.

28.   Rain & windy. I was at Haslehead to visit Mr Haigh's son Benjamin. I called at Milshaw at James Green's. I hear that Mr Pen, vicar of Emley was at Wakefield at the Visitation on friday the 25th and being overcome with wine got a fall from his horse & is dead.

30. Drisling rain. I was at Holme to visit Mrs. Earnshaw's son in the Measles. I called at Mr. Crosland's the schoolmaster.

July 2. Fair but cloudy. Mr Elston preached from . . . 3.16.

4. I was at the Chapel. Mr Elston preached in forenoon from . . . 3.16 in the afternoon from . . . 5.2.

6. Misty morning. I was at Halifax at Dr Nettleton's and got home at a quarter past 10.

11. Mr Elston preached from . . . 3.16.

12. I hear that Mr Bowman vicar of Dewsbury preached a sermon at the visitation on Friday 25 June last from Matt. 15.16, latter part. ' Thus have ye made the commandments of God of none effect by your traditions ', at which the clergy were very much offended.[6]

July 18. Fair. Mr Elston preached from Rom: 5.4.

19. Thornhill Feast & Races.[7]

23. Thunder, lightning & Rain.

25. Mr Dobson preached from Job. 28.28. I was at Stony Bank at night with Mr Dobson.

31. Excessively hot & Sultry. I was at Dammos[8] to visit Tho⁵ Littlewood's son. I paid Joseph Woodhead for a pair of New Shoes 4/-. Got the last of our Hay. This afternoon the lightning broke through the thatch, struck some of the plaster off, also struck off some of the plaster in other rooms. Broke a stone pan with some pots in but the pots were not broken, removed a little Box from one side of the Room to the other & set it upon a little Table &c. This was done at John Lockwood's of Woodend. I think lightning & rain at night. This was the hottest night that hath been for 20 years.

Aug. 1. Very hot, great showers thunder & lightning much rain at night. Mr Elston preached on the forenoon from . . . 2.11.

5. I was at Halifax at Dr Nettleton's and got home between 9 & 10.

6. Mr Bastow[9] minister at Elland is dead.

7. I was at Ranaw at Mr Joseph Greaves; and at Mr Hawks-withs of Netherdenby.

8. Mr Buck preached from Philip. 3.20.

[6] For some account of this Sermon see *Gent. Mag.*, Vol. I, pp. 333, 349, 366, 408, 414, 419. William Bowman, Deacon, 1727; Priest, 1729, Chichester. Emanuel, Cambridge B.A. 1727, M.A. 1731. Curate of Boroughbridge 1730; Vicar of Dewsbury 1729, and Chaplain to Earl of Hopetown.
[7] Thornhill Church was dedicated to St. Mary Magdalene. The feast-day would therefore fall on the 22nd if the date was strictly kept, but when the fair day was granted in 1317 it was appointed for the day before the vigil. This year it was a day early.
[8] Dammos, elsewhere called Dam House. A farmer still lives in Dam House, Cartworth, Holmfirth.
[9] Mr. Bastow of Elland. Jeremiah Bastow, minister at Elland, died July 28th, 1731.

10. I hear Dr Leigh[10] is appointed vicar of Halifax in the room of Mr Burton deceased.

12. I was at Stony Bank with a Book. Hot.

15. Some rain. No Sermon. Mr Elston is preaching at Elland.

22. A rainy day. Mr Crowder preached from Colos: 3.4.

26. Very rainy day.

29. Shower. Mr Elston preached from Psalm. 16. & much rain at night with thunder and lightning

Sepr 5. I was at Chapel. Mr Elston preached Titus 2.10.

11. We got in the last of our Corn.

12. Fair morning. Mr Elston preached from Eccles: 8.11.

19. I was at chapel. Mr Elston preached from Proverbs 22.6 Train up a child in the way he should go &c.

23. I bled . . . Roebuck of Hollin house the younger. Mr Dobson was here.

26. Mr Elston preached from Job. 5.17.

28. I was at Stony Bank to visit a child.

Oct. 1. Mr. Elston preached from Rev: 1.5.

3. Mr Elston preached from 3 John 22.

9. Frosty morning. I was at Haslehead to visit Mr Haighs son Jonathan aged 9. I was at Stony Bank at night.

10. Had no service at the chapel.

13. Fair. cold wind. I was at Cumberworth lane head to visit John Millomdew who is very ill.

16. Fair. pleasant. Holmfirth Fair.

17. Mr . . . preached from 2 K. 3.5.

24. Mr Elston preached from Psalm: 73.3.

29. I went this morning at Mr Ludlam's for my Book.

31. Fair. Mr White preached from H. 9.27. I was with Mr White at Stony Bank at night.

Nov. 7. I was not at the chapel. Mr Elston preached from 6 Micha 5.

15. Joseph Newton set out for London this morning.

21. Mr Elston preached from Mark 9.30 latter part. "Have peace one with another." I suppose will soon leave us Mr Dobson is about to leave Bullhouse and is going to Cockey (Moor) in Lancashire. I hear that Dr Nettleton is very much indisposed.

24. I called at Oldfield & left Joseph Swallow Mr Bowman's Sermon. I went to Woolstone to visit Ab^m Moorhouses. I went to Stony Bank to visit little Thomas.

Nov. 28. Very cold. Mr Elston preached from . . . 16.25. I was at Stony Bank at night. I hear Dr Nettleton has been very ill with a fever but is some better.

[10] Dr. Leigh or Legh. George Lee, Trin. Hall, Camb., LL.D. Deacon, 1727; Priest, 1728, Lincoln. Instituted to the Vicarage of Halifax 1731. Died December 1775.

30. I called at Mr Ludlams.

De^r 2. I went to Blackhouse with Mr Royston[11] vicar of Almondbury, Mr Brook Schoolmaster of Almondbury[12] and the curate of Marsden.

5. Had no sermon at chapel.

6. I was at Flashhouse[13] near Bullhouse to visit Joseph milnes.

10. windy & rain. Was at Stackwoodhill[14] to visit Mr Newton. I went to Totties at Mrs Jacksons'. It is one year since Mr Elihu Jackson died.

11. I was at Blackhouse in the evening with Mr Thomas Morehouse Mr Elston and Mr Ab^m Ludlam.

14. I was at Stackwood hill to visit Mr Newton. They have sent this morning for Dr Nettleton.

20. I was at Holmfirth at Daniel Sharps with Mr Thompson, Mr Kenworthy, Mr Thos Morehouse &c.

26. Sharp frost, exceedingly cold. Mr Elston preached from 2 Chr (?) 3.18.

31. Public worship. Mr Elston preached from . . . 15.14.

1731-2

Jany 2. Mr Elston preached Matt^r 26.39.

9. No service at the Chapel.

16. Sharp frost. Mr Elston preached afternoon from 2 . . . 3.5.

29. I heard yesterday that Dr Balderton[1] was dead but know not whether it be true.

30. Had no service.

Feby. 6. Mr Elston preached. I was at Stony Bank at night.

---

[11] This was Edward Rishton, Vicar of Almondbury from 1726. Deacon 1708; Priest 1710. He was of St. John's Coll., Cambridge. He was at Almondbury in 1743.

[12] Samuel Brook. B.A. St. John's Coll., Camb. Deacon 1730; Priest 1741, York. Curate of Flocton 1738. Licensed as Grammar School Master at Almondbury in July 1732. There was another Free School in the parish, at Holme, kept by James Crosland, who was licensed in 1727. In 1743 each school had about twenty boys.

[13] Flashouse or Floshouse in Penistone parish.

[14] The modern form of the name is Stagwoodhill.

[1] Dr. John Balderston, a medical man. He was the cousin of Dr. William Cooke, president and fellow of Jesus Coll., Cambridge. Balderston (his name is variously spelt Balderton, Balderson, and Balderston) married the daughter of Samuel Hobson, an apothecary of Leeds.

13. I was at chapel. Mr Elston preached from Micah 6.8.

14. I was called up on the night to visit Geo & Jnº Morehouse of Stony Bank.

15. I sent Mr Thompson Mr Isaac Smith's Sermon this day.

17. Dr Nettleton was at Stony Bank at Noon.

20. Sharp frost. I was at Stony Bank last night all night. I was at Stagwood hill this morning to visit Mr Newton. Dr Nettleton was at Stony Bank this forenoon made a short stay.

24. Penistone Great Fair.[2]

March 1. Mr Kay of Melsham is 21 years of age this day.

5. Mr Elston preached. fair cold wind.

12. Mr White preached from Ephes. 5.15.

19. I went to the Chapel. Mr Elston preached from Jeremiah 8.7.8.

25. Thomas Littlewood's son lost this afternoon.

26. I was at the Chapel in the forenoon. Mr Elston preached.

28. Thomas Littlewood's son Joseph aged 4 years & a half was lost on the 25th is not found.

30. Exceedingly cold I was at Almondbury at the funeral of Mr George Morehouse's daughter and got home about 8. snow rain & sleet. In the afternoon much rain. He hath buried 2 daughters before, called Eliz[th] and the latter Ellen, the former aged 17 weeks the latter near three quarters.

31. Small rain. Mr Elston preached from Psalms 25.11. I was at Stony Bank at night.

April 2. Mr Elston preached from Heb: 5.9. This is the last time of his preaching here but is going to Elland next Sunday. Mr Wadsworth was at chapel.

14. 3 corps were carried down here towards Benton this day. 1 from Hillos,[3] Jno Roberts daughter, two from Mr Littlewoods of Dammos both upon one Bier. I hear Jane Fitton of Kirk Burton the Midwife is dead.

16. Mr Lewin.

25. I have received a letter this day from Mr George Morehouse[4] with two enclosed, one from Mr Aldred and another from Mr Elston. Abraham Heeley was here.

26. Mr Green of Austonley was here and I lent him £12 for a year on a Note.

29. Holmfirth Fair.

30. Had no Service.

May 7. No sermon.

---

[2] The official date for this fair was the Thursday before Feb. 28th.

[3] Hill House at Cartworth.

[4] George Morehouse or Moorehouse of Stony Bank built Moorcroft about 1630. George Moorhouse of Moorcroft died in 1720 and devised it to his son John, who in 1748 sold it to his relative Thomas Moorhouse of Stoney Bank, when it became the residence of his elder son George.

11. I hear that Thomas Littlewood's Son who was lost of the 25 of March is found on Westnab it is between 6 & 7 weeks since he was lost. The child was found yesterday the 10 in the afternoon a good way beyond the Westnab. Its head was eaten off and its skull left bare, its hands were gone and its arms as far as could be seen for its waistcoat sleeves appeared to be empty it had its waistcoat on and cloth buttons but there were some ribs came out of its Breeches. its Hose & Shoes and its feet & legs were not touched. They brought & wrapped it in a blanket to Meltorn[5] Chapel.

13. I hear this afternoon that Thomas Hinchliff carpenter Son of Joseph Hinchliff of Anondyn is slain at Cartworth.

16. Thomas Hinchliff was buried this day Coroner's Inquest sat yesterday the 15th at Dammos.

21. Mr White preached from Lam. 1.9. I was with him at Stony Bank at night.

24. I was at the funeral of Mr Thos Hargh of Haslehead, and staid all night at Philip Mitchell with Mr Jnº Morehouse, Mr Green of Yaton[6], Robinson.

4. Very hot. Had no sermon.

11. Mr Lax[7] preached from 119 Psalm 6/18th. No service.

25. No service.

July 2. Mr White preached from 1. Cor 3.13

9th. No service.

16. Mr Denton preached from Psalm 9.10.

19. I dined with Mrs Jackson at Totties was at Stony Bank at night.

23. We had no Service we expected Mr White but he disappointed us.

30. No service.

Aug. 6. Had no service.

13. Mr Thornton preached from Philip 3.3.

18. Peniston Races.

31. Wakefield Races.

Sept. 1. Got in the last of our corn this day.

3. No service.

6. We had a swarm of Bees on the 16 of May which I took this day and it had twenty-two quarts of Honey in it. I had another swarm on the 28 of the same month out of the same Hive.

7. Barnsley Races.

10. Had no service.

17. Had no service. Much rain last night a windy turbulent weather about now.

[5] Meltham
[6] Yateholme or Yeatholm was a farm in the township of Holme and was in possession of the Green family for nearly three centuries.
[7] Thomas Lax became minister at Topcliffe 1726, and in 1736 of Lion Chapel, Bridlington.

C

24. Had no service. Rainy weather.

Oct. 1st. Fresh & cold. Mr Towers[8] minister at Hopton preached from 1 Peter 2.17. fear God. Mr Wordsworth was at our house yester night, and was at Chapel this day, both forenoon & after.

4. Some little rain. I was at Nether Cumberworth to visit Cotton Home. I heard yesterday that my Lord Luisham[9] is dead of the small pox and that Mr Dowden of Lockwood is dead & buried.

7. Extraordinarily much rain & a flood.

8. Mr Halliday[10] preached from Mark 1.15.

15. No service.

21. Holmfirth Fair.

22. We had no service. I hear that Dr Walker as he is commonly called formerly an Apothecary in Huddersfield is dead Much rain a flood.

25. I hear Dr Walker was buried yesterday.

29. Had no service.

Nov. 5. Had no service.

13. rainy day. I was at Stony Bank to visit Mr Tho More-house who is indisposed.

Nov. 19. Sharp fresh snow. Had no Service.

20. I saw the eclipse[11] in the morning very clear.

26. Fair. Mr Elston preached in the forenoon from 1 Titus 11 part of the 12 verse, afternoon from Isaiah 40.6.7. I was with Mr Elston at Stony Bank. At Totties to visit Mrs Jackson.

Dec. 3. Had no service. Frost.

7. I was at John Goddards & lent him £15.

10. Had no services. It is 2 years this day since Mr Elihu Jackson died.

16. very sharp frosty night. Mr Ainsworth who . . . Dr Nettle-ton some time small and set up at Stoppard[12] and is removed about 5 weeks since to Ashton came here late at night and said he had come purposely to see me, said he was in a great strait for money and brought 4 Books and some Physic to sell me. I told him I

[8] Mr. John Towers, minister at Hopton or Habton. The *Nonconf. Register* notes the death of his wife and daughter in May 1743.

[9] George, Viscount Lewisham, was the eldest son of William, first Earl of Dartmouth. He married Elizabeth, daughter and heir of Sir Walter Kaye, Bart., of Woodsome. George died of smallpox at his house in Hollis Street near Cavendish Square. William, the second Earl of Dartmouth, was his eldest son.

[10] William Halliday, minister at Bullhouse in Penistone, died Dec. 11th, 1741.

[11] There was a total lunar eclipse visible in England on Dec. 1, 1732 (Gregorian calendar). The Gregorian calendar not being in use in this country at that date, the eclipse would be recorded at the time as appearing on Nov. 20. The editor is indebted for this information to Mr. A. Hunter of the Greenwich Observatory.

[12] Stoppard is Stockport.

had just parted with my money and had none to spare and had no occasion for the physic so he pressed me to buy the Books and wanted 15/- for them. I gave him 12/- & said I had but 6^d left. How it came into his head to come here and how he found me I know not for I had little acquaintance with him but saw him sometimes when I went to Dr Nettletons.

17. Frost broke.

18. rain last night I was at Hagg[13] with Mr Lockwood, Mr Thomas Morehouse, Thomas Hobson and Mr Ludlam & got home a quarter past 8.

19. A rainy day. Mr Ludlam should go next week to speak to Mr Brook a minister in Nottinghamshire to get him to come and preach here. Mr Lockwood had promised to go to Mr Angier[14] minister at Cleckheaton who is boarded with Mr Brook's mother & to get a letter from him and directions for Mr Ludlam's to talk with him have also promised to speak to Mr George Moorhouse this day to get him to bring a letter to Mr Elston next Saturday for one Mr Low who . . . make is . . . me that part of the country where Mr Brook is, and with Mr Ludlam not a denial from Mr Brook some . . . is to . . . Mr Low.[15]

Dec. 31. No service.[16]

1732-3

Jan^{ry} 1st. Sharp frost.[1]

7. No Service.

14. No Service.

15. I was at Stony Bank with Mr Thompson.

20. Madam Crosland of Cartworth died on the 18th in the night.

21. Had no Service. Madam Crosland buried this day.

27. Had no service. Cold wind.

---

[13] Hagg near Honley.

[14] Mr. John Angier does not seem to have been the minister at Cleckheaton at this time. He had moved away to North Ferriby in 1728 and was succeeded by Evan Stock. At Cleckheaton at a hamlet called Swinley or Egypt there was a brick chapel called the Red Chapel.

[15] A very long prayer on the 22nd.

[16] Here follows a prayer of thanksgiving for having been spared to the end of another year and preserved from severe trials and danger during the year.

[1] A prayer for the commencement of the new year follows.

Feb^{ry} 1. Windy turbulent & rainy extraordinary great wind & rain. a great flood.

Feb. 3. I was at Thurlston to visit John Platt. I called at at Radmonyate.

4. Had no service.

8. I called at Mrs Jacksons and spoke to Mr Salkeld in Wooldale.

11. Mr Brook preached from Isaiah 5.4.

18. Had no service.

19. Windy & cold. Some rain. At Carlcoats. A great number of old people and such as are subject to shortness of breathing & stoppages in the Lungs carried off by this new fever which is so common.

25. Had no service.

26. Cold windy and turbulent and rain an extraordinary wet afternoon, a great flood.

Mar. 4. Had no Service.

11. Had no Service.

18. Had no Service.

23. Frost, there is a great deal of snow upon the moors great drifts. I had a terrible journey to Maythorne.[2]

25. Had no Service.

March 29. Rain & thunder much lightening very soon this morning, a flood. I went to Blackhouse this afternoon with Mr Thomas Morehouse to visit Mr Lockwood who is very much indisposed. He wished me to write a letter for him to Dr Nettleton to come to visit him and I did so. and he sent a Servant with it this night.

Ap^l 1. Had no Service.

2. I was at Blackhouse to meet Dr Nettleton got there about 1 stayed till 5 I was at Sudil[3] at Widow Berrys.

5. I was at Stony Bank at night with a design to speak to Dr Nettleton but he was not come.

8. Had no service.

14. Marsden Fair.

16. I was at Pairhill to visit Joseph Haigh & at Middlecliff to visit Wm Marsden.

22. Misty & Cloudy. Mr Denton preached from John 13.34. Love one another.

25. I was at Blackhouse this morning with a letter from Mr Brook. He acquaints us with his resolution to continue where he is, and not to come to us. Mr. Lockwood continues indisposed I went to Thurlstone to visit Jno Plat and got home about 11 at night.

26. Extremely cold wind. I was at Totties at Mrs Jackson's.

29. Had no service.

[2] Maythorne in Fulstone.
[3] Sudil, Sude Hill.

May 11. I was at Stony Bank last night with Dr Nettleton and got home at half past 12.

12. I was at Stony Bank this morning, but Dr Nettleton was gone.

20. No Service. Robert France has told us that his kinsman Mr Hadfield would come over and bring Mr Kelsall with him but we were disappointed.

27. Had no service.

29. I was at Halifax: and was at Mr Elston's and stayed whilst almost night before Dr Nettleton came home.

June 1. I was at Blackhouse this morning to visit Mr Lockwood.

3. Had no service.

June 10. Had no Service.

14. Lightning and thunder.

15. Extremely hot. I was at Moorcroft.

17. Had no service at Chapel. Mr Drayley[4] vicar of Kirkburton is come to preach at Holmfirth.

19. Rain last night. I was at Stony Bank much rain towards night. I was at Totties at Mrs Jacksons.

24. Had no service.

25. Excessive hot.

26. Thunder lightning & rain last night excessively hot. I hear a young man was struck with the lightening at Thomas Shaw's of Lingard's last night.

27. Thunder lightning & rain this afternoon there was a flood. I was at Stony Bank.

28. There was a young man killed yesterday in the afternoon on the common near Lingard's with the lightening, it is John Sykes of Oldfield's brother's son There was an oak split with the lightning on Monday in the night at Cavehull, and an Ash at Longley Hall.

30. I hear that 4 beasts of Henry Buckley's of Saddleworth were killed with the lightning last Monday and that a man was killed in Saddleworth the day before.

July 1. very hot. Mr Lax preached from 103 Psalm 2. I hear that last Wednesday there was a prodigious hail storm 6 miles beyond Stoppard[5] hail stones 7 inches about, that it killed several sheep and battered the wheat and quite spoiled it, so that they have turned cattle into it. Two miles on this side Ashton there came a terrible clap of thunder, so that it shook the house of one Lees . . . . . . went into the rooms and they found 3 doors split and in one of

---

[4] He means the Rev. Robert D'Oyley, Vicar of Kirkburton and Wickersley (Herring's *Visitation* II), but he was a non-resident and lived at Windsor (Morehouse, *Kirkburton*, p. 69). Died 1766.

[5] Stockport.

the 3 rooms a . . . of Pewter Dublers[6] were melted: but nobody in the house received any harm.

8. No service.

10. Some little rain windy. I went to Sheffield & bought 6 lancets. I bought a razor for 11^d, and a Wig for 10/- & got home a quarter before 11 o'clock. I stopped at Clothiers' Inn, and gave the landlord my riding coat & whip; and when I called for them about three o'clock in the afternoon, they brought me a wrong coat, a Gentleman from Tuxford, a Cloth buyer, had taken my Coat and was lately gone and had left his coat which was not so good by far as mine. I would not take it and came away without coat & both Landlord & Landlady promised to send for it and to send by Mr Joseph Greaves.

15. Mr Towers preached from Eph: 5.14; I was at Stony Bank with him at night.

16. I went to Blackhouse in the afternoon with Mr Thos Monkhouse to visit Mr Lockwood and wrote a letter for him to Dr Nettleton.

20. I was at Smithy Place this morning to visit Widow Bales. Her husband had been in the Royal Hospital at Greenwich, and was come down from London to Smithy Place.[7] She took a decoction of Foxglove yesterday for a vomit and a most enormous vomiting sickness & anxiety etc. followed. She died the next day and was buried on the 22^d.

24. Fair. Hot. This day I am 52 years of age.[8]

29. a very rainy day. Mr Renaw preached from Jerem. 30.21.

30. I was at Blackhouse to meet Dr Nettleton.

Aug. 3. I was at Blackhouse & wrote a letter to Dr Nettleton for Mr Lockwood.

5. No service. Much rain & thunder in the forenoon.

9. I hear that Mr Clough of Ealand is dead in London.

10. I was at Stony Bank with Mr Dobson & Mr Buck.

12. Mr Buck preached from 1 Peter 1.25.

14. I received my Coat which was taken from the Inn at Sheffield on the 10 July.

17. We got the last of our Corn.

Aug 18. Showers, thunder and heavy showers: a flood.

19. Mr Holden a young man which Mr Buck sent here from Bolton preached from John 3.16.

22. I hear that Mr Lockwood died this morning.

25. I was at the funeral of Mr Lockwood & got home between 9 & 10. The last time Mr Lockwood was at Chapel was on the

---

[6] Dublers, large dishes.
[7] In Honley.
[8] Here he writes down a prayer which is of considerable length.

25 July in the afternoon. The last time I visited Mr Lockwood was on Sunday the 19th at night.

26. Mr Holden preached from Psalm 37.5.

Sepr 2. Great tempests of rain & hail. Mr Holden preached from 1. Thes 4.13-4.

3. Mr Stephenson the old wandering person was here I gave him 6^d.

5. a very strong wind.

6. Wakefield Races this week.

9. Frosty morning. Mr Holden preached from 1 Thess 4.13-14.

13. A very wet day. Mr Holden was here.

14. Mr Holden preached from . . . 4.30.

17. A close day. Mr Holden was here. . I went to Stony Bank with Mr Holden.

23. Mr Holden preached.

24. Mr Holden goes back to Bolton this day and comes not again till the 4 November.

26. Strong wind last night, much rain a flood great storms of hail & rain during the day. I was at Blackhouse this afternoon to visit Mr Ludlam. I called at Stony Bank as I came back. Madam Horsefall held a Court[9] at Henry Pomfret's, and they walked their boundaries on Monday the 24th.

30. Had no service.

Oct. 7. Had no Service.

10. I went to Blackhouse to visit Mr Ludlam. Emley Races.

14. Had no Service.

21. Had no Service.

23. Frost broke. 6 sharp frosty nights together froze hard, the string [ended?] with last night which was the 7th.

25. Bailiffs Feast.

28. A Flood. Had no Service.

Novr 4. Mr Holden preached from 1 Sam 12.24. John Broadhead who comes to our Chapel is discomposed in his mind.

5. Mr Holden preached from 1 Sam 12.24 the latter part of the verse. Mr Holden was here.

6. I was at Totties to visit Mrs Salkeld.

11. Exception(al) rain. a flood. Mr Holden preached.

18. Had no sermon.

25. Had no sermon.

Decr 2. Had no Service.

6. I was at Totties & Dr Nettleton was there.

8. I was at Cubly beyond Peniston to visit John Senior & Joseph Micklethwaite.

[9] Within the Manor of Wakefield four Courts-leet were held—at Wakefield, Halifax, Brighouse and Holmfirth (Morehouse, *Hist. of Kirkburton*, 1851, p. 15).

9. Very sharp frost Mr Elston preached from Matt^w 5.17.
10. Frost broke last night. I was at Totties to visit Mr Salkeld. It is 3 years this day since Mr Elihu Jackson died:
14. Lightening & thunder.
23. Mr Holden preached.
30. I was not at Chapel in the forenoon Mr Holden preached, my head ached in the morning. My brother was seized very ill this morning went to the Chapel in the forenoon and was very ill. Staid at home in the afternoon and I bled him at night.
31. There was an Epidemical Catarrhous Fever in the beginning of this year. There was also an Epidemic in London from about the middle of January 1732-3 for about 3 weeks: The Bills of Mortality from tuesday the 23rd to tuesday the 30 of January contained in all 1588 being higher than any time since the plague. The remedies commonly successful were bleeding, sweating promoted by watery diaphoretics Blisters and the Common pectoral medicines and Febrifuge draughts of salts of wormwood Juice of lemons &c. Great numbers of old people carried off by it.

Great damage done by thunder and lightening last summer.

Oh Lord, I will bless & praise thee for all thy mercies in having preserved my life and brought me to the conclusion of another year.[10]

1734-5

Jan^{ry} 5. Had no service.
7. Boisterous wind much rain in the night a flood. Cold wind hail and snow.
12. A very great snow. Had no service.
19. Had no service.
24. cold wind, was at Blackhouse to visit Mr Ludlam.
26. very warm. Had no service.
27. I was a Stony Bank with two Books.
Feb^{ry} 2^d. Mr Eden[1] preached from Job 27.8.

[10] The year 1734 is lost. He commences the year 1734-5 with a prayer. The transcriber frequently omits these prayers.
[1] William Eden was there from 1734-46, after that he went to Elland. He seems to have been in the habit of preaching from the same text two or three times running. He raised and commanded a local force of volunteers against the Jacobites in 1745, and was afterwards commonly known as Captain Eden.

9. Had no Service.

17. I was at Delph[2] to visit Mary Danton.

23. Had no service, windy, raining & cold; a flood.

27. Windy, turbulent, rainy. Penistone Great Fair.

March 2. Had no service.

3. I was at Holmfirth at Mr Thompson's for a Book. I called at Dan Thorps spent 4ᵈ with Mr Thompson, Mr Kenworthy, Mr Radcliffe and young Mr Thompson were there.

6. A very wet tempestuous day, a very great flood.

9. Had no service.

11. I hear Dr Wilson broke his leg last night.

16. rain Mr Eden preached from Matt. 6.19-20-21. Lay not up for yourselves treasures upon earth &c. I wrote a paper at night to be subscribed and sent to London.

23ᵈ. no service.

27. I was at Halifax got home a little before 9 got very wet as I came home. I went and called at Eland to see Mr Elston.

Apˡ 4ᵗʰ. Joseph Taylor in discharging a Gun which . . . had broke his Teeth and slit his over lip. I stitched up the wound.

6. Had no service.

9. James Kenworthy buried this day. I was invited to the funeral.

11. Had no service.

16. Kirk Burton court.

20. Mr Eden preached from Matt 6.19-20-21. He's coming to settle with us.

26. Holmfirth Fair.

27. A rainy day. Mr Dawson[3] preached John 8.36. I was at Stony Bank at night.

May 4. Very cold wind Mr Eden preached from . . . 13.1.

5. I was at Jonas Hobsons of Wooldale at Auction of the Books belonging to the Club on thursday May 1ˢᵗ. Mr Thoˢ Moorhouse was there and was ordered to buy Pope's Homer if he could buy it for 8/- but Dr Nettleton bid 12/- for them and had them.

11. Mr Dawson preached from Phil: 4.11.

12. There was a shower of hail & snow last night. Holm Moss quite white this morning but it was soon gone.

17. A Horse race on Cartworth Moor this afternoon.

[2] Delph, in Saddleworth.

[3] Mr. Dawson, Eli Dawson, was minister of the Presbyterian Church at Halifax from 1728-44. He was educated at Frankland's Academy at Rothwell, with his brother Samuel. Six of his seven sons were brought up to the Nonconformist ministry. His son Samuel was minister at Wibsey Chapel, and another son, Joseph, was at Hull. The six all abandoned the ministry and five conformed, largely it is said, by the influence of Dr Legh the Anglican incumbent of Halifax, and much to the indignation of the Presbyterians generally.

18. I was at Chapel in the forenoon. Mr Eden preached from Jerem: 9 & latter part of the 5. v.

23. Mrs. Martha Jackson is married this day.

25. A very rainy morning. Hot in the afternoon. Thunder & lightening & rain & hail. Mr Aldred preached from Heb. 9 latter part of the 27, & the former part of the 28.

June 1. Mr Eden preached from Jerem. 2.5.

8. Mr Dawson preached in the forenoon from Ps 119.59. I was not at Chapel in the afternoon.

15. Mr Eden preached from Hos 8.7 I was [not at?] the chapel. It is 20 years since I left this country.

17. I was at Stony Bank and gave them a Bill of £1.7s.11½d. beside attendance.

20. I was at Blackhouse at night. I came with Mr Ludlam and Mr Etler to Thurstonland. I left 3 notes at Blackhouse one was a receipt signed by Mr Holden for Madam Hutton's Legacy. It was wrong dated in the January 1733-4. It was for two years and there was 2 years and a half due to us at that time. Another which showed according to Mr Elston's letter that there was 2 years and a half due to us at Martinmas 1733 according to which there was 4 years due last Whitsuntide. It had also the names of the Tenants. Another that showed that Mr Elston left in April 1732.

June 22. Mr Dawson preached from Col: 3.2.

29. Mr Buck preached from Psalm 119.92.

30. Some little rain in the morning. In the afternoon Mr Buck came here and my brother & Abraham Heeley and after some time Mr Thoˢ: Morehouse & Mrs Morehouse Mrs Aldred Mrs Buck and Mrs Summers called here, and went to Holmfirth, after some time Mr Buck and I went after them.

July 6. Mr Dawson preached from Job. 22.21.

7. I was at Blackhouse and paid Mr Eden 3.5.0 Mr Dawson was there and Mr Parkin of Penistone.

13. Mr Eden preached from Phil: 4.5. very wet day, a flood, windy turbulent day.

20. Mr Dawson preached from Mark 12.21 in the forenoon. In the afternoon from Heb: 12.9-10.

24. This day I am 53 years old.[4]

27. Mr Eden preached from Luke 6.41-42.

31. Thunder & much rain, a flood.

Aug. 3. Mr Dawson preached.

10. Mr Eden preached.

17. Mr Dawson preached from Heb: 12.9-10.

21. Dalton Races.

24. old Mr Dawson preached from Heb 4.9. very heavy rain in

[4] A prayer was added here.

the morning. It rained so excessively that the waters are so high that I was not at chapel in the afternoon.

30. I was at Middlecliff to visit Jnᵒ Thornton's daughter I went also to Haslehead.

31. Mr Eden preached

Sepʳ 4. Peniston Races.

7. afternon The younger of Mr Dawson's sons preached from Josh. 24.15.

9. Wakefield Races.

11. Mr Eden was here and I went with him to Stony Bank.

12. I was at Sofley to visit John Wadsworth's wives aunt.

14. Mr Eden preached from Job 1.9. I was not at Chapel in the forenoon.

Sepʳ 17. Mr Eden ordained at York this day.

19. We got in the last of our corn. Some few drops of rain.

20. I was at Stony Bank. I stayed up at night & saw the eclipse of the moon on the east side.

21. Strong wind and rain. We had no service at the chapel. Mr Eden is at York.

25. I was at Copthurst to see Josh Kaye. I called at Hades⁵ Mr Kenworthy was gone to Wakefield and staid there a good while. Linley Races.

28 Mr Dawson preached from Matt. 6.24. "Ye cannot serve God & mammon."

Oct. 5. Mr Eden preached from Coloss: 2.20.

12. Frost last night. Mr Stock⁶ preached from . . . 13.17.

18. Holmfirth Fair.

19. Mr Eden preached from 144 Psalm 15.

20. Mr Dobson was here & paid me £1. 5s. od. interest. Mr Thompson was here a good while.

26. Mr Eden preached from Gen: 1.31.

Nov. 2. Had no Service Mr Eden is at York.

9. Mr Eden preached from 1. Cor. 5.18.

16. Rain. Mr Abᵐ Dawson⁷ preached forenoon from Acts 26.20.

23. Mr Eden preached from Acts 17.29.

30. Rain last night. Mr Eden preached from Revel 3.15.

Dec. 3. Godfrey Charlesworth was here & gave me a new note. He owed me two years interest.

7. I was so ill all last night I did not go to the chapel in the forenoon. In the afternoon from Acts 17.30.

8. a deal of snow but no frost.

⁵ Hades. There is a Hades to-day in Marsden and another in Holmfirth. Probably the latter is meant. There is also a Hade-Edge in Cartworth, where there is a Methodist Chapel.
⁶ Mr Stock, Evan Stock from Cleckheaton.
⁷ Abraham Dawson, another of the sons of Eli Dawson.

14. Mr Samuel Dawson preached Matt 6.24. I called at Stony Bank at night.

15. Mr Ludlam paid me £2: 10s: od which he had borrowed of me in July. I gave him a Bill for physic for 8/6 & he gave me half a guinea.

21. Mr Eden preached from Acts 17.30.

28. Mr Sam Dawson preached 119 Psalm 60.

30. I was at Nab to visit Mr Wm Marsh who is very ill, and his neighbours advise him to send for Dr Nettleton and I have consented.

Dec. 31.[8]

1736

1. Commences the New Year.

4. Mr Eden preached from Luke 13.8.9.

11. Sleet, hail. Stormy cold wind. I was at the Chapel in the forenoon but was called out before service was done. Mr Farrar preached from 1 Sam¹. 15.22.

18. Cold wind & rainy day. Mr Eden preached from Acts 17.31.

21. On thursday the 15th the King's Speech was read.

25. Mr Eden preached from . . . 11.14.

Feb^ry 1. Mr Ab^m Dawson preached from Rom 12.18.

2. Much rain, a prodigious stormy wind, a great flood.

5. Abraham Lockwood of Brockholes[1] buried this day, my brother is gone to the funeral. Rain & cold.

6. I was at Jn° Goddards, he paid me 30/- interest. I lent him ten pounds more and he gave me a note.

8. Exceedingly cold & snowing morning. Mr Ab^m Dawson preached Philip: 3.20. Coldest day that hath been this winter. Sharp frost. Dr Nettleton was at Holm.

9. Snow last night & continued snowing all this day.

13. I was at Stockwood hill to visit Dame Newton.

15. Frost broke. Mr Ab^m Dawson preached from 10 Psalm 13.

18. I hear Mr Micklethwaite of Birchworth was buried on Monday the 16 of this inst.

22. Snow & sleet. Mr Eden preached from Matt. 7.24.25.26.27.

---

[8] Dec. 31. He wrote a short prayer here and another for New Year's Day.
[1] Brockholes in Thurstonland, and near to Honley.

I hear that Stapleton hath given in a list of 2000 who are suspected to have no vote and W . . . n[2] hath given in a list of 1700 the former hath only given in their names but the latter hath given in their places of abode.

29. Cold wind. Mr Sam¹ Dawson preached from Psalm 4.6.

March 4. Mr Buck, Mr Alred and Mr Thomas Morehouse called here.

7. Mr Eden preached from Matt^w 7.24.25.26.27. I was not at Chapel in the afternoon.

14. Mr Eden preached from Haggai: 1.7.

15. I saw the eclipse of the moon at night, it was a total eclipse.

21. Mr Eden preached from Hagg. 1.7. afternoon from 1 Cor 5.21. "Prove all things hold fast which is good."

Mar. 28. Mr Eden preached 1 Cor 5.21.

April 4. Mr Eden preached 90 Psalm 12.

11. Mr Eden preached in the forenoon from Psalm 90.

12. I was not at chapel in the afternoon.

15. Windy rainy tempestuous weather. I was at Edward Dickinson's of Huflatt. a great flood.

18. Mr Sam¹ Dawson preached from Lam: 3.24.

21. I hear that Joseph Firth of Lanehead departed this life this morning.

21. I hear that Sir George Armitage of Kirklees is dead.[3]

25. Cloudy, Windy, Storms. Lightening & thunder and rain. Mr Eden preached.

29. Dr Nettleton came over and I went with him and Mr Tho⁸ Morehouse to Stony Bank and got home at half past 12, at night.

30. I was at Stony Bank this morning and went with Dr Nettleton to see Henry Hinchliffe, and to the Cross to see George Tinker. I went with him as far as Honley where we parted. I went to Mr Armitages of Thickhollins.

May 2. Mr Sam¹ Dawson preached from Prov: 18.14. I was not at Chapel in the forenoon.

4. Mr Tho⁸ Crosland of Cartworth is married yesterday.

9. I was not at chapel in the forenoon. Mr Eden preached from Acts 26.28-29 afternoon.

11. It seems there is news that Sir Rowland Winn hath gone out and that the scrutiny is at an end, and Sir Miles Stapleton's friends had great rejoicing yesterday by ringing the Bells at Honly, Holmfirth, Benton, Almondbury, Huddersfield &c by bonfires and great rejoicings.

[2] Sir Roland Winn.
[3] Sir George Armytage, of Kirklees, fifth baronet, died unmarried, and was buried April 24th, 1736.

12. They had a very great stir in Scholes yesterday, had a bonfire and had the [effigy] of a man and stick in it.[4]

16. afternoon. Mr Ab^m Dawson preached from Psalm 16.3. I was called out of chapel before the sermon.

19. Burton Court.

23. Mr Eden preached from Acts 26.28-29.

30. Had no service.

June 6. Mr. Ab^m Dawson preached from Gen: 29.9.

13. Mr Saml Dawson preached from Job 28.28.

19. Ben Blackburn of Aldermans Head,[4a] Steward to the Duke of Norfolk, was buried at Sheffield last Tuesday.

20. Mr Eden preached from Acts 26.28-29. Mr Wadworth buried this day.

27th. Mr Saml Dawson preached from Psalm 90.12.

28. I was at Hades to visit Mrs Kenworthy. I went with Mr Kenworthy and his son up on to the Moss and I opened the grave of a man who it is believed hath been buried there about 60 years. the dogs had eaten off his left hand before he was found and his head off. His body and limbs were sound and uncorrupted.

July 4. Much rain. Continued all day, a flood. I was not at Chapel nor any of our family. Mr Zouch[5] Vicar of Sandal near Wakefield and Justice of the Peace preached at Holmfirth yesterday.

10. Jonathan Hinchliff brought me New Coat waistcoat and 2 pairs of Breeches, and I paid him 8/- for making them.

11. Much rain in the forenoon, a flood. In the afternoon I was not at chapel. In the forenoon Mr Saml Dawson preached.

12. I was at Stony Bank to visit George. I was at Blackhouse and Mr Ludlam gave me The Craftsmen[6] a Sermon or paraphrase on part of the 19th Acts.

[4] This was the close of the great Parliamentary contest of 1734. Sir George Saville, who had sat in the previous Parliament, retired, and Sir Roland Winn of Nostell, fourth baronet of that name, appeared on the ministerial side. The Tories were putting forward Sir Miles Stapleton of Myton. Cholmley Turner, Esq., of Kirkleathem, who had sat in Parliament since 1727, was also putting up. Turner and Winn united and issued a joint address. Almost at the last minute the Hon. Edward Wortley came forward and joined Stapleton. Large sums of money were squandered on both sides. The result was that Stapleton headed the poll and Turner was second. More money was wasted on a petition and the legal proceedings dragged on till 1736, when the Whigs finally dropped them. Hence the rejoicings mentioned here.

[4a] Alderman's Head, a farm in the township of Langsett.

[5] Charles Zouch, son of a Reading goldsmith, Christ's Hospital and Trinity Coll., Cambridge, B.A., 1715, M.A., 1718. Assistant master, Wakefield Gr. Sch. V. of Sandal. J.P. for the West Riding. d. 1754.

[6] The Craftsman, a Sermon or Paraphrase upon certain verses of the 19th chapter of the Acts of the Apostles. Composed by the late Daniel Burgess and intended to be preached by him in the high times, but prevented by the burning of his meeting-house. (By Thomas Gordon of Kirkcudbright, 3rd ed., 38 pp., London 1720). Other editions show some variations in the title.

16. I was at Deaconbrook to visit Wm Naylor's wife and was at Timothy Shirts as I went and called at Gunfit Mill⁷. I called at Mr Hawksworth's, I came back to Stony Bank and got my dinner there with Dr Nettleton and staid with him till almost 7 a clock.

July 18. very hot. I was at Stony Bank. Mr Ab^m Dawson preached in the forenoon from Psalm 33.1. In the afternoon from Gen: 39.9.

21. I was at Stony Bank to visit George. Mrs Morehouse gave me 5/- for visiting him. I had given him no physic.

23. I was at Blackhouse and gave Mr Eden £2 10s. od. quarter-age.

24. I am 54 years of age this day.⁸

25. Mr Samuel Dawson preached from . . . 16.26.

Aug. 1st. I was not at the chapel. Mr Eden preached from Luke 12.45-46.

8. I was not at chapel Mr Abraham Dawson preached from Proverbs 4.26.

15. Mr Eden preached from Luke 12.45-46.

16. Mr Burn brought me two young Pidgeons which came out of Almondbury Kirk Steeple.

17. A good shearing day.

21. This afternoon we got done Shearing.

22. Mr Samuel Dawson preached from . . . 7.21.

29. Mr Eden preached from . . . 1—1.16.

31. We got in the last of our corn.

Sepr 5. I was not at chapel. Mr Saml Dawson.

7. I was at Halifax and got home a quarter before 9. I bought Dr Nettleton's Treatise concerning virtue & Happiness price 4/- I bought a [book?] on Harrogate Spaw⁹ at 6d.

9. My brother & I were at Rushbearing at Lydgate and paid either of us 1/8 and got home at a quarter past 10.

12. Cold wind. Mr Eden preached.

19. Mr Saml Dawson preached from 119 Psalm 60. I was at Stony Bank at night.

26. afternon very hot. Mr Eden preached from Gal 6.3-4 in forenoon. I was not at the Chapel in the afternoon.

Oct. 3. Mr Ab^m Dawson preached from Heb: 13.16.

6. I hear of a truth that Richd Littlewood of Kilnhousebank was

⁷ Gunfit, Gunthwaite.
⁸ A prayer follows here.
⁹ *Spadacreni Anglica*, or The English Spaw: being an account of the situation, nature, physical use and admirable cures performed by the Waters of Harrogate and parts adjacent, by the late learned and eminent physician, Dr. Dean of York, and also the observations of the ingenious Dr. Stanhope. Leeds 1736.
The work was originally published without Michael Stanhope's observations.

found dead this morning, had fallen from his horse as he was crossing the water above Hinchliff Moor. He had been at Huddersfield.

Oct. 7.   I was at Blackhouse with some books and paid Mr Eden £2 10s. 0d. quarterage.

8.   Old Richard Littlewood of Kilnhousebank & James Hoyle of the Hill buried this day.

9.   I was at Stony Bank in the afternoon and Mrs Morehouse would have paid me for what I had done for her son Thomas, but I would take nothing for she had given me 5/- for attending upon George. a flood.

10.   Great showers of hail & rain. a flood. Mr Eden preached from Gal: 6.3-4.

17.   Mr Saml Dawson preached from . . . 7.21.

21.   Honly Court.

24.   Mr Eden preached from Gal: 6.3.4-5.

27.   Strong wind rain, a flood, lightning in the evening.

31.   Mr Ab^m Dawson preached from Proverbs 10.18.

Novr 7.   Mr Eden preached in the forenoon from Gal: 6.3-4-5. afternoon from Deuter: 33.29.

14.   Mr Saml Dawson preached.

20.   I was at Stony Bank to visit the children in the Measles.

21.   Much rain. a flood. I was not at the chapel. Mr Eden preached. I was at Stony Bank.

28.   Mr Eden preached.

Decr 25.   Mr Eden preached Deut 30.11-12-13-14.

7.   I hear Mr Wilkinson of Greenhead[10] departed this life on Sunday the 5th in the afternoon.

12.   Mr Saml Dawson preached from Rom: 14.17. Mr Newton Stockwood hill departed this life yeterday about half past 9.

15.   Great Snow. I was at the funeral of Mr Newton.

17.   A great flood.

18.   a very rainy day a great flood.

19.   rain Mr Eden preached Deut 13.11-12-13-14.

23.   A strong boisterous & extremely cold wind.

25.   I was at Stony Bank to visit Mr & Mrs Morehouse.

26.   much rain last night. Mr Ab^m Dawson preached.

Decr 28.   Much rain in the day. A very great flood. It came above 2 lands[11] into the . . . from the Newmill water to the yate.

30.   I was at Stony Bank to visit Mr Morehouse.

[10] A house at Meltham bore this name.

[11] A *land* was one of the strips into which a cornfield or pasture land which had been ploughed was divided by water-furrows. This was often taken as a measure of land area and of length, and of value, varying according to local custom. (N.E.D.) A small land is four yards wide. An ordinary land, as at Driffield, nine yards. A land at Elmswell was twelve yards wide.

31. Wind & rain. a very strong wind.[12]

Remarks upon the year. There was a very hot . . . Summer. Hath been a deal of snow, sleet, wind and rain, thus far this winter. The Small Pox were very mortal at Halifax, Honly and many other places this summer. The Small Pox are also at Newmill, Wooldale, Stackwoodhill &c. The Measles had been prevalent before then.

1736-7

Jan[ry] I.[1]

2. Windy, Some rain. Mr Eden preached from Luke 13.8-9.

9. Cloudy windy with some rain. Mr Farrar preached from Eccles: 12.14.

10. A windy rainy day. there was a great flood. There was lightning both on Saturday the 8th at night and yesternight.

16. I was at Kirk Bridge to visit Joseph Battey and his wife. Mr Eden preached from Ecles. 8.11-12-13-14. I was not at chapel in the afternoon.

18. I was at Buscar before Skelmanthorp to visit Joshua Armitage's wife.

21. Thomas Cattell of Holmfirth, his widow, hath killed a Bailiff, died upon the spot who was serving a writ upon her and suddenly run her penknife into his Belly and ripping it up.

23. An extraordinarily strong & cold wind. In the afternoon storms of rain & hail very boisterous, some thunder, at night a flood. Mr Sam[l] Dawson preached from Matt: 6.19-20.

27. Snow & hail. I was at Stony Bank to visit Mrs Morehouse, was at Totties at Mrs Jackson's

30. Mr Eden preached Ecles 8.11-12-13-14.

Feb[y] 6. Wind, rain, very turbulent. Mr Smith preached forenoon from Job 27.8. In the afternoon from Luke 17.8.

13. A very rainy turbulent day, a flood. Mr Sam[l] Dawson preached from Luke 22.42. I was not at chapel in the afternoon.

Feb[y] 16. Sleet, abundance of rain, a very rainy day, windy, a very great flood.

17. Windy. great tempests of rain & sleet some hail thunder lightning snow.

18. A prodigious strong wind last night, and rain a flood.

---

[12] He concludes the year with a short prayer.
[1] He commences the New Year as usual with a short prayer.

20. Mr Eden preached from . . . 18.33. I was not at the chapel in the forenoon.

22. Much rain last night a great flood.

24. A great tempest of rain and sleet.

27. Mr Sam¹ Dawson preached from

Mar. 6. Mr Eden preached from . . . 18.33.

13. Mr Eden preached from . . . 18.33. I was not a chapel in the forenoon.

16. Wet day, rain, sleet, hail, snow, a flood.

20. Sleet, rain. Mr Eden preached from Jerem: 4.22.

27. Mr Sam¹ Dawson preached from Heb: 3.13.

April 3. Mr Ab^m Dawson preached from Prov: 10.18.

9. misty morning, Dr Nettleton told me on tuesday last that he had² rec^d any [mother?] of pearle but . . .

10th. afternoon Mr Sam¹ Dawson preached from Heb 3.13.

17. Cold wind. Mr Eden preached from . . . 19.30.

22. I hear that Mr Buck is so ill that there was no hope of his recovery, there was a report that he was dead but hope it is not true. Joseph Swallow of Ellentree²ᵃ head buried this day.

23. Much rain a flood. I was at Stony Bank to visit Mrs Morehouse.

24. Mr Eden preached from John 15.13.

25. Holmfirth Fair.

May 1. Mr Sam¹ Dawson preached from Levit: 19.17.

8. a flood. Mr Eden preached from Prov: 17.17. a very wet day.

15. Mr Ab^m Dawson preached.

22. Extremely hot. Old Mr Dawson preached from Cor (2) 4.17.

29. Mr Doyley vicar of Kirkburton preached at Holmfirth this day. Whittsunday. Had no service at the Chapel.

June 5. A rainy morning. Mr Sam¹ Dawson preached from Proverbs 1.31.

12. A very strong turbulent wind Mr Eden preached from Rom: 2.12.

19. Mr Sam¹ Dawson preached.

26. Windy & cloudy. Mr Brooksbank preached.

July 1. Extremely hot. Thunder & rain.

3. Mr Sam¹ Dawson preached from Psalms 4.10.

10. Rainy morning. Mr Brooksbank preached from Psalm 101.5.

13. We got the last of our Hay and the pastures are burnt up.

17. Mr Eden preached from Rom: 2.12.

18. I hear they have begun to Shear at Almondbury and some other places last week.

² Not?

²ᵃ Formerly called Edentree head. It is in Holmfirth.

24. A rainy day. Mr Eden preached from Rom. 2.12.

30. cloudy, showers, windy. I was at Hades to visit Mrs. Kenworthy. I have been reading "An Enquiry into the Natural Rights of Mankind to debate freely concerning Religion, by a Gentleman of Lincoln's Inn, 1737."

31. Mr Eden preached from Rom. 2.12.

Augt 7. A rainy day. Mr Buck[3] preached from Prov: 27.1.

9. Mr Buck was here in the afternoon and staid a good while. I was at Stony Bank to visit the Company, Mrs Buck, Mrs Summers with others.

13. Townend Rushbearing.[4]

14. Mr Buck preached from Psalm 37.37.

15. We got done shearing.

21th. cloudy, rainy. Mr Buck preached from 2 Tim: 1.10, part of the verse "Who hath abolished death and hath brought life and immortality to light through the Gospel" An excellent Sermon.

22. I was at Stony Bank to visit George Morehouse. Mr Buck was there.

25. We got the last of our Corn.

Augt 25. I went to Almondbury to visit Mr George Morehouse's wife, I bled her. Mr & Mrs Aldred were there. Mr Eden, Mrs Summers, Mrs Esther, Sarah and Hannah Morehouse. Mr Buck and his family left Almondbury in the morning and set out for Bolton. I got home between 8 & 9.

28. Mr Eden preached from Rom: 2.12. I was not at Chapel in the afternoon.

Sepr 4. In the forenoon Mr Eden preached from Rom: 2.12.

6. Good harvest weather. Wakefield Races.

11. Mr Eden preached from Rom: 2.12.

18. Mr Eden preached from Phil: 4.11. I was at Stony Bank at night for a Book.

25. Mr Eden preached from Philip. 4.11. In the afternoon from Rom: 12.18.

27. Great showers. I went to Halifax and got home at a quarter before 8. It rained fast as I went and when I was there but was pretty fair as I came home. I paid Mr Richd Cook 2/- for forfits

---

[3] John Buck who was minister at Bolton.

[4] The rushbearing. As practised in West Yorkshire, a large amount of rushes was collected in bundles and heaped up in a large cart or waggon and usually overhanging at the ends which were ornamented by cutting a kind of pattern on the close-packed bundles. Then the whole was lavishly adorned with flowers. Young men in linen shirts decorated with ribbons of all colours, attended the waggon on foot or on horseback. When guns of any kind were available they were fired off and sometimes a drum was beaten. Arrived at the church or chapel, the rushes were strewn on the stone or earthen floor and formed some protection from the cold during the next winter.

for not going to the Club and spent there 2/6 in all 4/6.   Bought a pair of gloves 1/-.

30.   A very rainy day.

Oct. 2.   Mr Eden preached from Rom: 12.18.

5.   Burton Court.

9.   Mr Eden preached from Rom 12.18.

16.   Mr Eden preached from Heb. 2.15.   I was at Stony Bank at night.

19.   I was at Ranaw to visit Mr Joseph Greaves' daughter.   I called at Hazlehead both as I went and as I came back.   Thomas Haigh was not at home.

23.   Mr Eden preached.   I was not at the chapel I was at Stony Bank.

29.   Had no service.

Nov. 6.   I was at the Chapel in the forenoon.   Mr Dodge[5] of Sowerby preached from Coloss: 1.27 latter part.

10.   wind west.

13.   I was not at the chapel in the forenoon.   Mr Sam¹ Dawson preached from Prov. 1.31.

20.   Mr Eden preached from Prov: 3.13.

25.   I called at Mr. Ludlam.   Mr Eden and Mr Halliday were there.   he is come to preach at Bullhouse as a candidate.   I went to Farnley.   I called at Blackhouse as I came back and got my dinner with Mr Ludlam Mr Eden and Mr Halliday.   I called at Stony Bank in the morning.

26.   I hear that Madam Spencer[6] of Cannon Hall was buried on Wednesday the 23ʳᵈ of this instant.   I hear this morning that Queen Caroline[7] is dead.

27.   Mr Eden preached from Prov: 3.13.

30.   Queen Caroline died on Sunday 20th of this inst and I hear that the King is very much indisposed.

Decʳ 4.   Some rain.   Mr. Eden preached from Matt 5.77 (sic).[8]

6.   Some rain.   Dr Wilson was here.   He would be 58 years old at Christmas.   I was at Stony Bank.

7.   Windy, tempestuous.   Storms of rain hail Snow and Sleet very cold.

8.   A great snow fallen.

11.   Very sharp frost.   I was not at Chapel.   Mr Eden preached from Mt 5.47.   I was called to visit Dame Clark of Totties who is worse; as I went I met John Kaye coming for me.   I called first

---

[5] Mr. William Dodge.   Presbyterian minister at Sowerby.   "A useful preacher and physician."   He died July 14th, 1742.

[6] John Spencer of Cannon Hall, the second owner of that name, died April 13, 1729, aged 74, and was buried at Cawthorne.   This was his widow. The Hall was just north of Cawthorne.

[7] Queen Caroline, wife of George II.

[8] v. 47.

at Joshua Woodheads and then I heard that there was a running Dr[9] at Dame Clarks. I went there and found him there, I went into her chamber to visit her, and when I came down again he got up and went out and came in no more while I staid, but I spoke [about] employing him for . . . saith he had gone . . . Dame Clark asked me [what] . . . was [wrong] with it I told her I could say nothing in that case for most of such running D[rs] were cheats.

12. I called at Dame Clarks I told her I thought she had not been such a fool as to meddle with a running Dr who deserved whipping out of the town and had sent for Dr Thompson and . . . called there on Saturday at night after I was gone and after the running Dr was gone who was last there. He told her as I had done, that the distemper laid in her mind more than in her body, and that if she pleased he would meet me there and consult with me. I told her that I would have nothing to do with runnagates but would meet Mr Thompson or any Physician anytime but blamed her that she would not send for Dr Nettleton as I had advised her several times.

18. Cold wind. I was not at Chapel in the forenoon. Mr Eden preached from Matt 5.47 in the afternoon.

24. I hear Jn⁰ Hadfield of Shawhead who I visited the 17th inst, died yesterday.

25. Mr Eden preached from Matt. 5.47.

Remarks on the year.

Queen Caroline died on Sunday the 20 of November a princess of a bright shining character and universally lamented.

this year there was a very sickly spring a fever & pleurecies, the most sickly spring that hath been this four years.

A very sickly autumn fevers pleurisies & agues and Rheumatisms.

A very great drought this summer, a great Scarcity of Hay.

Bleeding & blistering were good for the fever. Sick persons seized with unusual symptoms.

[9] A wandering quack doctor.

END OF THE FIRST VOLUME

1737-8

Jan^{ry} 1st. I was not at chapel in the forenoon. Mr Eden preached from Matt: 5.4.

6. A very great wind last night great storms of hail and rain; in the evening lightening.

7. a prodigious strong wind & much rain.

8. much rain a terrible wind last night a great flood I was not at chapel.

10. ·In the afternon Snow and very turbulent. I was at Hades as I came home very windy the Snows continually and 3 flashes of lightening & 3 peals of thunder and very loud.

11. A snowy day.

13. Snow & Sleet, frost broke.

15. The Snow goes very gradually. Mr Saml Dawson preached Jerem: 13.23 an Excellent Sermon.

16. The snow goes apace.

22. Mr Eden preached from Rom: 6.21-22.

29. I was not at Chapel. Mr Halliday preached from 1 Col: 4.9.

Feb^r 5. Clear. cold wind. Mr Eden preached from Rom: 6. 21-22.

12. Mr Halliday preached from Prov: 10.22. I was at Stony Bank.

15. I paid Jonathan Hinchliff 5/- for making me a new Suit, Coat, Waistcoat and breeches.

19. Mr Eden preached from Rom 6.21-22.

23. Peniston Fair.

26. Windy, cold, rain. Mr Ab^m Dawson preached in the forenoon.

27. A great wind. Thunder & lightning in the night, and tempests of rain & hail.

March 5. Wind & rain. Mr Eden preached from Rom: 6.21-22. I hear that Dr Nettleton hath been extremely ill & kept his house a week.

9. Windy, rain. Some snow upon Holm moss this morning. I was at Stony Bank to return *Tacitus Annals*. A great hail shower in the afternoon.

12. I was not at Chapel, old Mr Dawson preached from Jude 25 verse.

19. Wind much rain. I was not at the Chapel in the forenoon. Mr Eden preached from Rom: 6.21-22. A prodigious strong wind last night & this morning, in the forenoon hath broken down a Bullace tree.

26. Frosty morning. Mr Halliday preached from Psalm 16.8.

April 2. Mr Eden preached from Matt. 4.7.

9. Mr Halliday preached from . . . 14.9.

12. Burton Court.

14. Lightning & thunder rain, a flood. I was at Stony Bank with a Book. Marsden Fair.

16. We had no Service. Mr Eden preached at Ealand.[1]

19. A good quantity of rain last night. Snow upon the hills this morning. Extremely cold wind.

23. I was not at Chapel. Mr Halliday preached in the morning from . . . 14.9.

25. I was at Ranaw. Frosty morning. There are drifts of Snow yet upon the hills.

29. Holmfirth Fair.

30. I was not at Chapel in the forenoon. In the afternoon Heb: 6.1.

May 4. I hear that Old John Haigh of Ranah Departed this life on Tuesday the 2nd about 5 in the afternoon. I was invited to the funeral.

5. Rainy morning. Cloudy & Showers through the day. Old Mr Haigh of Ranaw buried this day, I could not go to the funeral.

May 6. Thunder & lightning last night and rain.

7. S. Cloudy Extremely hot. It began to thunder, lighten and rain when we were in Chapel in the forenoon. Thunder lightening & very much rain, it continued raining all service time and was a very great flood. Newmill water was never so high in the memory of man. The water went, the Kirk Bridge of Holmfirth water had risen proportionably, it would have been the biggest flood that ever was seen here, but Holmfirth water kept pretty moderate so that it did but come a land and half into the next close where the waters meet and went out again at the yate. Holmfirth chapel was over-flowed as high as the stalls, which water came down by Dan Thorps. Abel Hobson of Underbank house was flooded the water broke through at the window and carried out goods so that he had [great?] damage. We could get home from Lydgate no way in than towards Wooldale, Stonybank or Newmill. We went to Joseph Broadheads of Lydgate and stay'd there. An excessive great shower towards night, the ways are very ill broken up and very bad. Mr Smith preached from Galat: 6.9. And be not weary of well doing for in due season ye shall reap if ye faint not.

14. Misty, some rain. Much Thunder lightning & rain in the afternoon and a great flood. Mr Eden preached from Luke 12.21.

16. I was at Charras[2] near Smawshaw to visit . . . Smith. I

---

[1] Elland.
[2] Charras, a house and farm near Smallshaw.

went from thence to Bullhouse to visit John Hadfields wife. I was at Ranaw to visit Mr Jos^h Greaves' wife.

21. I was not at Chapel Mr Halliday preached from Ecl: 8.11. Whitsunday.

23. Rain last night—A cold rainy day, a flood.

24. They are walking their boundaries this day. Set out this morning at Mytham Bridge a vast number of people.

25. I hear they finished their boundaries this day and ended at Mytham Bridge where they set out.

26. Mr Hearing came for the duke of Leeds,[3] and Holmfirth people met him, a vast number of people to Walk the Boundaries of Holmfirth and they began at Mytham Bridge on Wednesday the 24 of this inst and finished on thursday the 25 they began & ended at Mytham Bridge. They began on Wednesday morning & ended on thursday night.

28. Mr Eden preached from Luke 12.21. I was not at chapel in the afternoon.

June 3. Mrs Kenworthy departed this life about 7 at clock yesterday morning, in the 55 year of her age. Mr Kenworthy was 54 years old on the 2^d of Decr 1737.

4. Mr Smith preached from 2. Cor. 5.14.

6. I was at the funeral of Mrs Kenworthy, she was buried at Almondbury, James Kenworthy was buried the 9th April 1735.

11. We had no service. Mr Eden is gone into Lancashire.

18. Some rain. Old Mr Dawson preached from Isaiah 26.4. I was not at Chapel in the forenoon. I was at Stony Bank at night.

19. I called at Ben Greens of Newmill. Mr Kay of Milshaw was there and was very glad to see me.

20. I went to Mr Thompsons for a Book. Mr Kenworthy was there a while but went away. Mr Thomas Morehouse came hither and I staid late I got home about 12.

Halifax Races began this day.

25. Much rain a flood. Old Mr Dawson preached from Matt: 5.8.

26. Extremely hot. Lightning at night. I hear Mr Elston departed this life on Wednesday the 21 of this inst: & was buried on Saturday the 24.

27. Lightning most of the night, a close morning.

29. I was at Foster place to visit Christopher Tinker's wife who is dangerously ill. Mr Thompson came then and prayed with her whilst I staid. I was at Blackhouse at Mr Ludlam's Mr Halliday was there.

[3] Thomas Hyde, fourth Duke of Leeds, son of Peregrine, the third duke. Thomas was born in 1713, succeeded to the dukedom in 1731, and married in 1740 Mary, the second daughter of Francis, Earl of Godolphin and granddaughter of John Churchill, Duke of Marlborough. Duke Thomas died in 1789.

July 1. Misty morning. day extremely hot.

2. Extremely hot. Mr Saml Dawson preach^d from 2 Phi (?Cor) 1.4.

9. Very great showers & some hail. Mr Eden preached from Ephes 4. 25. I was at Stony Bank at night.

11. A rainy morning. Mr Ludlam & Mr Eden were netting & I went a little way with them. Mr Ludlam gave me 3 trouts.

13. I was at Carlcoats to visit Thos Rowley. I was at Cartworth to visit Madam Crosland.

13. The sessions at Halifax.

16. For the most part a very hot day. Mr Halliday preached.

18. Hot day I was at the funeral of Elizabeth Oldham I was called away soon after dinner before they set out with the corps and went to Waterside to visit Thos Bray's son. My brother was invited to the funeral but could not go. Mr Eden preached from Job 16.22. N.B. She had lived with Ab^m Healey.

23. Rainy morning Mr Eden preached I was not at the chapel in the afternoon.

24. This day I am 56 years of age.[4] Thornhill Races.

30. Mr Eden preached from Luke 14.21.23.24.

Augt 4. A very great wind which hath done damage to Corn.

6. Mr Halliday preached from Isaiah 44.20. Lightening at night.

13. I was not at Chapel in the forenoon. Mr Halliday preached from Isaiah 44.20.

20. Mr Eden preached from Luke 14.21.22.23.24.

26. I was at a Race on Cartworth Moor.

27. Mr Ab^m Dawson preached from Rom 14.12.

Sepr 1. We got the last of our Corn.

3. I was not at chapel. Mr Eden preached from Matt. 16.26.

4. Joshua Woofenden of Holmfirth came hither to fee a Council[5] with respect to the mending of Holm Causway.[6] And I gave him 1/6.

5. I hear that Matt^w Broadhead's wife of Knowl is very ill again after I was called away, she was very well & composed whilst I was there and talked with very . . . and . . . and was very good that she was better but soon after I came away she [began?] to be ill on a sudden. two men was forced to hold her, and she spit in their faces and called upon the Devil to come and fetch them all and said she saw the devil.

9. A prodigious stormy wind with rain.

10. Mr Halliday preached from Isaiah 44.20.

---

[4] A short prayer follows here.
[5] A counsellor-at-law.
[6] The road over Holme Moss, known as Holme Causeway, constructed of large stones.

17. Mr Eden preached from Matt^w: 16.26.

24. Mr Eden preached from Luke 17.21. I was at Stony Bank.

Octr 1. I was too late for the Chapel in the forenoon. Mr Halliday preached from Psalm 19.11.

6. I learn that the learned & excellent Dr Boerhaave[7] is dead

8. I was not at Chapel. Mr Eden preached from Job 20: 4.5.

15. Windy, Mr Halliday preached from Prov. 12.26. I was at Stony Bank at night there was no Service at Holmfirth Mr Thompson is in the Gout.

18. Burton Court.[8]

19. I went to Blackhouse to Mr Ludlam's to pay him for Summering my mare.[9]

21. Holmfirth Fair.

22. I was not at the Chapel. Mr Dobson preached from Psalm 116.7 in the afternoon.

23. The Statutes at Holmfirth. Young Mr Thompson is come to Holmfirth to see his father who is in the Gout.

29. Mr Farrar in the forenoon from James 1.4. The afternoon from Acts 10.38. I was not at Chapel in the afternoon. There was no Sermon at the Chapel at Holmfirth. Mr Thompson is very ill.

Nov. 5. Mr Halliday preached from . . . 6.13.

Nov. 5. Bonefires in Holmfirth.

12. Mr Saml Dawson preached from Luke 15.10. Mr Thompson preached again this day. He hath not preached since the 8 of last month.

18. I was at Rhoyd[10] to visit Wm Booth the Schoolmaster. I bled him.

19. Some little rain. Mr Halliday preached from Psalm 119.91.

26. I was not at the Chapel. Mr Eden preached from Job. 20.45.

Decr 3. a great flood. I was at Chapel in the afternoon. Mr Halliday preached from Psalm 46.1.

6. very much rain all the afternoon and very great flood. Lightning both morning & nights.

7. Lightening this morning. I was at Stackwoodhill and asked William Newton the price of Ab^m Heeley's farm. It is £6 rent and he saith he hath laid a little close to it near Kirkbridge which is 10/- per annum. but he asketh £240 for it. And for Joshua

---

[7] Dr. Boerhave. Herman Boerhave (1668-1739), celebrated Dutch physician and scientist, Doctor of Leyden University 1693, Lecturer in Medicine there 1701, professor of medicine and botany 1709, professor of chemistry 1718. Author of *Institutiones Medicae* and other works.

[8] The manor of Wakefield was of very wide extent and though the town of Wakefield was the administrative centre it was necessary to have other courts, such as that at Kirkburton, in the outlying parts.

[9] Keeping her at grass and looking after her during the summer.

[10] Rhoyd. Some property, belonging in the seventeenth century to the Woodhead family, situated near the chapel at Honley, bore the name of Royd.

Woodhead's of Totties farm which is but £3 10s. 0d. rent he asketh £160. for the Riding he demandeth £5 per Ann and with the building upon it, he will pay me interest for my money and set it up in the rent.

20. I hear Mr Kenworthy came back from London yesternight.
24. Mr Eden preached.
28. Wind Sleet & snow.
29. Frost. cold wind.

1738-9

Jany 1. A prodigious strong wind much sleet & rain last night, a great flood this morning.[1]
2. I hear there was an Earthquake in Halifax market place about 7 o'clock in the morning, of Saturday, the 30th of last month.
3. I was at Middop to visit Joshua Sanderson's wife. very sharp frost great drifts of snow upon the moors a fresh fall of snow & hail sleet & rain in great abundance and a very great boisterous wind and a great flood. I had an ill journey. They set up the Guide Stoops[2] in the lanes this day.
5. Blustering & stormy, cold. great showers of rain & sleet. very turbulent.
6. I was at Butterley to visit Mr Cowper.
7. Sharp frost very cold wind and some sleet & rain Mr Eden preached from Rom: 2.3. I was not at chapel in the forenoon.
12. I hear that Abel Tinker of Carr fell from his horse and was killed yesternight as he came from Penistone. He was killed in the fold of Edwd Batty's of Penistone where he set up his horse it is that when he got on horseback he touched the mare with the spurs & she threw him. a very strong wind rain & hail.
14. A very strong wind last night. Mr Eden preached from the first 13 verses of the 25 Matthew.
21. Mr Eden preached from Matt the first 13 verses of the 25 Chap.

[1] A short prayer of thanksgiving follows at this point.
[2] Guide stoops or mile stones due largely to an Act of 1698 ordering the J.P.'s to erect guide posts at crossways. The J.P.'s of the West Riding issued an order to the surveyors to set up such posts with the names of the nearest market towns. Further orders of the same kind were issued from time to time. When stone was available these "stoops" were six feet long, and square in section. (Crump, *Huddersfield Highways*, 1949, pp. 46-94.)

24.　Windy.　turbulent much rain.

27.　I was at Stony Bank with 2 of my Ld Shaftbury's Book[3] & for the 2 vols of the History of the Conqest of Mexico.[4]

28.　Mr Eden preached from Matt 5 & first 13 verses.

31.　I was at Stony Bank and Mr Morehouse paid me 7/6 for Physic.

Feby 1.　Very much rain. a great flood.

4.　A great flood very strong wind & much rain last night. Mr Eden preached from John 18.36.

11.　Wind & rain last night. much rain & wind. I was not at chapel in the forenoon. Mr Halliday preached from Prov. 20.27.

17.　Windy & rain. I was at Haslehead to visit Thomas Haigh I called at Ramah[5] at Joseph Greaves daughter at Carlcoats at Joseph Horsfall. I was at Meltom[6] to visit James Garlick's wife.

18.　I was not at Chapel in the forenoon. Mr Eden preached from John 18.36.

23.　I was at Stony Bank to visit Mrs Morehouse.

25.　Mr Halliday preached from Matt. 5.3.

March 4.　I was not at Chapel. Mr Eden preached from Eccles 12.14.

11.　Frost extremely cold wind. Storms of hail & snow. I was not at Chapel in the forenoon. Mr Halliday preached from Matt 5.4.

18.　I was not a chapel in the forenoon. Mr Eden preached, very cold. There was no service at Holmfirth. Mr Thompson is worse.

24.　Very cold wind. I was at Stony Bank. I hear it is not Turpin who is confined at York Castle.

25.　Mr Eden preached. I was not at chapel. There is no service at Holmfirth Chapel. Mr Thompson is ill of the Gout.

Mar. 29.　Emor Rich of Darrells was here, his daughter continuing very ill and he saith that Dr Cookson of Wakefield[7] is to come & visit her this afternoon.

Ap^l 1.　Rain, had no service. Mr Eden preached at Bullhouse.

2.　It is confirmed that it is Turpin who was confined in York

---

[3] Anthony Ashley Cooper (1671-1713) succeeded as third Earl of Shaftesbury in 1699 and wrote *Characteristics of Men* &c, in 1711.

[4] *The History of the Conquest of Mexico by the Spaniards*, Done into English from the original Spanish by T. Townsend, 3 parts, London, folio, 1724. Another edition, the translation revised and corrected by N. Hooke, 8vo, London, 1738.

[5] Ranaw.

[6] Meltham.

[7] Dr. Cookson was in his day the leading doctor in Wakefield. In 1747 he bought Cliff House in Westgate, pulled it down, and substituted a brick building, still called Cliff House. (Walker, *Wakefield*, p. 399.)

Castle, and hath took his trial for Horse stealing & is condemned.[8]

8. Strong blustering cold wind rain hail & snow. I was not at chapel Mr Eden preached.

15. I was not at chapel in the forenoon. Mr Halliday preached from Matt^w 5.5.

20. I was at Hades to visit John Kenworthy who is worse and hath sent for Dr Nettleton. cloudy, windy very cold.

22. Extremely cold wind. Snow upon the Hills rain & sleet all day. a very wet day, a flood. Mr Eden preached in the forenoon from Acts 2.36. I was not at chapel in the afternoon.

23. I was at Rough Birchworth to visit George Yates he was so very ill that he had sent for Mr Askin before I got thither & he had bled him and sent him some medicines. As I came home a little past Stony Bank I met Dr Nettleton & Mr Kenworthy, and turned back with them to Stony Bank, and got home about 3 a clock. Easter Monday.

28. Holmfirth Fair.

29. Mr Halliday preached from Prov: 14.32.

May 6. I was not at Chapel in the forenoon. Mr Eden preached from Philip 4.11.

13. Mr Halliday preached from Matt. 5.6. I was at Stony Bank to visit Thomas.

20. Mr Kenworthy was at my house this morning and desired me to go to Halifax to speak to Dr Nettleton about his son. I got to Halifax about 2 a clock. I was not at Chapel. Mr Ab^m Dawson preached.

23. Dr Boerhaave died Sept 23^d 1738, in the 70th year of his age. Dr Saunderson professor of the Mathematics at Cambridge died April 20th 1739.

27. I was not at chapel in the forenoon. Mr Stocks preached in the afternoon from Matt: 6.19-20.

June 3. Mr Buck preached from Titus 1.12. "and godly in this present world" Read both the 11th and 12 verses to complete the sense.

4. I called at the Stake-lane to see Barthol: Brays' maid.

5. I was at Halifax and got my dinner at Dr Nettleton's.

8. I hear that a Man was killed with the Lightening over Skipton on Tuesday the 22nd of last month he was on Horseback and the Horse was not hurt. I hear also of damage done at the same time with lightning burning housing.

10. I was not at Chapel in the forenoon. Mr Eden preached in the afternoon from Ephes. 5.4.

[8] Richard Turpin, the famous highwayman, son of an Essex innkeeper. While apprenticed to a butcher began by cattle stealing, ultimately convicted at York Assizes on a charge of horse stealing and hanged at the age of somewhere about 30. The famous ride to York, if it ever happened, was probably by John Nevinson (1639-84).

I hear that on tuesday the 22 of last month there was a haith[9] of Thomas Kays of Marsden burned with the lightning.

17. Mr Halliday preached from Matt^w 5.7 in the afternoon.

24. Mr Eden preached from Ephes: 5.4. I was not at Chapel in the forenoon.

25. I was at Scholes to visit John Tyas's son Christian. I hear they have fetched Dr Wilson to him. John Tyas is a conceited brutish rude unmannerly fellow.

26. Halifax Races this week.

28. John Moorhouse of Falstone the younger was here I bled him. a very hot afternoon. There was an oak split with the lightning yesterday at Falstone.

July 1. Mr Eden preached from Ephes: 5.4. I was not at chapel in the forenoon.

July 8. Mr Halliday preached from Matt 5.8.

10. I was at Mr Jacksons to visit widow Lister that is his Sister Martha who came from London to Totties yesterday.

15. Mr Eden preached from James 4.11. I was not at Chapel in the forenoon.

18. I was at the funeral of Jn° Kenworthy of Hades, he was buried at Almondbury this day, he died on the 14th.

22. Mr Halliday preached from Matt. 5-9.

24. I was at Thunnor[10] Bridge to visit John Smith's son. I saw the Eclipse of the sun very fair.

29. We had no Service Mr Eden is gone into Lancashire to his father's. In the afternoon one John North of Cawthorn who is in Service at Darrington below Pontefract, came hither and is very ill in the ague.

Aug. 2. Barnsley Races.

5. One Mr Liddon a young man from Bolton a candidate for the ministry preached in the forenoon from Prov: 3.17. Her ways are ways of pleasantness & all her paths are peace, in the afternoon from 2 . . . 5-10. two excellent sermons.

9. Began to shear.

11. Had no service at chapel.

12. I was not at Chapel in the forenoon. Mr Farrar[11] preached from Job. 2-10.

16. Mrs Mary Jackson married this day. Joseph Emmerson came to invite us to the supper at Mr Jackson's. I told him it was too late but he was very wishful for us all to go, and I told him

---

[9] Haith. The N.E.D. and the E.D.D. explain this as an exclamation, "By my faith! " Here is it probably a slip for laith or lathe, a word still in use in the North of England for a barn.

[10] Thunder Bridge.

[11] Thomas Farrar of the family of Farrar of Elland Park. He was minister at Eastwood and in 1739 went to Elland as minister. He died 1745. He seems to have been at some time at Warley in Halifax.

that my sisters were not well and could not go so late. I went with him and there was Joshua Woodhead and his wife, James Miller & a Boy there &c and I sat at an . . . in the back kitchen and they were warming meat. I said it was very far of the night and I thought they had been . . . for . . . but they carried it to their friends and relations and they set at supper and had but . . . had their dinner. I said they might almost have boiled a piece of beef. there came in Joseph said if they had brought some Tobacco and some drink they might have done better but he had done all he could for us and could get none so that there was no help that he . . . [knew?] of I told him there was no remedy but peace [and?] there was always a fast before a feast. at last between 9-10 Mr Jackson and the bride and the Groom and some others sat down to [eat] again and they called me out of the back kitchen to sit down with them, and I got my supper and then went into the far kitchen & drank punch and some claret and my brother and Joshua Woodhead and the rest went to supper. We came away a little after 11. They call the Bridegroom Mr Ardinton.

17. Mr Ardinton & his bride accompanied by their friends and Mr Jackson are set off from Totties this day after dinner for Leeds.

19. Mr Halliday preached. I was not at Chapel in the afternoon.

26 Mr Eden preached from James 4.11. I was not a chapel in the forenoon.

29. very much rain a great flood.

31. boisterous great tempests of rain windy very much rain Some thunder & lightening.

Sepr 5. I was at Blackhouse. Mr Ludlam was gone with his brother to Wakefield Races.

6. My brother was at Mixenden yesterday at the ordination of Mr John Smith.

9. Wind & rain last night. Exceeding much rain and a very great flood. Mr Stocks[12] preached from Luke 13.24. Very bad Harvest weather.

11. Much rain last night, thunder & lightning a very rainy day & great flood.

14. very bad harvest weather.

18. I was at Mr Jacksons to visit Widow Lister who is come back from Leeds. Mr Herring of Horbury, Mrs Radcliffe of Almondbury and old Mrs Appleyard buried yesterday.

23. Rain last night. Some thunder & much lightening great showers Mr Ab^m Dawson preached from Joshua 24.15 (the former part).

25. John Kaye of Netherthong was married to Eliz. Oxley yesterday.

[12] Evan Stock.

26.   a very rainy day & flood.

28.   Much rain in the morning very heavy rain in the afternoon. I was at Mr George Morehouse of Almondbury.   Gave him a Bill of 16/- for what I had done for his family & he gave me a guinea.

30.   Mr Eden preached from James 4.11.   I was not at chapel in the afternoon.

October 7.   Mr Halliday preached from Col: 1.12.

14.   Mr Eden preached from James 4.11.

20.   Holmfirth Fair.

21.   Mr Eden preached Col. 3.12.

25.   I was at Hollinhouse to meet old John Roebuck.

28.   Mr Halliday preached from Jerem: 23.23-24.   The wild creature that hath done so much damage by worrying sheep was taken alive at Carlcoats.

Oct. 28 1739.   I hear that Enoch Armitage died last Spring. It was 20 years last Spring since they went from Lydgate.[13]

Decr 2^d.   Extremely frosty.   Mr Eden preached from Matt: 5.33. 34.35.36.37.

3.   a stormy blustering day.   Exceedingly slippery.

4.   Much rain.   John Maxon of Kirkburton buried yesterday.

5.   Old Henry Horn buried this day.

9.   Mr Halliday preached.

16.   Mr Eden preached from Matt 5.33.34.35.36.37.

23.   Mr Halliday preached from Eccles: 12-14.   I was not at the Chapel in the forenoon.

27.   Very sharp frost. Extremely cold wind. I met Dr Thompson —he goeth back to Bingley today.

30.   Mr Eden preached from Heb: 2.15.   I was not at chapel in the afternoon.   Excessively cold.

31.   Snow showers very cold.   Exceeding sharp frost.

1739-40

Janry 1.   Sharp frost very cold, misty.   Snow most parts of the day.

6.   very sharp riming frost.   Some snow.   Mr Halliday preached from Jerem: 18.7-8.   I was not at the Chapel in the afternoon.

9.   Sharp frost.   This being the day appointed by Authority for a general Fast Mr Eden preached from 1 Sam: 7.12.   Hitherto the Lord hath helped.

[13] The November part is lost.

13. Frost. Great snow showers. Mr Eden preached from Matt 5.34.35.36.37.

20. Sharp frost. A young man from Hunchill[1] near Leeds preached in the forenoon from Ps. 73.25-26. In the afternoon from Heb: 4.7. His name is Mr Garrett.

27. Sharp frost very cold. Afternoon Mr Eden preached from Matt: 5.34-35-36-37. They had no service at Holmfirth in the afternoon Mr Thompson is in the Gout. Mr Hodgson of Cumberworth preached at Holmfirth in the forenoon.

Feb[ry] 3. Snow storms. Mr Garrett a young man from Hunchliff preached in the forenoon from 1 . . . 1.9. In the afternoon from 1 Peter 1.4.

10. Frost last night. frost broke this morning. I was at Cartworth to visit old Mr Crosland.

13. Exceeding sharp frost. Extremely cold wind almost as cold as on the 29 & 30 of December last. I was at Halifax to speak to Dr Nettleton about old Mr Crosland, a very bad cold slippery dangerous journey.

14. Sharp frost. A Snowy day, a good deal of Snow.

16. very cold, frost broke and a great deal of snow gone. I was at Blackhouses to visit Mr Ludlam and got my dinner there.

17. Some rain the snow goes a pace & the waters are risen. Mr Halliday preached from Matt 7.13.14. I was not at Chapel in the forenoon.

19. Great tempests of snow in the afternoon extremely cold. Feb[y] 21. Peniston Fair. Sharp Frost.

24. Some rain. a cold east wind Mr Eden preached from . . . 3.2.

Mar. 2. Rain, afternoon Mr. Halliday preached I was not at Chapel nor any of our family.

7. Sharp frost extremely cold wind. Snow sleet rain very tempestuous I was at Carlcoats to visit Joseph Horsfalls' son. I had a very cold bad journey.

9. Sleet rain & windy tempestuous day, great showers of rain towards night and a prodigious Strong wind very blustering & turbulent. Mr Eden preached from Prov: 17.17. I was not at Chapel in the forenoon.

16. Some rain Mr Eden preached from Acts 26.28-29. I was not at Chapel in the forenoon.

23. Mr Brooksbank preached but none of our family was at the Chapel myself & my Sister Mary were so ill.

30. Mr Dobson preached, but none of our family were at Chapel myself and my sister Mary were so ill.

31. Mr Eden was here.

Ap[1] 1. Frosty morning, my brother was at the funeral of old

---

[1] Hunslet.

E

Caleb Broadhead. I hear that old Jonathan Firth died about Michaelmas last, and Mr Tinker of Cross[2] and several others.

3. my sister Mary is extremely weak. I rode to Scholes[3]

Ap[1] 4. My sister Mary is very ill almost expiring. Lord Jesus receive her spirit!

5. Hannah Taylor & Rachel Bower sat up with my sister Mary last night and she departed this life . . . about 6 of the clock this morning very quietly was sensible to the last and longed to die, and had good hope . . .. for she hath been very ill and not fit for business many years, hath had many dangerous illnesses that we did not expect her recovery and always both under her afflictions and that all her behaviour was patient almost beyond example. Some rain very cold.

6. Some rain very cold. Mr Eden preached from Acts 26.28-9. My brother was at the chapel in the forenoon to speak to Mr Eden to preach a sermon at the funeral of my Sister and to speak to John Townsend to make a grave. Easter Sunday.

8. very cold wind. We buried Sister Mary at Lydgate in my Sister Rachael's grave. Mr Eden read the 14 Chapter of Job and the 15 chapter of 1 Corinth, and he preached an Excellent Sermon from 1 Cor 15.55-56-57 O death where is thy sting O grave where is thy victory &c It is appointed to all men once to die, the apostle brings in death yet our victory over it is assured and that so the sting of Death to cease and makes it may have no Power over us, and that leading a virtuous and Christian life makes death comfortable. We went to the Chapel by Wooldale and carried the corps with napkins and had no Bier. Some frost this morning. Wid[w] Hopkins of Wooldale departed this life this afternoon.

9. very cold wind Joseph Emmerson left Totties this day & came to our house to take leave of us.

My sister Mary came from Mythom Bridge to Totties on the 5 May 1739 and departed this life the 5 April 1740.

10. Called at Mr Jacksons of Totties to buy some oats. this is the first time I have been there since I was ill.

Ap[1] 11. A cold wind a great drought and I think there is a frost almost every morning a very backward Spring. Old widow Hobson buried this day. my brother is gone to the funeral. The wind is continually East or north east.

12. I rode to Stackwoodhill to visit Dame Newton but dared not venture by myself and my brother went with me.

13. An extremely cold wind. Mr Ab[m] Dawson preached from Colos: 4.11. My brother was at Chapel.

[2] Cross, close by Cartworth.
[3] Jessop appears to have been confined to the house from March 17th to this day.

14. I sent for Mr Eden to be so good as to come up and smoke a pipe with me, and he came up this afternoon and staid a good while, and I gave him two crown pieces that is 10/-.

14. very sharp frost cold wind a very great drought and backward Spring.

20. wind & rain last night, a windy blustering day, great showers of rain & hail. Mr Eden preached from Acts 26.28-29. My brother was at Chapel in the afternoon.

21. A great snow fallen last night. Snowing this morning & frost extremely cold & strong wind. Large iceicles at the eaves of the house all day, and as cold as the depth of winter.

23. I hear that Widow Gream sister to Mrs Morehouse of Stony Bank is buried this day.

24. I hear that Widow Greame is buried this day & not yesterday. Mr Ludlam is under confinement at Wm Shackleton's. He came over on tuesday. Mr Wm Radcliffe hath arrested him for £200.

26. Showers of hail & snow, cold wind Holmfirth Fair. I was at Stony Bank with a Book.

27. None of our Family was at Chapel. I hear Mr Dawson preached.

30. I hear that Robert Swallow of Ellen tree head was buried on Sunday last.

May 1. Cold wind. I was yesterday at Hepworth to visit John Marsh who fell off his Horse as he came home on Saturday from Holmfirth Fair & hath broke his collar bone & hath a large wound in the head. There hath been a vast great Mob up some days who I hear pulled up several Mills were [sic] there was Bluestones under . . . that they grind packs and send them away oversea & they take away all the corn at such mills.[4] I hear that Dr Thompson took Mr Hopkins shop at Huthersfield and remained there last month, & is my . . . in Holmfirth, he staid about 2 years at Bingley.

2. cold wind but the wind is turned westward.

4. Cold wind. Mr Eden preached from John 6.54. my brother & sister were at the Chapel. Hail afternon then it got to snow very fast, frost and Snow, a good deal of snow fell, a very backward spring.

5. There is a deal of snow upon the moors, great showers of large hail, and great tempests of Snow. Some thunder.

11. I was at chapel this forenoon I have not been there this

---

[4] The "blue stones underneath", can hardly have been the millstones. Most of these came from Derbyshire and were fawn coloured. They were certainly not stones from the Blue John mine, which were of brittle fluorspar. Some superstitious reverence was frequently paid to blue stones. They were used, too, as boundary stones, as sanctuaries for criminals, and wealthy people frequently desired to be buried underneath such. (N & Q. Ser. VIII. I. 150, 217, 378, clx. 33, 106. cxli. 124.)

8 weeks but at the funeral of my sister Mr Eden preached from James 3.2.

12. A rainy morning very warm rain blessed be God for the same Extraordinary rich day.

14. I was at Cors[5] Bowers butcher for a Leg of mutton 8¼ lbs at 2s. 9d. that is 4^d a pound and a Loin of Veal 7¼ lbs at 1s. 9d. that is 3^d a pound, the dearest meat we ever had Extremely cold as Christmas.

17. I did not turn to grass until this day and still a very bare pasture. frosty morning.

18. I was not at chapel. Mr Eden preached from James 3.2.

May 19. frosty morning for the most part a great drought. cold wind.

25. very cold wind, as cold as winter yesterday & this day Mr Eden preached from James 3.2. Whitsunday.

28. Cold wind. I hear there is a frost almost every morning I was at Hollingreaves to visit Joseph Heeleys apprentice & called at Stony Bank for some Books.

June 1. For the most part an east wind and very great drought. Mr Eden preached from 2 Phr 1.10.11.[6] I was not a chapel in the forenoon. Trinity Sunday.

4. For the most part extremely hot wind south-east which hath been so East or Northeast.

5. A great shower last night, cloudy, great showers, plentiful rain.

8. Showers. Mr Farrar preached in the forenoon from 1 Phr 4.18 and in the afternoon from Heb. 13.5. I was not at chapel in the forenoon.

9. Great Showers. Thunder & lightning & some hail.

15. Some little rain. Old Mr Dawson preached from . . . 5.9.

17. Halifax Races began.

19. I was at John Morehouses of Moorcroft for some mint, and his wife gave me a paper to keep a Covenant between her Husband & her.

22. Mr Saml Dawson preached from 24 Josh. 15.

29. Mr Eden preached from 2 Phr. 1.10.11.

July 1. I was at Stony Bank in the afternoon & took Dence (a dog) with me and left her there to be hanged because she is unsound & not fit to be kept.

6. Little rain. Mr Eden preached. I paid him £2 10s. 0d.

[5] Cornelius.

[6] It is difficult to know what text is meant. If Phr is a mistake for Chr (Chronicles) then the first text seems impossible. If it is a mistake for Philippians (see July 20) then there are no first and second books of Philippians. It *might* mean Phil. II, vv. 1-10.11.

13. Raining, thunder, great Showers, I was not at Chapel. Mr Eden preached.

15. Samuel Kinder an old man at Overthong hanged himself last Sunday at night when his wife was gone to milk.

17. Showers. A very strong wind.

20. Great showers. Mr Eden preached from Phil 1.10. I was not at Chapel.

July 27. Mr Eden preached from Luke 15.23.

31. At this York assizes there are some of the rioters at Dewsbury &c. ordered for transportation and some to be imprisoned for some time.

Augt 3. Misty rainy day. Mr Eden preached from Luke 15.22. I was at chapel in the afternoon.

6. A very strong wind.

7. A prodigious strong wind, very tempestuous and excessive great showers, much rain. I hear Mr Abraham Ludlam departed this life sometime yesterday night.

8. Mr Ludlam died about 12 a clock on Wednesday at night aged about 39.

9. Mr Ab^m Ludlam buried at Barnsley this day. I was not invited to the funeral.

10. Mr Eden preached from 1 Peter 1.16.

11. I was at John Goddards of Scholes & he gave me a note for £30 which he had of me on 9th inst.

12. I was at Hall near Crosland to visit John Crosby's wife & at Thickhollins to visit Mrs Armitage. wind & rain last night.

15. I was at Holme to visit John Green's son John. I bled him. I called at Matt^w Hadfield's. I called at Wm Booth's the Londoner Madam Thompson was at John Green's a very positive woman, and said she knew as well as any Physician in England what should be done for the Boy. She is Mr Thompson's wife of London where Dr Thompson of Holmfirth served out his apprenticeship.

17. Mr Eden preached from 1. Peter. 1.16.

18. We began to shear off the White oats & the Friezland oats.

24. Mr Eden preached from Matt^w 12.7.

30. I was at Thurstonland at Wid^w Morehouses. Mr & Mrs Buck &c were there and I accompanied them to Stony Bank.

Aug. 31. A cloudy rainy day. Mr Buck preached from Titus 2.11-12.

Sepr 1. Wakefield Races. A fine day.

3. Mr Buck was here yesterday in the afternoon & staid a good while.

4. We got in our white oats this day.

6. A very rainy day. Hepworth Rush-bearing.

7. Mr Eden preached from Matt^w 12.7.

8. A prodigious strong wind and much rain. I hear that Mr

Matthewman departed his life on Friday the 5th and is buried this day. Great showers, I was at Elihu Hopkins' with Mr Eden & John Morehouse.

10. Showers, a very great wind, and very tempestuous very bad harvest weather.

11. A very wet day and an extreme great wind & showers.

12. Showers, windy, very tempestuous. I was at Scholihill near Peniston to visit John Haigh.

13. A very great wind last night.

14. Mr Eden preached from Mark 12, the first 9 verses. Honley Feast.

17. I gave young Joseph Woodhead a halfpenny for one of Nicholas Greaves of Almondbury's Halfpennys[7] which was coined in 1668 when Shopkeepers had liberty to coin halfpennys.

18. I was at Stackwood hill to visit Jonas Kennedy, he has got some medicine from Dr Holland.[8] I called at Newmills and Staid a while with Mr Hardy & Wm Newton. Wm Newton paid the shot.

19. Calm Sultry.

21. Mr Eden preached from Mark 12 & first nine verses.

28. Frosty morning. there was ice. Mr Aldred preached from Job 35.8.

29. Storms of Hail. Cold wind. At Stony Bank to visit Mr Morehouse's Son Thomas.

October 1. Hail rain & snow, very cold wind, frosty morning, there was ice.

4. A rainy day. I was at Moorcroft at John Morehouse's to visit his son George and at Stony Bank to visit.

5. Frosty very cold. I was at Stony Bank and at Moorcroft. A Stranger preached from Psalm. 19.11.

7. Mr brother is making[9] at Thongsbridge. We did 6 strikes[9a] and a peck of Friezland Oats and made 15 Strike and a peck. We did Sow 8 strikes of the Black Oats and made 12 Strikes & a peck but they were very ill shaken.

12. Mr Eden preached from Mark 12 and the first nine verses.

13. I hear that Old Mr Crosland of Cartworth departed this life about 6 o clock yester night.

15. Frosty misty morning. I was at the funeral of old Mr Cros-

---

[7] These shopkeepers' tokens for halfpennies were once fairly common. Nicholas Greaves who kept a shop in Almondbury was the son of the Rev. Nicholas Greaves, rector successively of Holmfirth and Tankersley.

[8] This Dr. Holland died May 1st, 1741.

[9] *Making* oats means threshing.

[9a] *Strike* is the name of a dry measure, usually a bushel, but in some districts half a bushel, and in others, two or four bushels. The contents of the round wooden measure used, have a "strickle" drawn over the top, so that they are level with the top and not heaped up.

land and we had our dinners at the Clarks and got home about 7.

17. There was much lightning yesternight.

18. Holmfirth Fair.

19. Some little rain. I was not at chapel in the forenoon. Mr Eden preached from Isaiah 55.6.

21. Thunder & lightning towards night.

22. Burton Court. Jonathan Wadsworth of Meltham house died yesternight. Thunder in the forenoon.

26. Frosty & misty morning. Mr Eden preached from Joshua 24.15.

31. I was at Denby dike side near Denby Mill to visit John Mosley's son. I called at John Earnshaw's the Clerk of Cumberworth and at Caleb Marsden's of Bursedge[10] to visit his mother. There is Corn to Shear at Cumberworth.

Nov[r] 1 Much rain a great flood. wind rain snow & sleet. very tempestuous a very wet turbulent day.

2. very sharp frost. Extremely cold strong wind. Mr Eden preached from Joshua 24.15.

Nov. 9. For the most part rain. I was at Honley. Mr Eden preached from Matt: 23.8.

15. Dark cloudy rainy day I was at Newmill at Ben Green's to meet Joshua Bailey & dan Battys Boy came there and after the Surrender to John Morehouse of Moorcroft he surrendered his house to me and I was to give him £25 on Monday morning. John Morehouse is to keep the surrender & court it. Old Mr Empson buried this day.

16. Rainy day. Mr Eden preached from Matt 5.17.

21. Rain wind hail turbulent last night & this morning. Rotherham Fair.[11]

23. Mr Halliday preached from James 5.11 I was at Ben Green's with him at noon: and one Mr Hanson who came with him from Halifax, and we had some dinner there and Mr Hanson paid 1/5 and would let me spend nothing.

24. Sharp frost. I hear Dr Thompson was married at Honley yesterday and was at Holmfirth at his Father's this day with his Bride.

28. Wind & rain last night, wind rain & very tempestuous forenoon. very much rain. A very great flood.

30. Mr Eden preached from Rom: 9.30-31. I was not at chapel in the forenoon.

Dec[r] 2. A prodigious wind last night, windy turbulent tempests. Great storms of rain lightening at night. I was at Nether Denby

[10] Bursedge, in the parish of Silkstone.
[11] Rotherham Fair was held on the day before the Vigil, the day of the Vigil, the Feast of St. Edmund the bishop, and five days later, Nov. 18-25 inclusive, and there was another fair on Dec. 1st for cattle and horses.

to visit Mr Hawkesworth & he gave me 2/6 for my visit & 1/- for a bottle of physic.

3. Windy rainy great showers very tempestuous, a prodigious strong wind.

5. Windy. tempestuous, rain snow & sleet.

7. Cold, Snowing in the afternoon. Mr Eden preached from Rom. 9.30.31.

8. Snow last night a very great snow fallen: sleet rain & frost all day, a great snow. I was as far as Wooldale to go to Thurstonland but the snow was so deep & there came so much sleet & rain that I turned again & went no further for the snow was so deep that I should have been very long riding thither and should have been very ill wet.

9. Frosty snowing morning. Afternoon there is a great snow.

14. Mr Eden preached from Coloss: 8.11-12-13.

15. A sharp frost. I was at Thurstonland Mr J^{no} Ludlam and Jonas Walker came with me to Stony Bank and I got home about 12 at night.

16. Sharp frost. I was at Edgend to visit Robert Francis daughter Anne.

18. Exceedingly sharp frost.

20. Exceedingly sharp frost. Some snow. Holmfirth Flesh Day.[12]

21. Exceedingly sharp frost, an exceeding cold winter almost as cold as the latter end of last year. Mr Eden preached from Luke 16.8.

22. An exceedingly blustering wind, snow last night, there was a great snow before which fell on Sunday 7th in the night and the last night another great snow so that there is a prodigious great snow and some drifted the frost giving back.

24. a clear day, some snow or sleet. I was at Cross to visit Mr Joshua Earnshaw. the snow goes away very moderately. there is so much snow.

25. Sharp frost. I was at the funeral of Daniel Newton. we set up 9 horses at the Clarks and spent 6^d. I came home with Mr Tinker & Mr Crosland. Dan Thorp fell into the pond on the top of Stocks moor and we were long hindered with him.

26. It began to thaw about noon, windy turbulent rain at night a very great blustering wind. I was at Cross in the forenoon to visit Mr Joshua Earnshaw.

28. There is abundance of snow gone. Mr Eden preached from . . . 8.11-12-13-14.

31. A prodigious strong wind.

[12] Holmfirth Feast Day was kept on Ascension Day and the following Sunday. The name *Flesh Day* seems now unknown there. Here the date of the *Flesh Day* is December 20th, so possibly this was a second Feast Day.

1741

Jany 2. Some rain. I was at Netherthong[1] to visit Adam Beaumont & I called at Abraham Woodhead's.

4. Small rain. Had no service.

8. Jonathon Hinchliff was here and brought my new coat & Breeches and I paid him 8/- for making them.

10. Sharp frost extremely cold.

11. Some snow extremely Cold wind. Mr Eden preached from Rom: 14.17.

12. Extremely cold, sharp frost. I was at Ben Green's with Mr Eden, Mr Thomas Morehouse, Mr George Morehouse, Mr Saml Hall and Mr Isaac Hanson, and got home between 5 & 6.

13. Sharp frost, snow last night extremely cold. I was at Stackwoodhill to visit Wm Newton's son William.

18. Wind & rain a very wet day. The Snow is going very fast. Mr Eden preached in the forenoon from Rom: 14.17. & in the afternoon from 2. Cor: 5.11. Mr Morehouse of Stony Bank was here at night.

23. Windy rainy very turbulent a prodigious strong wind & much rain.

25. A prodigious strong wind, storms of sleet in the afternoon. I was not at chapel in the forenoon. Mr Eden preached from 2 Cor 5.11.

26. A very great wind, snow sleet tempestuous a very ragged forenoon rain afternoon.

29. Some rain & sleet. I called at Godfrey Charlesworths and told him I would either have my money or better security.

Feby 1. Frosty morning, a fine day. Mr Eden preached from John 14.21.

4. Sharp frost, this is the day appointed for a General Fast. Mr Eden left us without service. My brother went to Holmfirth Chapel. I went to High Flatts to visit Elihu Dickinson.

7. I was at Holmfirth to speak with Mr Thompson we were speaking of setting up a Club for Books in Holmfirth. Mr Thompson would have us continue in the Halifax Club. I called at Danl Thorp's.

Feby 8. Mr Saml Dawson preached from 2 Cor: 7.1. I was not at Chapel in the afternoon. My sister went.

14. Mr Dobson came here and left me 5/- for interest. I was not at home.

[1] In Huddersfield.

15. Mr Eden preached from Ioh 5.21[2] above all things hold fast to that which is good: I was not at chapel in the afternoon my brother & sister were.

16. Old Anne Morehouse is dead and is to be buried on Wednesday the 18th day.

18. Cold day rain & snow. I lent to Mr Joshua Earnshaw an English Terrence & Virgil.

22. Extremely cold sharp frost. Mr Eden preached from Ioh 5.21.[3]

24. I went to Leak Hall to visit Joseph Firth. I bled him Christopher Tinker of Foster Place died this day & William Booth in the afternoon (of Holmfirth).

25. James Bradley of Choppards[4] buried this day.

26. Penistone Fair.

28. a pleasant day.

March 1. Mr Eden preached from Prov: 21.21.

7. old Mother Eastwood buried this day.

8. The Schoolmaster of Hepworth's mother buried (on Sunday) this day. She came over to see her daughter and sat her down in a chair and died suddenly without any previous illness or complaint. I was at Haslehead to visit Thomas Haigh's wife. I was not at Chapel. Mr Eden preached from Job 20.4,5.

12. The Schoolmaster of Hepworth's wife died of a fit on Monday the 9th in the night & buried at Almondbury this day.

13. I was called up between 2 & 3 a clock this morning to visit Mr Thomas Morehouse of Stony Banks son Thomas. I got home between 5 & 6. I went to Cawthorn to visit Thomas Smith. I went into the Church. Sharp frost extremely cold.

14. Cold wind. I called at Stony Bank on my return from Thurstonland. They have sent for Dr Nettleton.

15. I was at Stony Banks in the afternoon to meet Dr Nettleton. I was not at chapel. Sharp frost. misty very cold.

16. Snow sleet very cold. I was at Hepworth to visit Francis Tinker's son Francis, I found him dangerously ill. Mr Thompson was there & prayed for him whilst I was there. I was at Stony Bank to visit Thomas.

18. Frost, a snowy day. cold wind. tempests of snow & hail. I was at Hepworth to visit Francis Tinker's son, he is speechless.

19. Frosty morning & the ground is covered with snow. Francis Tinker's son Francis died this day being the 5 day of his illness. I was at Dan¹ Thorp's in the afternoon to reckon with Mr Hardy for 2 years since I came to Totties.

[2] The correct words should begin "Prove all things" and are from 1 Thessalonians 5.21.

[3] I presume Ioh is a sign that he did not remember the reference, which is 1 Thess. 5.21.

[4] Choppards in Holmfirth.

21. I called at Stony Bank to visit little Thomas Morehouse.

22. very cold wind Mr Eden preached.

23. Francis Tinker's son Francis Buried this day.

24. I was at Newmill to speak to Mr Eden about Articles for our club and spent 4ᵈ. We are to meet at Arthur Hobson's the first thursday in April. very cold. frost all day.

25. Mr Armitage of Blackhouse had an heir born this morning, since dead.

27. Some flaques of snow & some hail. I was at Joseph Goddard's. he is out of this way and I fear there will be a great loss by him.

28. Storms of hail & snow. exceedingly cold day.

29. Sharp frost exceedingly cold wind hail & snow. I was at Stony Bank in the morning to visit Thomas I was there again at night. Mr Eden preached from John 6.54 'Whosoever eateth my flesh & drinketh my blood hath eternal life: and I will raise him at the last day.'

Oh Lord forgive my sins be merciful and grant that this for ordinance may make it more an essential to help to my acceptance of Christ &c. easther sunday.

30. Jonothan Robuck died (on Monday) this day in the morning.

April 2. Exceedingly sharp frost I was at Hollingscove to visit Joseph Hedley. I was at Arthur Hudson's at the Club and by vote was chosen Book-Keeper we made Laws and there was 21 members and I received 3/- of every one of them in all £3 3s. od. and I paid Joshua Wilson 9ᵈ for a Quire of Paper for a Book we spent 6ᵈ a piece & I got home a quarter after 11.

3. I was at Stony Bank in the afternoon to speak to Mr Croft to write a letter to Swale of Leeds⁵ of whom we should have our Books. I was at Wooldale with a letter for Halifax.

4. Honley Fair. The first fair at Honley I was at Honley fair. Abᵐ Woodhead put 3/- in my hand for the Club.

5. They had no service at Holmfirth. Mr Thompson is in the Gout. Mr Haliday preached at Lydgate Chapel from Num: 32.23. we had a full congregation.

6. I was at Mr Thompsons and we sent for a quart of ale at 3½.

6. I paid Mr Eden £2 10s. od. Abraham Rhodes of Hepworth buried on Saturday the 4ᵗʰ. He died of fits.

11. I hear that Dr Holland was buried on Saturday the 4ᵗʰ of this instant.

12. I was not at chapel. Mr Eden preached.

18. I was called out of Bed last night & went to Grice to visit John Knott. I bled him & got home about 3 a clock this morning. Sharp frost a strong cold wind as cold as winter.

⁵ Mr. John Swale, bookseller, Leeds, had a shop at the back of the Shambles there.

19. Mr Eden preached from Rom 6.21-22. I was not at Chapel in the afternoon. Storms of Hail. It is as cold as the depth of winter.

25. There was a fair Shower last night. Holmfirth Fair. Mr Eden was here.

26. Mr Halliday preached from John 9.2-3. I was not at chapel. There was some frost upon the hills.

28. Cold wind. I was at Holmfirth to visit Mr Bray's son he . . . on friday morning had been under Dr Wilson and they sent for me this afternoon he was worse than ever he had been and could not make water & very feverish.

29. I was at Holmfirth to visit Mr Bray's son. he is a good deal better.

30. very cold wind. I hear 4 children at Denby are dead of the small Pox and three children at Shipley are dead of the same distemper.

May 3. Some warm showers the wind is turned South or South-west. Mr Eden preached from Rom 6.21.22.

4. Huddersfield Fair. My brother was there.

5. I was at Holmfirth feast day & bought a pair of gloves at 6ᵈ.

6. I was at Meltom to visit John Osterfield the Schoolmaster's child.

7. Fine showers, hot, Thunder a fine growing day. I was at Holmfirth at the Club at Danˡ Thorp's. I paid nothing, John Booth of Holmfirth was admitted into the Club and paid me 3/- I receive 6d of Lawrence Lockwood and 6ᵈ of John Goddard for forfits because they came too late. I got home about 9.

10. Extremely cold strong wind. Mr Eden preached in the afternoon from Rom. 6.21-22. I was not at the Chapel in the forenoon.

12. I was at Stony Bank to visit George & Thomas Morehouse.

May 10. I hear that Robert Smith of Smithy Place his son who had Epileptick fits a long time was coming from Honley and had a fit and fell into the water and was drowned yesterday.

13. Cold wind. I was at Stony Bank to visit the Boys, the small pox are coming out of George. Thomas is very ill. I paid Mr Jackson 2/- for Newspaper. Some snow or very small hail.

14. Snow and hail. In the morning the ground was covered with Snow. I was at Stony Bank to visit the Boys. The small pox appear upon Thomas. I received the Books from Leeds this night for the Club.

17. Showers. I was at Stony Bank this morning to visit Thomas. I was not at Chapel in the forenoon. Mr Eden preached from . . . 6.21-22. Whitsunday.

19. I was at Stony Bank again at night to meet Dr Nettleton and

got home a little before two. Some thunder. Old John Donkersley of Honly is dead.

20. I was at Stony Bank this morning & staid a good while before Dr Nettleton got up. I hear that the Election for the City of York is over[6] and that Sir John Kaye is outed.[7]

23. I hear that Admiral Vernon hath taken Carthagenia[8] and they have been Ringing the Bells & making great rejoicings in all the great towns and in Holmfirth.

24. Mr Eden preached from Is. 6.6. Trinity Sunday.

26. I was at Halifax and staid while 6 a clock. Dr Nettleton did not come home & I did not see him, it was a quarter past 6 when I left Halifax and about a quarter past 10 when I got home.

27. Windy. hot. I called at Ben Green's, Mrs Hanson, Mr Brooksbank Mrs Nettleton and another Gentlewoman, Miss Cotton and another person are come to see Mr Eden and I smoked a pipe with them. I was at Stony Bank. Mrs Morehouse is very much indisposed.

28. I was at Stony Bank to visit Mrs Morehouse. I bled her.

29. I was at Wooldale at Jonas Hobsons and sent money by him to Leeds to pay Mr Swale for the Club Books.

30. I hear as one of Thomas Heaton's sons was riding full speed the Horse fell with him and the young man was slain. It was last week.

30. Mr Eden preached from Is. 6.6. I was not at Chapel in the forenoon.

June 3. Hot. I was at Stony Bank. Mrs Morehouse gave me some Sage to set, some Tea Sage. Thunder.

4. I was at Holmfirth at Wm Shackleton's at the Club we received new members Mr. Thompson, Mr Bray, Joseph Goddard, Joshua Woofenden, James Crosland Schoolmaster of Holme and Mr Crosland of Cartworth. The Schoolmaster & Mr Crosland of Cartworth were not there, but Mr Shackleton paid me 3/- for the Schoolmaster & Mr Tinker paid me 3/- for Mr Crosland of Cartworth. The rest gave me 3/- a piece. So that I received 18/-, and Jonas Hobson

[6] At York in 1741 there was an uncontested election in May. Sir Miles Stapleton and Lord Morpeth were elected, the latter succeeding Turner. Henry, the fourth Earl of Carlisle, succeeded to the title in 1738 and his son Frederick became the Lord Morpeth here mentioned. Frederick, however, died of consumption in August 1741, which necessitated a second election early in 1742.

[7] On the death of Sir Arthur Kaye, the third baronet, his nephew, John Kaye of Denby Grange, succeeded to the baronetcy. On the death of his uncle Thomas Lister, whose heir he was, he became Sir John Lister Kaye of Denby Grange. He was sometimes M.P. for York City. He died April 5th, 1752, and was succeeded by his son, Sir John Lister Kaye, the fifth baronet.

[8] Vernon had not taken Carthagena. In spite of having a large fleet and army, Admiral Vernon and General Wentworth could not work together and their quarrels resulted in a disastrous failure.

& John Battye paid their forfits for being absent last Club and Jonas Eastwood and Joshua Wilson for not coming in time this Club, so that I received 2/- forfits in all £1. I got home between 9 & 10.

5. I was at Stony Bank. very hot. In the afternoon thunder lightning & rain. Much lightning & thunder exceeding great thunder claps very terrible, and exceeding much rain. I question whether ever I saw it rain faster and it continued a long while. Some hail at night.

6. I was at Cumberworth to visit Norton's wife. I paid Jonathan Hinchliff 1/2 for making me a pair of leather Breeches.

7. Mr Ab^m Dawson preached from Gen: 20.11. Surely the fear of God is in this place. I was not at Chapel.

8. I was at Moorcroft to visit little George Morehouse in the measles. I was at Stony Bank to visit George & Thomas (Morehouse) Storms last night. a very fine growing day.

10. Much rain last night and heavy rain & hail and very tempestuous this morning.

11. A cold wind. I was at Stony Bank and Staid there all day. They say there was frost this morning.

13. I was at Banksmill. I spoke to Dr Thompson this afternoon he was riding towards Newmill.

14. Mr Brooksbank preached in the afternoon from Matt^w 11.28. Come unto me &c in the afternoon from Prov. 14.32 but the righteous hath hope in death. Old Widow Dyson of Hepworth buried this day.

16. Hot. very fine showers.

17. I was at Oxpring to visit Cornelius Bower I set out about 8 at night and got home about 3 in the morning old James Bower went with me, & James Bower & Wren Bower came back with me, windy rainy, very great showers.

21. Had no service at the Chapel. Mr Eden is gone into Lancashire. Old Mr Jackson is come to Totties.

23. For the most part extremely hot. I was at Shipley Lane head. I was at Cartworth & at Cross. I got my dinner at Cross. I was at Mr Jackson's to visit the late Mrs Jackson now Mrs Ellwood who is come over.

25. Extreme hot. There was thunder & lightning & rain last night. I was at Hollinhouse to visit John Robuck. I was at Moorcroft & at Stony Bank to visit Mrs Morehouse she was not at home. She had gone visiting to Totties.

28. Mr Eden preached from Job 1.9 doth Job fear God for nought. I hear old John Robuck of Hollinhouses departed this life last night about half past 10.

30. I was at the funeral of Old John Robuck, I got home between 8 and 9.

July 1st. I was at Snowgatehead to visit old John Starkey.

2. I was at John Booth's of Holmfirth at the Club and went up to Stubbin[9] to visit John Croslands Daughter and came back again to John Booth's. I got home between 10 & 11. Received forfits Mr Morehouse 6^d. Benjn Woodhead 6^d.

5. Some little rain. Mr Eden preached in the afternoon from Job 1.9.

6. Some thunder. Old Alice Beaumont of Smithy Place buried yesterday.

7. I was at Newmill and paid Mr Eden £2 10s. 0d., I called at Moorcroft.

9. For the most part hot. I was at Stack wood hill I was at Middop[10] to visit John Earnshaw Daniel Firth of Netherthong died at Wm Newtons of Thongs Bridge last night. We got done mowing. The Monthly Meeting at Wooldale.

10. I was at Thurstonland at Wid^w Morehouse's and saw Mr Ludlam & Mr Eden there.

11. We got in our Hay. Joshua Bower brought in a load of Peats.

12. Mr Eden preached from Acts 16.30. I was not at chapel.

13. I was at Middop to visit John Marsden's Daughter & John Earnshaw.

July 15. A fine Hay Day notwithstanding there was a Rainbow this morning.

18. Thunder & rain. afternoon great showers.

19. Rain last night. A rainy day. Mr Eden preached from Matt^w 12.41-42.

23. Edward Eastwood of Hagg[11] did shear Oats in the Broad-hills last week and hath been shearing this week.

24. I have completed the 59th year of my age.

25. Some showers and thunder. very hot day.

26. Some showers. Mr. Eden preached from Matt. 12.41-42.

28. Extremely hot, great showers & Thunder.

29. Mrs Kaye of Butterley was here & her niece and she had a small bottle of Sal. Vol: ol[12] for Mr Kaye.

30. They are shearing in several places.

31. Mr Doyley vicar of Kirkburton is come over and preached at Kirkburton last Sunday.

Aug. 2. Mr Halliday preached from Revel: 14.13. I was invited to the Christening at Moorcroft but was not there.

9. Mr Eden preached from Matt: 12.41.42. I was at chapel in the forenoon, and was fetched out just before service began. I was at chapel in the afternoon and went to Stony Bank at night

[9] In Austonley.
[10] In Langsett.
[11] Hagg in Honley.
[12] Sal volatile oil.

for a Book. Mrs Kaye & her niece were here to ask after Betty Turner.

11. I was at Scholes at John Batty's to get him to go to Bark[13] (near Cawthorn) to speak to the Landlord of Wilberclough about the farm. He says he will go on Wednesday the 12th.

12. I was at Stony Bank and gave Mrs Morehouse a Bill for 5ˢ 1ᵈ and she gave me 10ˢ 1ᵈ. I was at Jonas Hobsons of Wooldale with a letter from Mr Swale of Leeds and with 10/- for the last books he sent for the Club.

14. I was at John Batty's to know what answer he received about Wilberclough. He went on Wednesday the 12 and the Landlord says I shall have the first refusal of it; he shall treat with nobody else until he hath done with me. very strong wind.

15. I was at Carlcoats town head at Wᵐ Stacks. I called at Sofley.[14]

16. Mr Eden preached from Matt 12.41-42.

18. Hot, I was at Halifax, I paid Dr Nettleton 9/- for Mr Joshua Earnshaw.

20. I was at Mr Jackson's and at Moorcroft to visit John Morehouses's son John in the Small pox.

21. Rain. some thunder a flood.

22. A rainy day. Much rain great storms. The Rushbearing at Lydgate this day. Neither my brother nor I was there.

23. A fine day. Mr. Eden preached from 2 Cor. 10.17.18.

24. I was at Mealhill at Joshua Booths. I was at Holmfirth at Danˡ Thorps with a book from Mr Thompson belonging to the Halifax Club.

26. I went with John Batty of Scholes to Bark to speak to John Dupledge about Wilberclough farm. He was gone to Barnsley and we went after him. He asked £10 for the farm which was but £7 before I bid him £8 10s. but he would not take it. We had our dinners at Barnsley and it cost me 1ˢ 4ᵈ got home a little after 8.

27. we got done shearing we should have finished shearing last week but it rained.

30. Mr Samˡ Dawson preached from Heb. 13.15.

31. We got our corn this day.

Sept. 2ⁿᵈ. John Beaumont of Netherthong died this day.

6. Mr Brooksbank preached from Luke 15.2. I was not at chapel in the forenoon.

7. They have been very busy in making interest this last week for a member to represent the county of York in the room of the Lord Morpeth deceased. The candidates are Mr Fox and Mr Turner.

8. much rain. a flood.

[13] Bark, Barg, Barugh or Barch, village two and a half miles north-east of Cawthorne.
[14] Sofley, Softley, a village south-east of Carlcoates.

10. Rainy day exceeding great showers, a flood.

Sep[r] 13th. fine day. I was not at chapel Mr Eden preached. Honley feast Sunday.

16. Some rain. Much rain exceeding great showers.

17. I was at Birchworth to visit John Ellis Mason, much rain in the afternoon. Old Joseph Mallison buried yesterday.

20. Mr Alred preached from Job 11.14-15.

23[d]. I was at Netherthong at Ab[m] Woodheads and bought a weather glass I gave 6/- for it. I brought it home with me. The mercury is about the 2[d] stroke below 30.

26. I was at Jonas Hobson's of Wooldale & received some books from Leeds.

27. I was not at chapel in the forenoon. Mr Eden preached from Matt: 16.26.

28. Wakefield Races this day & on the 30.

29. Rain last night. Mrs. Tinker of Cross,[15] sent Josias Hadfield to tell me that Abel Hobson's farm is to let, he hath taken a farm at Oldfield; and she would fain have me to take it.

30. I was at Cinderhills to speak to Joshua Cuthill about Abel Hobson's farm. He saith he heareth that Abel hath taken a farm at Oldfield, but he hath said nothing to him and he thinks he shall now have Underbank but if he doth he will let me have the first refusal of it. I was at Ecklands to visit Francis Askham's wife at John Hadfield's of Bullhouse. Much rain a very strong cold wind as I came home.

Oct. 1. I was at Holmfirth at Joshua Earnshaw's at the Club and got home a quarter before 9.

2. Cold wind: fair, the mercury is risen to 29.

4. Frosty morning, strong wind. Some thunder great storms of Hail and rain a wet turbulent day. Mr Eden preached from 1 John 3.20-21. I was not at chapel in the afternoon.

10. Honley fair. The second fair. My brother was at Honley fair.

Oct. 11. Mr Eden preached from Gal: 6.3.4.5.

17. Holmfirth Fair.

18. Mr Eden preached from Gal: 6.3.4.5. Old John Thorp buried this day.

21. Burton Court. Huddersfield Statutes.[16]

[15] There was a place called Cross in Saddleworth and another in Lydgate and another in Halifax. The first would seem to be the one referred to here.

[16] In various places statute fairs were held where servants hoped to be hired for the next year. They stood about in groups, each wearing something to denote the particular work to which he was accustomed. Some days after the statute fair a second fair was held, known as the Mop, to give an opportunity to those who had not been hired "to mop up what was left".

F

25. Mr Farrar preached in the forenoon from Luke 11.2, afternoon from the same. I was not at Chapel in the afternoon.

26. Much rain great showers. I was at Holme to visit Mr Green's Sons in the Small pox and had my dinner there, and next went with Mr Kennedy to Matt: Hadfield's to smoke a pipe and spent nothing. I was at the Schoolmaster's to visit a child in the small-pox.

28. I hear that John Duplege hath let the farm at Wildberclough to Wortley contrary to his most solemn promises to me on 26 Aug^t.

Novr 1. Mr John Green of Holme's son Thomas died on friday the 30th and his son John died on the 31, about 9 at night. Mr Green buried both his sons this day. much rain a tempestuous day a very strong wind. I was not at chapel. Mr Eden preached from Gal: 6.3.4.5.

3. I was at Scholey and left a letter with John Batty for John Duplege of Barke to reproach his conduct about his farm.

4. I was at Meltom. I called at the School but Mr Osterfield is removed to Huddersfield. Abraham Heeley left Wooldale this day.

5. I received 3/- of Arthur Hudson for John Castle of Brigg who is admitted into the Club in the room of Ab^m Woodhead who hath gone out.

6. I was at Thongs Bridge at Wm Newton's to speak to him about Abraham Heeley's farm. Abraham Heeley hath left Wooldale & is gone to Wood-nook.

7. Warm day. I was at Thurstonland at Dame Morehouses. I bled her.

Nov. 8. Mr Eden preached from Matt: 23.8. I was not at chapel in the forenoon.

13. I was at Stony Bank. Mr Radcliffe is come to Wm Shackleton's to make interest for Mr Turner.[17]

14. Frosty morning. I was at Wm Shackleton's and spent 2^d. Mr Wm Radcliffe and his son the Justice of Peace was there yesterday and a great number of persons met him there and promised their votes to Mr Turner. I was at Wm Newton's about the farm, he asked me £7 for it and I would have given him the old rent, that is £6. for there is but 12 day work.[18]

15. Much rain an Exceeding high wind, excessively turbulent & tempestuous. Mr Eden preached from Gal: 3.4-5. I was not at chapel in the afternoon. I was at Cartworth & at Cross where I staid till the moon rose, but I had an ill gate home.

[17] At the York election.
[18] Day work, a measure of land, one tenth of an acre, the area that one man could plough in a day, a term in use since the thirteenth century. Up to modern times used by farmers in the neighbourhood as a measure for seed oats, barley, wheat, etc.

16. Snow shower. Sir John Kaye[19] is coming to Holmfirth to Wm Shackleton's to get votes for Mr Fox.

17. Frost. I was at Brinkhouse to visit young John Charlesworth's wife I went by Lankside as I came back I called at Joseph Greaves' of Ranaw.

19. Sir John Kaye was not himself at Holmfirth on Monday the 16th, but Mr Pollard.

22. frosty morning, a very cold wind. Mr Eden preached from 1 John 3.21-22. I was not at chapel in the afternoon.

25. Stormy blustering, rainy turbulent. This being the day appointed for a Public fast, Mr Eden preached from 1 Samuel 7.12. "Hither [to] hath the Lord helped us." I was at chapel and I went with Mr Eden, Mr Thomas & George Morehouse and Mr Scott to Ben Green's and spent 6d.

Novr 26. Wm Newtons daughter Lydia married this day (Thursday) to a Boy (Mr Empson of Gool Hall) about 16 years of age, who is said to have an estate of £450 per Ann: besides a vast sum of money (The united ages of Mr Empson & his wife did not amount to 32 years!)

Novr 27. I hear that a man was lost in the way near Woodhead on Sunday the 15th at night and was found dead on Monday morning. They say he came from Ecclesfield.

On thursday the 17th Mr Radcliffe treated the Electors at his own house and one Ramsden that lived at the Mill a little above was drowned as he went home and was not found of several days after; and I have not yet heard whether he be found or not.

I hear another man was pulling wood out of the water at Rippenden which was brought down in a flood, and was drawing out a great piece, and fell into the water & was drowned.

29. Mr Halliday preached from Heb: 9.26.

30. A very pleasant day. I hear that Ramshaw that was drowned when he had been at the Treat at Mill-bridge on thursday the 17th and was long before he was found was buried on the 28th.

Decr 6. I was not at chapel. Mr Halliday preached from Jonah 1.17.

8. Windy great storms of rain. hail and snow towards night And in the morning there is a little snow fallen.

11. Mr John Ludlam came hither & paid me £1.14.7. I hear that Mr. Halliday went to Bed well yesternight was taken very ill and died this morning at Halifax. He preached at Lydgate the two last Sundays. I hear Esther Beaumont of Netherthong died yesterday.

---

[19] Sir John Lister Kaye, fourth baronet, of Grange, Alderman of York. Lord Mayor in 1737. Died April 5, 1752. He was nephew and heir of Sir John Kaye, M.P. for York 1713, 1714-22.

13. very sharp frost. Mr Eden preached from Jeremiah 17.7. I was not at Chapel.

14. Very sharp frost. Mr Halliday buried this day, who died as I hear suddenly of an hour & a half or two hours illness.

Dec. 17. frost, rain & sleet.

20. Mr Eden preached from Rom: 12.18. I was not at chapel. I feel much indisposed.

21. I hear one Mosley of Shipley hanged himself on Monday the 14ᵗʰ at night.

22. Mr Eden was here. I continue indisposed. I hear Dr Nettleton is very ill of a fever.

25. Sharp frost, flaques of snow.

26. Sharp frost. I was at Cinderhills at Joshua Cuthills and took the farm at Underbank of him at £8 8s. od. for six years and I may have as long as I live and his sons do not want it.

27. Sharp fresh extreme cold wind I was at Chapel in the forenoon, but it was so very cold I did not go in the afternoon. Mr Eden preached from Rom: 12.18.

29. A pretty great snow fallen last night.

30. frost. cold, snow most of the day. There is a great snow.

31. There is a prodigious great snow & very great drifts. I was at Holmfirth I left 4 magazines at Josʰ Woofenden's for Mr Thompson.

Old Joshua Smith of Holmfirth buried this day.

1742

January 1. Frost, snow windy turbulent. Excessive cold a Strong wind which blows the snow about and fills the Barns. The most turbulent forenoon that hath been seen this long time. Frost Broke & rain in the afternoon.

2. Windy blustering rainy day. the snow goes apace.

3. Some rain. I went to Scholes but I could not get up Syke lane for the Snow drifts there was a great drift of snow in the lane by Joshua Woodhead's between here and Scholes, the mare was fast in it several times and I thought I could not have gotten through it. I left the mare at the workhouse for the lane was so full of snow that I could take her no further. I rode back through Joseph Woodhead's Close and so mist the snowdrift between here & Scholes. Mr Eden preached from 6 Matt 32. I was not at Chapel.

6. Robert Frances wife buried this day. I was invited to the funeral but could not go. She died in the 78 year of her age.

9. Frost & snow. I called at Newmill at John Goddards, he departed this life about 2 a clock this morning.

11. Frost broke, wind rain forenoon much rain towards night. The snow goes fast. I hear that Dr Nettleton was so ill on Saturday the 9th that he was thought to be in a dying state.

12. Much rain, then snow. Snow all day a very ill day, the great drifts of the old snow are not gone. I was at Mr Jackson's but he is set off towards York for the Election begins to-morrow.[1]

13. Snow goes apace. We hear from Halifax that on Sunday 10th in the morning died there the Learned and Ingenious Dr Thomas Nettleton very much lamented. He was the author of a *Treatise on Virtue & Happiness*. He was born on the 4th of November 1682, and died on the 10th of this instant so that he was 59 years 9 weeks and about 4 days old. He was buried at Dewsbury yesterday the 12th inst.

Jan^{ry} 13. The Election at York begins this day. A tempestuous day of wind and rain.

14. Much rain a prodigious wind, rainy & tempestuous most of the day. Second day of Election.

16. I hear Mr Turner gets on successfully.

17. Windy tempestuous, very cold, great showers and some hail. Mr Eden preached from 90 Psalm 12. I was not at chapel it was so very cold and rainy. I hear that Mr Turner was about 700 before Mr Fox on thursday night, and that Mr Fox was almost come up to him, or was 2 or 3 before him on friday night. How the votes stood yesterday I have not heard. John Goddard's wife of Newmill died yesterday (the 16th). Her husband died on the 9th inst.

18. I hear that Mr Fox's party are insolent and abusive. They threw dirt upon Mr Turner's party abused them ill as they go to York.

20. Great showers I was at Stony Bank with letters. They are riding about to pick up votes for Mr Fox, and report that Mr Fox is but 100 behind Mr Turner. The seventh day of the election.

21. Very cold. Mr Turner I hear was 755 before Mr Fox on monday night.

23. A man came into Barnsley yesterday and said that Mr

[1] The death of Lord Morpeth had necessitated a bye-election, the polling for which began on Jan. 13th, 1742, and lasted eight days. Turner appeared again and was opposed by George Fox. The voting was Turner 8005, Fox 7049. (*Parliamentary Representation of Yorkshire*, Record Series, Y.A.S., II, p. 145.) Very much money had been wasted on the county elections in recent times, which probably explains why after this there was no contested election in York for many years.

Turner was Chaired on thursday at night and all the Town said the Election was over.

24. Mr Eden preached in the forenoon from the 90 Psalm 12. In the afternoon from Eccles 11:9. I hear of a certain truth that the Election ended on thursday and Mr Turner was chaired at 3 in the afternoon, and had a majority of 956.

25. I called at Mr Thompsons I was at the Cross and got my dinner there. Mr Foxes party are very much out of humour and complain very much of foul play and tell abundance of lies and impossible stories.

27. A prodigious strong wind.

28. A Snowstorm a Strong blustering & very cold wind, with some sleet. Much lightning in the evening.

29. Windy, blustering showery. I was at Netherthong to visit Ab^m Woodhead. He was dead when I got thither. The Election at York ended on thursday the 21. Mr Turner polled 8005. Mr Fox polled 7049, so that Mr Turner had a majority of 956.

31. Cold wind Mr Eden preached from Eccles: 11.9. I called with Mr Eden at Ben Greens and he gave me a receipt which he brought from Halifax for Mr George Morehouse how those pills are made which did him so much good from the gravel.

Feby. 2. I was at the funeral of Abraham Woodhead of Netherthong (at Almondbury). I set up my mare at Mr George Morehouses and came home with Wid^w Morehouse of Thurstonland.

4. I was at the Club at Wm Shackleton's & got home a little before 8.

7. Sharp frost all day, a strong & exceeding cold wind snow & hail. Mr Eden preached from Matt 5.47.

13. Hail & rain. I was at Jonas Hobson's of Wooldale for the Life of Lady Betty Hastings[2] which he had brought from Leeds.

14. There is very great rejoicing that Sir Robt Walpole now made Earl of Orford hath resigned his office. The Tories are desperately insolent and are making Bonfires on every side and burning him in Effigy.

[2] Lady Elizabeth Hastings. This is the lady of whom Richard Steele said that "to love her was a liberal education". She was the daughter of Theophilus, seventh Earl of Huntingdon, and on the death of her mother she inherited many Yorkshire estates. Few people have been so universally admired, and she had many distinguished friends, especially among the clergy. Ralph Thoresby frequently visited "the most pious and excellent Lady Elizabeth Hastings". She was the sister-in-law of Selina, Countess of Huntingdon, but though influenced at one time by the Methodist movement, she would not allow it to undermine her zeal for the Church of England. She was rich and generous: the York Hospital, the Charity School at Ledsham, and Queen's College, Oxford, owe much to her charitable work. She was buried at Ledsham Church, where her monument is still to be seen. The book referred to is *An historical character . . . of Lady Elizabeth Hastings*, by Thomas Barnard, Leeds, 1742.

16. I was at Sofley to visit John Wadsworth's wife.

21. I was not at Chapel Mr Eden preached from Matt: 5.47.

28. Mr Samuel Dawson preached from 2 Peter 1.10. I was not at Chapel in the forenoon.

March 5. I was at Morecroft to visit John Morehouse's son John. I was at Stony Bank to visit Mrs Morehouse.

8. I was at Butterley³ to visit Mr Kaye.

11. I was at Halifax and bought Drugs of Madam Nettleton. Abraham Ibbotsons wife of Bankend died on the 9th for which I paid £2 19s. 6d. and I bought medicines of Mr Hulm who is come there and hath Dr Nettleton's physic room, for which I paid 19ˢ 6ᵈ.

14. I was not at chapel in the forenoon Mr Eden preached from Matt: 5.47.

15. The Assizes at York this week. John Beever of Deirshaw buried this day.

22. I was at Yatom to visit Mr Greens Eldest son John. Storms of Hail & Snow a very cold & Strong wind.

27. I was at Moorcroft, John Morehouse was at Wakefield yesterday and Swore in the Surrender for Joshua Bailey's house, he paid 2/6 to the Steward of the Court and 6ᵈ to the Bailiff.

28. Mr Eden preached from Ezek: 18.2.3. very cold wind John Gledhill's wife of Cinder hills died on the 24ᵗʰ.

30. Cold wind. I was at Jouthouse³ᵃ to visit John Rich who is now past recovery.

31. Joshua Smith of Wooldale died on Monday the first inst. He was seized in Totties Lane and died in 29 hours.

April 1ˢᵗ. I was at Holmfirth at the Club at Josh Woofendens and reckoned with the Club. I received 3/- for forfits and 15/- before in all 18/- I have 7ˢ 7ᵈ in hand.

2. Windy. I was at Sofley to visit John Wadsworths Daughter. I called at Carlcoats at Mr Empson's.

3. Honley Fair. John Rich of Jouthouse died on the 1ˢᵗ inst.

4. Some frost. Mr Eden preached from Ezek. 18:2.3. I was at Newmills and paid Mr Eden his quarterage and spent 2ᵈ with Mr Eden & the Bullhouse people.

8. I was at Holmfirth at Dan Thorp's to reckon with Mr Hardy I paid him 6ᵈ offerings, 2½ᵈ House Custom 1½ᵈ for the Cow in all 10ᵈ, and for the Clark 2ᵈ altogether 1/-.

Apˡ 9. Wᵐ Swallow's 2 children of Holmfirth buried this day in one coffin. They died on the 6ᵗʰ.

11. Mr Eden preached from Luke 12.21.

18. Mr Eden preached from Luke 12.21. Esther Sunday.

20. I was at Carlcoats called at Mr Empson's, John Wadsworth of Scholes Buried this day.

³ Butterley was in the township of Foulstone.
³ᵃ There is a Jowit House to-day about a mile west of Cawthorn.

22. I was at Shelley at Thomas Shaw's. A fine growing day. John Smith of Honley died the 7ᵗʰ inst.

24. Holmfirth Fair. Robin Ellis's wife Wooldale died 10ᵗʰ inst.

25. Extreme cold wind. As cold as the depth of winter. I was not at chapel in the forenoon. Mr Eden preached in the afternoon from John 6.54. Whosoever eateth my flesh & drinketh my blood &c. We had the communion & John Townsend paid me 1ˢ 7ᵈ that spared after the Bread & Wine was paid for.

26. I was at Deanhead to visit Elias Robinson.

30. Elias Robinson of Deanhead buried this day, died on the 27 inst.

May 1ˢᵗ. George Beaumont of Netherthong died on Wednesday the 28ᵗʰ inst; buried this day. I sent my brother to the funeral in my stead.

2. I was not at chapel in the forenoon. Mr Eden preached from Matt: 11.28.29.30.

5. We removed from Totties to Underbank this day. Wᵐ Newton sent up 2 draughts & 2 Servants and a Boy. they went 3 times, that is 6 Wainloads. I gave this even either of them 4ᵈ, and the Boy 2ᵈ and 8 quarts & 3 gills of ale.

6. The Club day at Robert Hursts of Honley, I could not go but sent the Book by Wᵐ Shackleton.

9. A very strong wind N.W. I was at chapel in the forenoon. Mr Eden preached from Matt 7.21.

16. Mr Brooksbank preached from Job 1.22.

21. very much rain. a flood. Wᵐ Burn set up my Bees.

22. I was at Gunfit⁴ yate to visit Wᵐ Gaunt.

23. Much rain last night. Hot & Sultry. Mr Eden preached from Matt. 7.21.

30. Mr Joseph Dawson preached from Psalm 119.165.

June 6ᵗʰ. Mr Abᵐ Dawson preached in the forenoon from Eccles. 5 afternoon from Eccles. 12.1. two excellent discourses. Whitsunday.

13. I hear Matthew Armitage of Oaks died on the 11ᵗʰ. I was invited for the funeral for tomorrow. I had given him up some time since but Mr Croft⁵ called there on the 2ⁿᵈ of this inst. and told him his condition was not so bad but he might be cured and he sent for Dr Thompson on thursday the 3ʳᵈ and he gave him some medicine but he lived but a week after. Mr Joseph Dawson preached. I was not at Chapel.

14. My brother is gone to the funeral of Mattʷ Armitage in my

⁴ Gunthwaite.
⁵ William Croft. Deacon, Chester, 1731; Priest, York, 1733; Grammar School Master at South Crosland, 1734; Curate of Honley in the parish of Almondbury, 1734.

stead. I hear that a Child at Holstage fell into a Stone pan full of hot water and is scalded to death.

18. Some rain & thunder There was much rain in some places. Mr Buck came hither about noon and had his dinner here and staid about 4 hours. I was at Thurstonland and as I came back I called at Stony Bank to visit Mrs Morehouse.

19. Some little rain here but there was rain upon Holm moss & Meltom Some thunder There was great thundershowers at Nunbrook at Leeds and Wakefield yesterday and as near as Shawhead. It rained very fast.

20. Mr Buck preached from 2 Cor. 5. first part of the 11th verse.

23. I have hitherto set the account of the barometer at Bedtime but now begin to set it for the morning. I was at Stony Bank at Moorcroft & Newmills.

24. I was at Almondbury at Mr George Morehouses there was Mr Thomas Morehouse & wife, Mr Buck & wife, Mr Alred and Wife. Mrs Summers, Mr Ludlam and a Gentleman he brought with him that they called Mr Dawson, Mr Scot. I got home at 11 a clock.

27. Thunder lightning & rain last night. Mr Saml Dawson preached from Acts 17.30.

July 4. Some thunder rainy. In the afternoon much rain. Mr Jos^h Dawson preached from Isaiah 57.20.21.

5. Matthew Hadfield of Holm died on friday the 2^d. a very rainy day.

8. The Monthly Meeting at Wooldale this day. Matt^w Hadfield buried on Sunday the 4th.

11. Mr Shaw preached from Heb: 12.14.

17. I was at Stony Bank to visit George Morehouse.

18. A very rainy day. Mr Eden preached from . . . 5.4. I was not at chapel in the forenoon it rained so fast.

20. very bad hay weather.

24. I am 60 years of age this day.

26. Edm^d Eastwood of Hag, and Joseph Haigh of Newmill did shear some Oats about a week since.

Augt 1. Mr Eden preached from . . . 5.4.

3. I was at Middlecliff to visit Jos^h Matthewman's wife. I was at Stony Bank their two sons went yesterday to School at Shipley.

8. Mr Eden preached from . . . 4.25.

13. I was at Foxhouse at Aaron Hursts'. I went forwards to Carlcoats to Mr Empsons.

15. Mr Eden preached from . . . 4.25.

21. Austonley Rushbearing.

22. Mr Shaw preached from . . . 10.31. I was not at chapel in the forenoon.

29. Mr Eden preached from Eccles: 3.15.

Sepr 1. I was at Almondbury at Mr George Morehouses & gave him a Bill of 17/- and he gave me a guinea.

5. Mr Eden preached from Heb. 4.9.

9. Great hail storm at Penistone. Old Arthur Kaye buried this day (of Choppards).

19. Mr Eden preached.

20. I called at Wm Shackleton's of Holmfirth and Dr Thompson was there and left his company and went with me by myself and desired to talk with me and said he would have a friendly correspondence with me, and would assist me in any case and would never speak one word against me Thomas Crosland of Biggin died this morning.

26. Mr Alred preached from Heb: 4.1. Abraham Haigh of Fulstone died on the 22nd. Thomas Haigh of Cowdill buried on the 22^d.

28. great Showers. Some thunder afternoon much rain.

Oct. 3. The mercury this morning was at the line at 26, the lowest that it hath been since I had the Glass. A prodigious strong wind, the strongest perhaps it hath been for some years very turbulent none of our family were at Chapel.

4. I was at Thurstonland and called as I returned at Stony Bank, there was Mr Ludlam Mr Eden and Jonas Walker there and were drinking much punch. I got home about 12 o'clock a very strong wind I hear Joseph Midgley the Landlord at the Buck in Halifax was buried yesterday.

10. Mr Eden preached from Mark 12 first 9 verses.

11. I was at Newmill I called on the Schoolmaster and paid him 1/- which Mr Kenworthy gave me towards repairing the School.

13. Aaron Hursts son brought a wainload of coals 10 loads at 4$\frac{1}{2}$^{d} a load. I paid him 3/9. Burton Court.

16. Holmfirth Fair.

17. Mr Eden preached from Mark 12 first 9 verses. I was at Ben Greens and paid Mr Eden 2.10.0. I hear that Nicholas Brammer of Huthesfeild[6] was buried on the 11th inst.

21. Jonas Walker of Thurstonland was here & gave me a note for £7 10s. 0d. The Bailey[7] feast begins this day.

23. A tempestuous day. I was at Pighill[8] to visit Mr Nath Dyson's wife & I called at Thick Hollins to visit Anthony Armitage's wife.

24. Mr Shaw preached. I was not at Chapel in the forenoon.

28. Snow this morning.

29. Exceeding sharp frost.

30. A great deal of snow now gone. Very rainy afternoon.

[6] Huddersfield.
[7] The Bailiffs' Feast.
[8] There was a Pighill at Sowerby.

31. Mr Eden preached from Mark 12 first nine verses. James Cook of . . . died on the 22. George Hirst of Liphill died this day.

Nov. 3. Old Mrs Batty of Scholes died on the 31 of last month and was buried this day. I was at the funeral. She was 78 years old.

7. There is a great deal of Snow fallen. Mr Eden preached . . . 8.28.

10. The day appointed for a General Fast. Mr Eden preached from Judges 2.10.

11. Exceding cold wind very sharp frost. I was at Newhouse to visit Ab^m Woods son Joseph. Old Judith Broadhead of Wooldale died yesternight.

14. I was not at chapel.

16. A snowy day and very cold.

21. Mr Eden preached from Luke 15.32.

24. Joseph Wood of Newhouse died yesterday.

26. Wid^w Tinker of Car died yesterday.

28. Mr Shaw preached from 12 Eccles: 8.

Dec. 5. Mr Eden preached from Luke 15.32, afternoon from John 7.24.

12. Mr Eden preached from John 4: 23-24.

19. Frosty morning. Mr Eden preached from Deuter 30.11.12. 13.14.

25. Jonas Holdsworth of Netherthong buried this day.

26. Sharp frost. Mr Eden preached from Deuter. 30.11.12.13. 14.

31. John Heward of Greave died yesterday.

1743

Jan^ry 1. Windy rainy tempestuous. great hail Showers thunder & lightning.

2. Windy tempestuous day. Mr Eden preached from Matt 5. 33.34.35.36.37.

3. Much rain a very great wind last night. hail tempestuous day. I was at Mr Thompson's who is ill. I spoke to him about the £4 which he owes me. He would not let me acquaint Mrs Tompson with it but said he had told his son of it, and when his son came he would tell him of it before me.

5. Windy tempestuous. A very wet turbulent day.

6. I was at Dan Thorp's at the Club and Auction we sold up all the Books. I went with Mr Tinker & rode home behind him. I had 4/7 in my hands and I sold the books for £2 15s. 6d. so that I have £3 0s. 1d. in stock to get the new Club with besides 2/6 which Jnº Tinker paid who was admitted a member. I hear Anthony Armitage's wife of Thick hollins died yesterday morning. Mr George Armitage of Huroyd[1] died very suddenly in a minutes time in the 69 year of his age.

9. Frost. Mr Eden preached from Matt 5.33.34.35.36.37. I paid Mr Eden £2 10s. od. Mr Armitage of Huroyd was buried yesterday.

16. Mr Farrar preached from Matt^w 6.33 an excellent sermon. I was not at Chapel in the forenoon.

23. Mr. Shaw preached from Titus 2.11.12 Cold wind rain last night.

25. Joseph Hinchliff of Longley his son Jonas the Butcher and Arthur Kaye of Bairshaw who were taken up for Sheep stealing were carried before a Justice of Peace this day. and are both committed to York Much rain sleet, tempestuous.

29. cold windy great Storms of rain & hail. Wren Bower had spoke to Dr Brook of Wakefield to come to visit her son this day. I heard that Dr Thompson was come to see his father in the afternoon. I went to desire him to go with me and we went up together and when we came there Brook and his Son was there and were got to order about the Leg as soon as we went in Brook began to abuse me and said Mr Thompson might stay if he pleased but he had no business with me I was no Surgeon. He was ordering some warm water to foment it with. Thompson said I was an honester man than he, and could talk better both of Physic & Surgery, but he was a rascal and a quack and had killed a woman at Ryley and they fell out very ill. We staid a while and came away together.

30. A prodigious stormy wind very cold Mr Shaw preached from Titus 2.13.14 I was not at Chapel in the afternoon. a large congregation, they had no service at Holmfirth. Mr Thompson is very ill.

Feb^ry 5. John Goddard & I went down to Greens & spent 8^d I came away & mist my way. I walked a vast way. the wind blew my Hat off my head and I lost it. It was so very dark and there was a House by but I knew not where. I called & wanted a light to seek my hat but they would not open the door. I sought it long, but could not find it. I went forward I knew not where and thought I had been towards Hinchliff Mill at last I called at a little House and asked what they called the place and they said Cawswayfoot. I went forwards a far as Ryley then I knew where I was and turned again and had many a weary step home. I got home about

[1] Highroyd.

6 a clock. I had gone a great many miles but I knew not where I went.

Febry 6. Cold wind. Storms of hail & rain. I was at Blackhouse at Mr Armitages to visit Benjamin Lockwood's Daughter of Height who lives there. Mr Oates the Tanner Mrs Armitage's father of Blackhouse buried yesterday. I was at Mr Thompson's at night. Mr Eden preached from Matt: 5.33.34.35.36.37.

7. Extremely cold a very strong wind some snow last night.

10. Old Philip Earnshaw of Holmwoods buried yesterday died on the 4th inst aged about 95 years.

13. Sharp fresh cold wind Mr Eden preached from the last mentioned text I was not at chapel in the afternoon.

20. Cold wind Mr Eden preached from 118 Psalm 6. I was not at chapel in the afternoon.

23. Barnsley Fair,[2] extremely cold wind.

24. Penistone Fair.

27. Cold wind & rain. I was not at chapel in the forenoon. Mr Eden preached from John 8.34. John Haigh of Smithy Place who now lived in the Hagwood died suddenly on the way about Banks as he was going to Honley on Wednesday 16th & was buried the 19th inst.

March 2. frosty morning very great wind. much rain very turbulent I was at Mr Kay's of Butterly. I was at Shore Hall[3] to visit John Wainwright & at Ecklands to visit a Boy of Wid^w Appleyard I called at Bullhouse and at Flash house at John Pashley's and at Askhams the Comb maker.

3. I was at Holmfirth at John Booths at the Club we received two new members Mr Armitage and Mr Haigh of Honley and they each paid 2/6.

6. Frosty cold wind some hail rain & snow. Mr Eden preached from Luke 16.18. They had no service in Holmfirth in the afternoon.

7. York Assizes this week.

8th. I was at Holmfirth to visit Mr Thompson who is very ill. Sharp frost, cold.

10. frost. The ground is covered with snow this morning Snow & hail Stormy very cold winds.

13. I hear Jonas Hinchliff is come off for Sheepstealing having turned evidence against Arthur Kaye who is put into the condemned hole. I was not at chapel in the forenoon. Mr Eden preached from James 3.2.

---

[2] Barnsley Fair was held on the last Wednesday preceding Feb. 28th. If the 28th fell on a Wednesday, the fair was held on the previous Wednesday. A great fair for cattle and swine. Other fair days, May the 12th and October 10th.
[3] Shore Hall and Ecklands were both close to Penistone.

16. I was at Mr Thompson's with a Book. He is very ill and not likely to recover. Old Mr Holdsworth came thither and Mr Thompson and I and he sent every one of us 2^d for Ale.

17. Some small rain. I hear that Mr Thompson departed this life about 7 or 8 this morning. He hath been minister of Holmfirth 30 years.

18. Cold east wind. I am invited to the funeral of Mr Thompson.

19. William Newton of Thongs Bridge had 2 Horses stole last night out of the Stable. I was at the funeral of Mr Thompson.[4] I was in the Chamber with the Priests & Gentlemen, there was 10 Priests we had gloves wine & Biscuit who were in the Chamber & the rest had 6^d a piece. Mr Croft preached an excellent sermon from Psalm 90.12. The Clergy had hatbands. The names of the clergy who were at the funeral were Mr Marsden, Mr Dawbas, Mr Smith, Mr Thomas, Mr Hardy, Mr Haigh, Mr Hodgson, Mr Wood, Mr Royston, & Mr Croft who preached the Sermon and read the Office at the Burial. Mr Thompson was buried under the Communion Table in the Chancel. Mr Thompson had the Gift of Holmfirth from Mr Briggs on palm Sunday the 25th of March 1711 and read his orders & took possession of the place on Whitsunday the 20 May, so that he hath been Minister at Holmfirth almost 32 years. He died aged about 60 years.

20. I was not at chapel in the forenoon Mr Shaw[5] preached from . . . 12.2. They had no service at Holmfirth in the forenoon but Mr Hodgson preached in the afternoon

21. I hear Wm Newton hath found his Horses but the Saddles are gone. Eli Penny's pieces are not heard of.

22. I was at Holmfirth at Dan Thorps and paid Mr Ha[igh?] 11^d and Clark 2^d in all 1/1.

27. Extremely cold very great wind Mr Eden preached from James 3.2.

Apl. 2. Honley Fair, very strong wind, as cold as the depth of winter.

3. Frost very cold Mr Eden preached from John 6.54. The Sacrament Day. Lord forgive my sins and grant that this . . . for ordinance and make it essential to my good. Esther Sunday.

6. Sharp frost. Extremely cold wind much snow in the afternoon.

7. Exceeding Sharp frost as the depth of winter. I hear old Aaron Hurst of Foxhouse died last night. I was at the Club at Joshua Woofendens and received 2/6 forfitures and 4^d for swearing

---

[4] William Thompson. Deacon, Chester, 1705. He appears to have been admitted 12th Aug., 1727 (Herring's, *Visitation Returns*, II, p. 222), though the diarist gives a probable story, especially as he seems to have known Mr. Thompson well. He says without hesitation that Thompson had been at Holmfirth.

[5] Probably Benjamin Shaw, minister at Bullhouse, Penistone.

in the Club time and met with Dr Thompson & went with him to John Booths. I came home with Mr Tinker & got home about one.

10. Mr Eden preached in the forenoon from Acts 16.30 afternoon from Matt: 5.17 much rain blustering cold day.

11. An exceeding strong boisterous wind.

14. Marsden fair.

17. Mr Eden preached from James 3.2.

24. I was at Stony Bank at night to visit Mr Morehouse. I was not at Chapel nor any of our family.

27. Fine growing day. Burton Court.

28. Old James Dearnley of Townend died yesterday James Heward of Holmwoods died yesterday.

30. Holmfirth Fair. John Brown at the Abbey, Shipley,[6] buried on 27th.

May 1. I was at chapel in the forenoon. Mr Eden preached from Luke 12.15. Old James Dearnley buried this day.

3. I was at Wardnook to visit Abm Heeley who is very ill. Elizabeth Hobson died this forenoon.

6. Extremely hot. I was at Holmfirth to visit Mrs Thompson. I was at Stony Bank to visit Mr Morehouse. Elizabeth Hobson buried at Lydgate this day. Mr Eden preached from Mark 13.37.

8. I was at Edge End to visit Robert France the younger. Old John Morton of Wooldale who died on the 6th buried this day. Also Old Thomas Mettrick of Holmfirth buried this day. I was not at Chapel. Mr Shaw preached from Mark 8.38.

14. I hear Old Abraham Heeley died yesterday about noon. He was 84 years of age on the 2: February last.

15. Mr Eden preached from Luke 12.15.

16. Abraham Heely, late of Wooldale, buried at Lydgate this day. I was not invited to the funeral and my brother was at Chapel. Mr Eden preached from Mattw 25.46.

20. I was at Mrs Thompsons and met Mr Thompson and one Dr Jackson of Halifax who had been to see her. I called at Mr Shackleton's for a Surrender which he had brought me from Wakefield Court.

22. Mr Shaw preached from Eccles: 7.2. I was not at Chapel in the forenoon. There was a very good congregation for they had no service at Holmfirth. I hear Joshua Jagger of Smithy Place died on Monday the 16th & buried on the 18th. I was at Stony Bank after Service to see Mr Morehouse. Whitsunday. Rain & wind.

26th. I was called up this morning about 4 of the clock to visit Dr Wilson who is very ill of the cholic.

28. I was at Holmfirth to visit Dr Wilson and called to see Mrs Thompson.

6 No religious house is known to have existed at Shipley. Esholt Priory was not far from Shipley. Perhaps that is meant.

29. Mr Eden preached from 2. Cor 10.16.17. I was at Chapel in the forenoon. I called to visit Dr Wilson. Trinity Sunday. Old Sarah Moresden of Wooldale buried on Sunday 8th inst I hear W[m] North who married Mrs Kaye was buried on the 21st inst. Thomas Robert of Low in Holmfirth his wife buried on the 30th inst.

June 2nd. I was at Cross Mr Tinker is got home from Cambridge whither he had gone with Mr Joshua Earnshaw.

5. very black clouds extremely hot. Mr Eden is gone into Lancashire Mr Ab[m] Dawson preached from Malachy. 1.6.

12. Mr Joseph Dawson preached from 1 Kings 8.27: in the afternoon after service I was at Stony Bank. In the afternoon thunder and much rain, I borrowed a coat but got ill wet. They had no service at Holmfirth in the forenoon.

19. Mr Shaw preached from Rom: 2.16 I was not at Chapel in the afternoon.

21. I was at Halifax and bought a Hat at 5/6.

26. Mr Eden preached. There was no service at Holmfirth.

27. They have been ringing at Holmfirth this afternoon for a victory.[7] Sir W[m] Wentworth of Bretton Hall sent them 1/- to ring, and it was the Steward Mr Witten.

28. Holmfirth People have sent John Battye of Scholes to Windsor to speak to Mr Doyley[8] about a parson for Holmfirth.

30. Some thunder rain in the afternoon. The visitation at Wakefield on the 22[d] inst the Archbishop of York Dr Herring was there and the Bishop of Chichester and they both confirmed.

July 3. Mr Eden preached from Prov: 21.21 in the afternoon from Haggai 1.7. I paid Mr Eden £2 10s. od.

July 8. It is now confirmed that there was a Battle at Dettingen on June 16th between the British forces under the Earl of Stair, the Hanoverians and Austrians on one side, and the French under the Command of Marshal Noailles on the other. The French were several thousands Superior in Number. It was a long & bloody action. His Britannic Majesty was in the Heat of the action the whole time of its continuance, sometime on Horseback, but mostly on foot. His royal Highness the Duke of Cumberland had his horse shot under him, and was shot through the leg with a Musket-Ball. Great numbers of the French were killed wounded and taken prisoners, and they were quite driven out of the field of Battle. There hath been great rejoicing all over the nation for this victory over the French. A rainy day, very bad Hay weather.

[7] The rejoicings were for the battle of Dettingen.
[8] Robert D'Oyley, M.A., Merton Coll., Oxford; deacon, London, 1711; priest, Lincoln, 1713, held the benefices of Kirk Burton and Wickersley in Yorkshire, but had a dispensation for non-residence in both, dating in each case from September 1727. He lived at Windsor where he had an assistant curacy. The congregation of Holmfirth chapel were anxious to fill the gap caused by the death of the Rev. William Thompson.

9. Jonathan Wadsworth the Schoolmaster at Newmill paid me 7ˢ 0ᵈ in full for a long table of ours which he fetched from Mytham Bridge to the School.

10. Showers. Mr Eden preached from Haggai 1.7. There was no service at Holmfirth.

11. A very rainy day, very bad hay weather.

14. I met with Mr Dobson at Totties, he paid me £1 interest. I hear that Mr Dodge a Dissenter minister at Sowerby was buried this day.

17. Mr Eden preached from Psalm 90.12.

24. Mr Eden preached forenoon from Psalm 90.12. In the afternon from 2. Cor: 5.11. No service at Holmfirth.

31. Mr Shaw preached from Matt 25.46. Mr Harrop⁹ a young man whom they have chosen for their minister preached at Holmfirth this day.

Augᵗ 3. We finished getting our Hay. We have a deal of hay & very well got.

4. I was at the Club at Newmill. I got home between 9 & 10. I received 1/- forfitures.

Aug. 7ᵗʰ. Mr Eden preached from 2. Cor. 5.11. There was no service at Holmfirth in the forenoon.

9. I was at Huddersfield at Dr Thompsons where I had not been of many years before.

11. I was at Stony Bank and Mrs Morehouse gave me a little chicken of the Spanish kind.

12. Penistone Races yesterday and to-day.

14. We had no service Mr Eden is gone to preach for Mr Dodge's widow and there is no service at Holmfirth.

15. I was at Moorcroft to Bleed John Morehouse's wife. Amos Bower brought us a load of Peats. Lightening in the morning & rain at night.

21. Mr Eden preached from Mattʷ 7.21. We had a very good congregation There was no service at Holmfirth.

24. I was at Holmfirth at Dan Thorp's with Mr Kenworthy and we had five pints of wine and he paid for them.

26. The Rushbearing at Lydgate yesterday. John Bray and James Brown were at our house yesterday morning and I gave them 6ᵈ but they would not go to the Rushbearing.

27. Longley Rushbearing.

28. Hot. Mr Eden preached from Mattʷ 7.21.

30. I was at Butterley at Mr Kays.

Sept. 3. Cartworth Rushbearing.

4. A very strong wind. Mr Eden preached Gal: 4.18. Mr Harrop who hath now got the place at Holmfirth preached there this day.

⁹ John Harrop., B.A., St. Cath., Cambridge; Deacon, Ely, 1742; Priest, York, 1748. Licensed 14th Sept., 1743. Died 1795 aged 75.

G

7. Cold wind, frosty morning.

10. I was at Butterley to visit Mr Kaye. Holmfirth Rush-bearing. John Hird of Foxhouse brought us a wain load of coals 12 load for which we paid 4/6.

11. Hot clear day. Mr Eden preached from Gal 4.18. I was not at Chapel. Honley Feast Sunday.

12. Wakefield Races.

13. I was at Butterley to visit Mr Kaye.

14. Wakefield Races this day & on the 12th.

18. Mr Aldred (of Morley) preached from 14 (   ) 32. In the afternoon from Gen. 18.19.

24. A very great Drought. I was at Stony Bank.

25. Mr Alred of Wakefield preached from . . . 4.18. A Close day.

30. Old Martha Haigh of Hagwood buried yesterday in the 89 year of her age. She lived last at Bank End and died there.

On Sunday the 4 inst: Mr Harrop enterd to the place at Holmfirth to be their settled minister.

On the 5th inst. we got done shearing.

I got a white Rose in the Garden on the 29th inst and pricked it in my Bosom and took it to Butterley and Mr Kaye & the Mrs wondered to see a fine Rose at Michaelmas & Mrs Kaye took it. There are several yet upon the Tree though it hath born a prodigious quantity in Summer.

Oct 2d. Mr Eden preached from James 4.11. I took a white Rose with me to Cartworth yesterday and my brother & I each took a Rose to the Chapel this day.

6th the first Cloth Market at Penistone, my brother was there. I was at the Club at John Booth's and I received 4/- forfitures and 2/6 of Mr Harrop who was admitted a member of the Club and 8d for swearing.

7th yesterday I took a fresh white Rose in my bosom to the Club Sir George Savile buried at Thornhill on Sunday the 25th of September.[10] Widow Lawton of Nab. buried on the 6th inst.

8th Honley fair. great Showers. I hear that Squire Beaumont of Whitley Hall is dead.

9th. Mr Eden preached from James 4.11. I was at Benj Green's and paid Mr Eden £2 10s. od. quarterage.

10. We had some White Roses stolen off the Rose Tree in the Garden yesterday in the afternoon.

13. I hear that Squire Beaumont of Whitley Hall died on Sunday the 9th in the morning. Cold wind. drisling rain. I was at Mrs Thompsons to visit Mr Harrop who hath hurt his arm.

15. Jonn Hinchliffe was here & brought Coat waistcoat & Breeches for me & for my brother and I paid him 6s 6d a suit in all

[10] Sir George Savile of Rufford, Notts, died at Thornhill on Sept. 16th.

13/- and I paid him 1/- for making me a pair of breeches and 1/4 for half a quarter of plush in all 15/4.

16. Mr Eden preached from James 4.11. I was at chapel in the forenoon.

17. I was at Holmfirth with Mr Kenworthy. I got the letter which is sent into Holmfirth about Symony &c.

19. Burton Court.

22. I was at Cross at Mr Tinker's. I was at Holmfirth at Wm Shackleton's with Thomas Firth. I was at Jos^h Earnshaw's and Joseph Haigh of Holmwoods treated me, when I was coming away I met Mr Crosland of Cartworth and he would needs have me to turn again with him and we had a Tankard of drink. I spent 2^d & got home between 6 & 7. Holmfirth Fair.

23. Mr Shaw preached from Acts 26.28.

25. A prodigious strong wind, and rain towards night.

27. The Bailiff Feast begins this day.

30. Cold strong wind. Mr Eden preached from James 4.11. much rain a flood.

31. A very strong wind very turbulent wind. Dr Thompson came to the Cross and brought a Dr with him in a Red coat who had a servant.

Nov. 2. Great storms of Hail & rain very tempestuous. Dr Jackson who came to the Cross on Monday the 31st of last month says that Mr Tinker's distemper is the Dropsy.

6. A very rainy day. much rain all day, very windy & tempestuous. I was not at Chapel nor my family. I visited Mr Tinker of Cross who is very weak. A prodigious wind yesterday.

10. I hear Mr Tinker departed this life yesternight. It is 18 weeks since he fell from his Horse as he was coming from Woodhead. A terrible wind & very tempestuous, much hail & rain at night. I was at Stony Bank. Mrs Morehouse was not at home. I left a Bill of 14^s 9^d.

11. I was at Cross to visit Mrs Tinker rainy & tempestuous.

12. I was at the funeral of Mr Tinker. We had the dinner at the Clarks & I got home a quarter before 8.

13. Mr Shaw preached from Numbers 32.23.

18. I hear Mrs Lister was married yesterday.

20. Much rain last night, wind rain, a flood. I was at Chapel in the forenoon and was ill wet. Mr Eden preached from Matt. 7.24. 25.26.27.

27. Mr Eden preached from Matt 7. 24.25.26.27.

30. There is a Sale today at Cross for Horses, Beasts, Husbandry, Grass, Hay &c,

Dec. 1. I was at Arthur Hudson's and got home at 9 the schoolmaster of Holmfirth was there and sang a song which they have made of Holmfirth.

3. I was at Stony Bank Mrs Morehouse is at Halifax I staid some time with Mr Morehouse.

4. Mr Eden preached from Rom: 2.10.

7. Sharp frost riming misty for the most part. I was at Cartworth at Mr Croslands. I came by Holmfirth and called at Joshua Woofenden's & spent 2ᵈ, and got the Ballad of him which is made about Holmfirth affairs and I transcribed it.

11. Mr Eden preached from Prov: 6.6. I called as I went to Chapel at Jonas Hobson's of Wooldale.

15. A little sprinkling of snow upon the Hills. I was at Hades at my dinner I was invited to the eating of a Hare. I came home with Mr Harrop and was called at Cross & got home between 9 & 10.

16. A snowy day.

18. very sharp frost. Mr Shaw preached from John 3.16.

22. Abraham Berry of Thurstonland buried on the 15 inst.

Decʳ 25. Mr Eden preached from Jer. 17.7. I was not at chapel in the afternoon.

26. Mr Armitage of Huroyd buried this day.

27. Sharp frost.

28. Exceeding sharp frost. Some drisling rain.

29. Frosty, very cold. I hear that Mr Dickinson[11] a dissenting minister at Northowram was buried this day.

30. I was invited to Cartworth to dinner. I did not go.

31. Some snow, frost, cold.

1744

Jan 1. Frost misty some rain & sleet very cold Mr Eden preached from Luke 13.8.9.

4. Sharp frost. I was at Cartworth & staid the afternoon with Mr Crosland.

5. Sharp frost very cold I was at the Club at Dan Thorps. I received 2/6 for forfitures & 2/6 of James Booth who was admitted into the Club. Mr Batty read us some papers about Mr Croft, They are very severe upon him.

6. I hear old Mr Dawson of Halifax was buried on Tuesday 3ʳᵈ

[11] Thomas Dickinson, educated at Franklin's Academy, became minister of Northowram in 1702. "A valuable and devoted minister." He died at Northowram on Dec. 26th, 1743, aged 73. (*The Nonconformist Register*, Brighouse, 1881, p. 335.)

7. Rain, windy. I was at Cross. Mr Crosland & Mr Harrop were there.

8. Rainy. cold wind. Mr Eden preached from Prov. 6.6. I was at Benj. Greens & paid Mr Eden £2 10s. od. quarterage.

9. Cold wind. I was at Scholes at John Batty's and got the paper to take a copy of it which was read last Club.

15. Mr Shaw preached from Isaiah 5.3.4: Frost broke.

21. We see a small Comet every night westward when there is a clear sky.

22. Cold wind. We had no Service. Mr Eden is at Halifax.

23. Frost. cold Snowy.

26. Sharp frost. some snow.

29. very sharp frost. I was at the chapel in the forenoon. I was not there in the afternoon. Mr Eden preached from Heb. 15. The Comet shined gloriously yesternight and this night. It hath been cloudy some nights.

30. Sharp frost. I was invited to Dinner to Stony Bank but I did not get to go.

Feby. 1. Frost last night. There is a great Snow.

2. Frosty night. the Comet is glorious.

3. A Thaw. the snow goes fast. I went to the Cross in the afternoon. Mr Hardy came there & I staid and got my Supper with them and was lost as I came home and went a vast way and the first time I knew where I was I was coming on the lane from Choppards & it was after 2 when I got home.

5. The Comet appeared glowing[2] a while in the morning Mr Eden preached from Job 27.8.

7. A sharp frost, exceedingly cold wind, storm of snow, strong wind very tempestuous My brother & I were at Sinder hills at our Supper at the Spare rib eating.

12. Mr Shaw preached from Luke 13.24. The comet shines gloriously & hath a very long tail.

19. Prodigious strong wind, I was not at Chapel in the forenoon. Mr Eden preached from James 1.17.

20. I was at Mr Kays' at Butterley.

23. Peniston Fair.

26. Mr Eden preached 1 James 17. I was not at Chapel I was at Home all day being ill in a cold. I have not seen the Comet since Sunday 12 inst.

29. Storms of Hail.

March 2nd. Storms of Snow & rain & Sleet frosty morning. Old John Charlesworth of Swinden formerly of Bruckhouse,[3] buried yesterday.

[2] The Comet was probably that known as the Comet of Cheseaux, remarkable for its brightness and for its tail. It appeared in 1744.

[3] Brookhouse, a farm in the township of Langsett.

3. Frosty. I was at Cross & Bled Miss Earnshaw.

4. Great storms of Snow & Sleet. A very cold wind & very tempestuous Mr Eden preached from Prov: 13.1.

5. Exceeding much rain, Sleet & Snow, windy, & tempestuous. A very wet day, a great flood Huddersfield Bridge taken down.

6. The biggest flood yesternight that hath been there many years Storms of Snow & sleet, very cold.

11. Hail & Sleet. Mr Eden preached. I hear there hath been a terrible sea fight between the French & us[4] and they are securing the Papists in England.

Mar. 16. Old Susan Burn . . . died the 13th buried this day.

17. Rain & hail. I was at Mrs Thompson's in the afternoon and Mr Harrop sent for some Ale.

18. Frosty. cold, I was not at Chapel in the forenoon. Mr Shaw preached from Malachi 1.6.

19. Thomas Littlewood of Dammos came to plough for us. Mrs Tinker & Miss Earnshaw came and sat here a good while this morning.

22. Sharp frost. I was at Hollingrove & Thurstonland & I called at Stony Bank as I returned but staid none for neither Mr nor Mrs Morehouse were in the house..

25. as I went to chapel at noon I called at John Brays of Townend & bled his wife. Mr Eden preached in the forenoon from John 19.11. In the afternoon from Acts 24.25. The Sacrament day. Esther Sunday.

27. Old James Armitage of Brockholes who died on the 24th buried this day. Much rain.

28. Old Sarah Woodhead wife of Joseph Woodhead who died on the 24th buried at Lydgate this day.

29. Mrs Tinker left Cross this day.

30. They have been taking account of the Papists & disarming them this month.

April 1. Snow & sleet, very cold. Mr Eden preached from 1 Th. 5.21. Prove all things hold fast that which is good. I was at Stony Bank at night.

2. Windy, tempestuous very cold a very turbulent day Snow & Sleet all day.

3. Snow last night & frost as cold as the depth of winter.

4. very sharp frost, cold windy & snow showers, as cold as the depth of winter. There is a very great snow upon the moors.

[4] The action off Toulon, sometimes known as the Battle of Hyères was fought on February 22nd, 1744. The English fleet under Admiral Mathews numbered 29 ships, the French and Spanish numbered 15 sail and 12 respectively. The action was muddled and indecisive. The English Vice-Admiral, Lestock, never came into the fight at all. Mathews retreated and in 1747 was by court martial dismissed from the Navy for retreating before an inferior enemy.

7. I was at Austonley to visit Christopher Green, he was dead before I got thither. Honley Fair.

8. Wind, showers, some hail. Mr Eden preached in the forenoon from 1 Thess 5.21 prove all things &c. in the afternoon from Acts 24.25. paid Mr Eden £2 10s. od. quarterage.

10. Mr Morehouse paid me £100 which he had promised.

11. Thomas Plat died on the 9ᵗʰ inst. I was at the funeral of Christopher Green and got home about 9 o'clock. This being the day appointed for a Public Fast Mr Eden preached from Judges 2.10, And there arose another Generation after them which knew not the Lord nor yet the works he had done for Israel.

12. I was at Thongs Bridge at Wᵐ Newton's and lent him £100 for which he gave me a note & promised me a bond.

15ᵗʰ. Mr Eden preached from John 19.11.

16. I was at Ellen treehead to visit Josʰ Danbys' wife as I went I called at Hades at Mr Kenworthy's. cold wind.

20. I was at Holmfirth and spent 2ᵈ with Mr Kemp and Eli Penny.

22. Mr Shaw preached from Luke 14.11.

24. I hear there are press warrants⁵ came into Holmfirth & other places hereabouts. Wᵐ Newton sent me a load of white wheat, the half of it ground at 10/-.

25. Burton Court.

28. Much rain last night. Holmfirth Fair.

29. Mr Eden preached from 2 Col. 8. Beware lest any.

30. Much rain this morning. There is snow upon the Moors. In the afternoon I was at Mr Thompson's to leave Mr Harrop the Magazine for March.⁶ We went to Mr Shackletons and staid awhile. There was Mr Winterbottom. I spent 2ᵈ.

May 3. Dark misty day. Drisling rain. I was at Holmfirth at Arthur Hudson's at the Club. I received 1/- for forfitures. Holy Thursday.

5. I bled Jonas Hinchliffe the Clark of Holmfirth.

6. Mr Eden preached from Phil: 4.11.

May 10. I was at Whickleden⁷ to visit Jonathan Eastwood who is senseless & speechless. I was at Holmfirth. I was at Stony Bank and met with Mr Wadsworth and came with him to Holmfirth to William Shackleton's. he paid the shot, it cost me nothing.

11. I was at Cartworth to account with Mʳ Crosland but he was gone to Foulby.

⁵ Press warrants, warrants for pressing for the navy.
⁶ The Magazine. This might have been either (a) *The Gentleman's Magazine; or Monthly Intelligence*, first published 1731 and continued until 1783. This is the first periodical in England to take the name "Magazine"; or (b) *The London Magazine; or Gentleman's Monthly Intelligence*, first published 1732, ended 1775.
⁷ Whickleden, in Scholes.

13.   Old Thomas Hobson died yesterday morning. Misty rainy day. Mr Eden preached from John 7.24. afternoon from Eccles: 8.15.   I was at Stony Bank at night. Whitsunday.

14.   I was at Cartworth at Mr Croslands and accounted with him. He paid me £4 17s. 0d. and also gave me a note for £6.   Mrs Tinker of Cross removes this day, from Denby to Sandel.   I was at Digley royd to visit John Littlewood.

15.   Mr Crosland removes from Cartworth to Foulby this day. I was at the funeral of Old Thomas Hobson of Mytham Bridge.   He was buried at Leedyate.   Mr Eden preached from Deuter: 32.29. we had the doings at Thongs Bridge, the Company which I was with had our Dinner's at Wm Newton's.

20.   Mr Eden preached from Eccles: 3.15 in the afternoon from Philip: 4.11.

21.   The man which Jonas Eastwod pressed was brother to Wm Sykes of Newmill, Miller.   He is got off, he would not pass.

24.   I was at Wooldale in the morning to visit Abraham Crosley but he was dead before I got thither, he died of a rupture.   He hath had it a long time.

27.   Mr Shaw preached from Rev. 14.13.   Blessed are the dead which die in the Lord &c.

29.   A very great drought.

30.   I was at Yatom to visit Mrs Green.

31.   I was at Hades to dinner with old Mr Holdsworth[8] Mr Harrop came thither in the afternoon.   Mr Holdsworth & I came home together.

June 2nd.   very hot day.   I was at Joseph Woodhead's for a pair of shoes for which I paid him 3^s 8^d.

3.   Mr Ab^m Dawson preached from Malach: 1.6.

5.   I was at Moorcroft to visit Mally Morehouse John Morehouses sister.   Some thunder and rain.

7.   I was at Honley at the Club at James Englands and got home about 11 o'clock.   I received 1/- forfitures.

8.   I was at Yatom to visit Mrs Green it rained very fast & Mr Green lent me a riding coat.

10.   Forenoon windy rainy.   Mr Aldred of Wakefield preached from Luke 12.48.   I was not at chapel in the forenoon.

17.   Mr Ab^m Dawson preached from Psalm 119.136.   In the morning as I went to chapel I called & bled William Turner's wife.

18.   I was at Edge End to reckon with old Robert France but he was not at home.   I called at John Greens of Cawell[9] he paid

---

[8] John Holdsworth. B.A., St. John's, Cambridge, 1710; M.A., 1717; Deacon, 1711; priest, York, 1712; Head Master of the Queen Elizabeth Free School, Halifax.
[9] Cawell is one and a half miles WSW. of Holmfirth.

me 6/-. I heard when I got home that Robert France had been here.

20. I was at Over Denby to visit John Woods' Daughter. I went to Nether Denby to see Benjn Sanderson's wife & I called at Wm Gaunts of Denby yate.

21. I was at Butterly and bled Mr Kaye and he gave me 2/6. Much rain.

23. I hear that when Mrs Kaye came home on Thursday at night after I was come away she was very much displeased that Mr Kaye had been bled and said she would not have had him bled for £20 and sent Robin away to Wakefield yesterday morning for Mr Hardcastle and he was there yesternight at 6 of the clock and whether he staid all night or not I cannot tell. He said it was a very bad thing to bleed Mr Kaye who was in danger of a Dropsy. I would loath have bled him and desired him to consider better of it, but he forced me to bleed him against my mind, and held the vessel himself and would take . . . whether I would or no and he bled a very large quantity. I was at Thomas Fawley's. I was at Holm-firth this afternoon and he told me Mr Kaye slept and he could not be awaked and they sent for Mr Hardcastle.

24. Midsummer day. Much rain towards night. Mr Eden preached from Matt 25 & the 13 first verses the Parable of the 10 Virgins.

25. I hear that Mr Farrar the Dissenting Minister at Ealand was buried on Wednesday the 20th of this instant. I was at Holmfirth at Joseph Woofenden's, spent 3^d. Robert Middleton was there on the 23^d and said I had been at Butterly and I had taken xx ounces of Blood from Mr Kaye besides some that was spilt upon the floor, and said did they think his Master had occasion to lose so much blood and parted with blood every day at stool. Mrs Kaye was at Holmfirth Chapel yesterday in the forenoon and both her maids in the afternoon and the maids were at Joseph Woofendens and never mentioned Mr Kaye so that I suppose it is well.

26. Old Robert France was here and I accounted with him and he oweth me £152 2s. od. I would have had him to have given me a note for £112 2s. od. and I had a Bond for £40 which I have had 32 years without interest but he run away in haste and would not set his hand to the Note which looks very ill. I was at Mrs Thompsons to visit her. I was sent for, Dr Jackson hath been there this day and she sent for me to look at the receipts.

27. very hot. I was at Zacheus Hinchcliff's near Sofley to visit his wife.

28. Thunder & rain. I was at Joseph Firth's of Lane head and hear that Robert Middleton says that they make a greater noise about his master being bled than there was occasion for. Hardcastle went home on the friday he did not stay all night.

31. Windy great showers of rain & hail much rain.

July 1ˢᵗ. A very rainy day. much rain all day. I was not at Chapel in the forenoon. Mr Eden preached from Matt: 25. The first 13 verses. I paid Mr Eden £2 10s. 0d. quarterage.

2. John Battye of Scholes sent me a dish of Fish yesternight. I met Robin Middleton yesternight and asked him how Mr Kaye did, he said he was pretty well; said I what meant all that stir & noise about him. He said that Hardcastle had told him before that Mr Kaye might as well have his throat cut as be bled, and he would fain have been bled last year at Buxton but nobody would bleed him, and therefore Mrs Kaye was very uneasy and would have had him to have gone to Wakefield for Hardcastle that night. Much rain in the forenoon.

5. I was at Newmill last night and met Betty Horsfall the maid at Butterley and asked her how Mr Kaye did, and she said he was well. I said what meant all that stir and she said when Mrs. Kaye came home she was very angry that Mr Kaye had been bled, and that so much had been spoken to him, and the maid told her that I would loath have bled him and would have stopt. She said I should have mastered him. The maid said he got as drunk as a witch at night and went to Bed and slept soundly, and the Mrs was angry he would not wake, and sent Robin to Wakefield for Hardcastle early in the morning without Mr Kaye's knowledge, and Mr Kaye was up at 8 a clock in the morning and was hearty. I hear this day that Robin Middleton said this foolish Doctor would do anything for half a crown, but Mr Kaye had given me half a crown for bleeding him.

6. I was at Holmfirth at Wm Shackleton's Mr Green of Yatom was there and I helped him to drink part of a Tanker[10] of Punch. He was drunk and paid 3/- and went away. Wᵐ Shackleton was fuddled and must needs have me to join with him at another Tanker and I paid 6ᵈ. I was at Yatom to visit Mrs Green.

8. Mr Shaw preached from 1. Peter 3.13.

9. Mr Thompson hath subpana'd several of Holmfirth people to go to York. York Assizes this week.

10. Mr Thompson hath sent subpanas to Mr Harrop, Joshua Wilson, Jonas Eastwood, Daniel Thorp Joseph Eastwoods wife in the Ginnil in the Low at Holmfirth and Mr Bray's wife of Hepworth.

11. Bad hay weather. Mr Bray is gone to York.

15. There was a mighty great storm at Shipley on Saturday at night, that is yesternight, and it rained exceeding fast at Woodsome. Mr Scott never saw it rain faster. For most part hot. Mr Eden preached in the forenoon from Matt. 25.13.

17. The visitations at Pontefract.

19. I hear that the difference between Mr Thompson & Holm-

10 Tankard.

firth people was referred to Lawyer Stanhope & Lawyer Wilson and they have deemed Holmfirth people to pay Mr Thompson £22 besides paying their own charges, so that they had better have tried the cause. Mr Harrop the parson turned tail and proved the greatest enemy to Holmfirth.

22. Mr Eden preached from Eccles. 11.9.

24. I have finished the 62 year of my age.

29. Mr Eden preached from 1 Peter 1.16. I was not at chapel in the afternoon.

30. We finished getting in our Hay. James Senior the Mole Catcher was brought distracted to Holmfirth and is chained in the Workhouse.

Augt. 2^d. I was at Newmill at the Club we spent 3^d a piece after the club and I got home between 12 & 1 o'clock. I received one forfiture.

5. Mr Shaw preached from Matt 6.33.

6. I hear that Mr Crosland buried Dolly his youngest daughter on Saturday the 4th inst.

12. Thunder and rain in the afternoon. Lightening at Night with much rain. Mr Eden preached from 1. Peter. 1.16. I was at Stony Bank.

14. Thunder & Rain. I was at Stony Bank with Mr Morehouse.

Augt. 15. I was at Shore hall to visit Dame Wainwright. I bled her; I was at Stony Bank to visit Mr Morehouse.

16. Much rain very rainy day. I was at Stony Bank this morning to visit Mr Morehouse. I was there again at night, and was ill wet.

18. I was at Mrs Thompson's to visit Mr Harrop. I was at Wm Burns of Mynilane I went over Robert Bower's close and as I got over the wall into the Thongs (c)hurch I fell and hurt my back very ill, that I could hardly go. I went to Stony Bank to visit Mr Morehouse.

19. Windy raining stormy, tempestuous. Great showers and a prodigious strong wind. I was at Mrs Thompsons in the forenoon to visit Mr Harrop. I bled him. I was at Stony Bank in the afternoon to meet Dr Hulm there. Mr Eden was there yesternight & persuaded them to send for him. Mr Eden preached from Matt. 11.28.29.30. There was no service at Holmfirth There was a very large congregation at Lydgate in the afternoon.

21. I was at Stony Bank in the morning. I was at Shore hall. I was at Stony Bank again at night to visit Mr Morehouse who is worse and I wrote a letter to Dr Hulm. A flood.

22. I was at Stony Bank at noon to meet Dr Hulm and we went to Newmill with Mr Eden and Staid awhile there.

24. I was at Stony Bank to visit Mr Morehouse who hath had a better night and is rather better.

26. I was at Stony Bank in the morning to visit Mr Morehouse. I was there again at night to visit him. Mr Eden preached from Luke 12.21.

27. A very great wind.

29. Great storms of rain and a prodigious strong wind a very rough blustering day. very bad Hay weather Great damage done to corn. I was at Stony Bank to visit Mr Morehouse and to meet Dr Hulm.

30. Thomas Harland, miller, departed this life yesterday. We began to shear today.

Sep. 2^d. Showers. windy I was at Stony Bank both forenoon & after to visit Mr Morehouse. We had no service at Lydgate. Mr Eden preached at Ealand.

4. I have heard that Mr Wadsworth got a fall from his Horse and died several weeks since very much lamented.

6. I was at Stony Bank to visit Mr Morehouse. I was at Holmfirth at the Club at Wm Shackleton's. I received 2/6 forfitures and 2^d for swearing.

8. Some showers. There was a Rushbearing from Hades to Holmfirth and Mr Harrop kept them out and they had a great stir to get into the Chapel.

9. A very rainy day, much rain Mr Eden preached from Luke 12.21. I was at Stony Bank after service to visit Mr Morehouse who hath a sore throat.

10. Showers windy, exceedingly turbulent much rain very tempestuous. I was at Stony Bank in the morning, and again at night with Dr Hulme.

11. Much rain, a very great wind last night and a great flood this morning. windy & tempestuous, much rain. I was at Stony Bank both forenoon & after.

12. Windy much rain. Wakefield Races this day and on monday the 10th inst.

13. Last night exceedingly much rain & this forenoon and a very great flood. the water was at the highest half past 10 o clock. I was at Overthong at Jos^h Earnshaws to visit him. I was forced to go up the Butrocher and turn down by George Beaumont and got over into Dr Wilson's croft to get to the Overthong I was at Stony Bank to visit Mr Morehouse.

14. I hear that Huddersfield Bridge which was taken down on Monday the 5th of March last and was rebuilt was taken down again yesterday.

16. I was at Stony Bank in the morning & again at night after the service. Mr Eden preached from Acts 17.29.

17. We got done shearing.

18th a cloudy day, rain afternoon. I was at Holmfirth at Joshua Bencrofts and at Mrs Thompsons at night. They lent me a Lanthorn I was fuddled and was sat down on the side of the bank and Mr Kenworthy and another man came by and would have carried me home on Horseback but I would not ride but came with them home.

23. A very rainy day. Mr Aldred preached from Prov. 3.6 I was not at chapel my brother was there in the forenoon. Some thunder I hear that Henry Pontefract of Thurstonland departed this life yesterday in the afternoon aged about 57 years. a great flood.

28. I hear that Mr Bowman vicar of Dewsbury died on Esther Sunday.

30. I was called up this morning about 4 o'clock and went to Ranaw to visit a young woman there. I was at Stony Bank to visit Mr Morehouse. Mr Eden preached from Acts 17.29 in the forenoon. in the afternoon from 17.29.

Octr 1st. I was at Birkhouse near Shore hall and at Renaw to visit John Hall of Skirhall his daughter and Joseph Greaves paid me 4/6 for what I had done for her.

7. I was not at chapel in the forenoon. Mr Eden preached from Acts 17.30. I paid him £2 10s. od.

8. We got in the last of our Corn.

9. Thunder in the afternoon but I suppose there was much rain in some places. Thomas Charlesworth of Ryecroft who died on the 6th buried this day.

13. sharp Frost. very cold wind. Honley Fair.

14. I hear Mally Morehouse of Moorcroft died yesterday. Mr Shaw preached from Psalm 139.7.8.9.10.

15. A very rainy day. Mr Kenworthy tells me that a writ was served upon Dan Thorp at the suit of Mr Harrop.

16. Mally Morehouse of Moorcroft buried this day. I was not invited to the funeral.

Oct. 17. I was at Meltom to visit Jonas Garbetts' wife.

18. Burton Court yesterday.

19. I hear Mr Harrop & Dan Thorp have agreed.

20. Holmfirth Fair.

21. Mr Eden preached from Acts 17.30.31. Mr Thos Morehouse was at chapel in the afternoon he hath not been there of a very long time before.

24. I was at Stony Bank. Mrs Morehouse gave me some apples.

28. Blustering very strong wind. Mr Eden preached from 1. Tim. 6.17-18-19. Charge them that are rich in this world &c. I was not at chapel in the forenoon.

31. I was at Hades at my Dinner. Mr Kenworthy invited me to a Hare eating there was Dolly Thorp and Jonas Eastwood at dinner. I got home about half past 7. Mr Kenworthy hath a writ for Mr Harrop.

Novr 2^d. A writ was served yesterday upon Mr Harrop at the suit of Mr Kenworthy. windy much rain and great storms of Hail a very story tempestuous day. Thunder & lightning in the morning a prodigious strong wind. A very great flood.

4. Cold wind. Mr Eden preached from 1 Tim 6.17-18-19.

8. Snow & hail.

9. A sprinkling of snow upon the Hills. Snow sleet & rain a very ill day.

11. Mr Eden preached from Rom: 8.28. I was not at chapel in the afternoon.

12. Joshua Earnshaw of Overbridge buried this day he died on the 10.

13. A drisling rainy day. I was at Butterly & Mr Kaye paid me 7/2. Mr Kaye was very kind but when I went up into the room to Dinner Mrs Kaye was very angry and asked me if I was come to bleed Mr Kaye again and was in such a passion that she left the room and would not sit at Dinner with us. Mr Kaye said that bleeding did him the most good of anything, and he was got very drunk when Mrs Kaye came home which made him so ill, and said Hardcastle was a damnable liar, and his physic made his legs to swell and that bleeding had done him more good than all Hardcastle's physic; and we parted very kindly and he thanked me for my visit.

17. I was at Cross to visit Ursula Tinker's sister and Ebenezer.

18. Sharp frost very cold wind a snowy day. Mr Shaw preached from Matt 22.11.12. I was not at chapel in the afternoon.
On Thursday the 18 Octr died the Dutchess Dowager of Marlborough in the 85 year of her age.[11]   more snow.

19. Snow extremely cold.

21. I was at John Batty's, he was at Butterly on the 15th at Dinner, and they never once named Madam Kaye's difference with me on the 13th. Sharp frost, snow, showers.

24 Martha Tyas married to John Green of Oxlees' son Joseph this day.

26. Abundance of snow, sleet & rain all day. a very ill day.

27. I had a stroke of Apples from Stony Bank.

28. Sharp frost all day. very cold wind.
On Saturday the 3 inst Mr Kenworthy and Mr Danl Batty made a wager of either of them £20 whether Mr Kenworthy be a Trustee about the Chapel or not, to be determined by Lawyer Wilson.

Dec. 2nd. Cold rain dark day. Mr Shaw preached from Matt. 22.11-12. I was called out of chapel soon in the afternoon to visit John Woodheads wife at the Holebottom. I came back to Moorcroft

---

[11] This, of course, was Sarah Jennings, the widow of the famous John Churchill, Duke of Marlborough, who had predeceased her in 1722.

to see John Morehouse's wife. Mr Croft was there & I staid a while with him.

Decr 7. Dark rainy day, wind turbulent & cold with wind.

9. Exceeding sharp frost. Mr Eden preached from Matt: 5.47. Timothy Eastwood of Holmfirth buried this day.

12. Exceedingly sharp frost: a very stormy cold wind the coldest day that hath been this winter.

15. I was at John Batty's of Scholes. I was at Mr Newton's of Stack Woodhill. I called at Ben Green's and spent 2^d. as I came home I mist my way in the westfield and fell into a Stone-pit on my back and leg, was so hurt that I could not stir, but was forced to lye there. I supose it was about 6 of the clock when I fell in and it was so extremely dark that other people were lost and could not hit their way. Very cold & some rain.

16. I lay in the Stonepit in the Cliff until Service was done at Holmfirth in the afternoon and then Elias Radcliffe found me and it was thought that about 200 people came to me and they carried me home, for I could neither go nor stand, and was almost frozen to death besides my hurt. they got me into bed but did not expect that I should live. a frosty very cold day.

17. Had 2 persons to wake with me, they are hard put to it to turn me in Bed.

21. A warm day. Mr Thompson came to see me.

22. A strong south wind and rain.

29. High wind, showers.

31. very great wind and rain. On Saturday the 15th I fell a vast way into a Stone pit in the cliff where I lay till the next day in the afternoon before I was found a great many people had been seeking me and when I was found it was thought about 200 persons were gathered together to carry me home.

Abraham Beaumont of Stanbank died and was buried since I was hurt.

1745

Jany 2. Wm Newton sent me a Rabit & Mr Kenworthy some oysters. Some little snow & frost.

5. Mr Green of Yatom sent me a Hare.

8. Frost and very strong cold wind.

9. An extremely cold and great wind. A General Frost.

10. Abraham Booth of Shipley lost & died on the Common near

Haddenley[1] & was found on Saturday 12th. Extremely hard frost.

11. A misty morning sharp frost rain & sleet freezing on the ground exceedingly slippery & very dangerous walking.

12. Frost Broke last night, dark misty & a rainy morning.

14. A cold dark misty day W[m] Burn brought me 2 Crutches.

15. James Bower brought me a Hare.

16. A snow fall last night.

21. Strong cold wind and snow a very turbulent day.

31. Snow, cold frost wind.

Feb[y] 7. Sharp frost clear day very cold.

10. Had no service at Lydgate. Mr Eden is gone into Lancashire. Sharp frost.

11. Sharp frost. Joseph Swallows wife of Scholes-Town head who died on the 8th inst buried this day.

12. Sharp frost. Mr Kenworthy was here, and had sent me a Flaquet[2] of Ale. Dan Thorp came with him in the afternoon to drink with me.

14. The snow goes away very moderately.

17. Sharp frost. Extremely cold wind. My Brother was at Chapel, and hath not been there before since I was hurt. Mr Eden preached from Eccles 8.11.12.13.14.

20. I took a walk to Josh Cuttells which is the first House I have been in since I was Hurt.

Feb[y] 20. Barnsley Fair.[3]

21. Penistone Fair. Frost & some snow.

24. Very sharp frost. Mr Eden preached from John 14.21.

25. Exceedingly sharp frost. extremely cold Our well in the Bank was frozen which was never seen frozen before Since we came hither.

27. Sharp frost. Some flaques of snow fell a good deal of snow fell in some places.

28. Extremely sharp frost. very cold. The well in the Bank is frozen again. Mr Eden gave me a Pidgeon. John Battys' wife sent me some minced pies & cakes, some Tarts and made wine.

Marst 1st. A snowy day.

3. Mr Eden preached from John 4.23-24. Joshua Tinker married Hannah Tinker Sister of Uriah Tinker of Cross the 28 of last month.

5. A thaw, the snow goes fast. John Kayes wife of Netherthong

---

[1] Haddenley, probably Hadingley is meant, two and three quarter miles east of Holmfirth.

[2] A flaquet or flasket was a small barrel with a handle, used by labourers to carry beer to the harvest field.

[3] The appointed days for Barnsley Fair were the Feast of the Conversion of St. Paul and the two days following (Jan. 25-7).

who died on the 3rd buried this day. Joshua Robuck's wife of Holmfirth who died on the 2nd buried this day.

8.   A warm & pleasant day.   I rode to the Cross & down Scholes moor and so home by Shaley Sinderhills[4] this is the first time I have been on Horseback since my hurt.

10.   I heard yesterday that Mr Hardcastle of Wakefield was very ill & it was thought he would not recover.   misty cold rainy day. sleet. Mr Eden preached.

13.   Edward Jagger of Shawhead died on Sunday the 10th and buried this day. much rain. the snow goes fast. I was at Newmill to visit Benj. Green's wife who is speechless. This is the first patient I have visited since I was hurt. I was ill wet and would loth have gone.

14.   I hear Ben Green's wife died yesternight she was here on Feby 22^d last & very hearty. I am invited to the funeral.

Mar. 14.   We had Thomas Littlewood of Damhouse to plow for us & we found him meat drink & hay.

15.   Ben Green's wife buried this day at Lydgate. I was not at the funeral. I durst not venture.

17.   Much rain a very strong wind. very turbulent. Mr Kendal[5] the minister of Ealand, a young man preached from 2. Cor: 7.10.

19.   Old Joshua Berry of Hepworth died yesterday. A man was lost and found dead near Woodhead on the 13th he was coming from Barnsley.

19.   I hear that Mr Hardcastle of Wakefield is dead and was buried last week. Since I was hurt he said he heard I had a good character and was very sorry for my misfortune and could well find in his heart to come see me.

20.   I hear Mr Hardcastle was buried on friday 15th. It was his grandfather that took Nevison.[6] We got done sowing this day, very hot, thunder & lightening.

21.   In the afternoon I was walking in the Bank and met with Mr Kenworthy and he alighted off horseback and forced me to get on and would have me go with him to Dan Thorp's and we had 3 pints of Ale. I paid nothing. This is the first time I have been at Holmfirth since I was hurt. Old Joshua Berry of Hepworth buried yesterday.

23.   I was at Stony Bank this is the first time I have been there since I was hurt.

24.   Mr Eden preached from . . . 3.20-21.

----

[4] Cinderhills.
[5] Mr. Kendal succeeded Mr. Hesketh at Elland Chapel this year.
[6] John Nevison (1639-85). A soldier who had served in France, and became a highwayman in 1660. Imprisoned at York in 1676 he escaped and was finally arrested at York in 1685 and hanged. Probably he was the person who took the ride to York wrongly ascribed to Dick Turpin.

29. I hear Sir Robt Walpole Earl of Orford is dead. He died on Monday the 18th aged 71.

31. Mr Shaw preached from Micah 6.9. Hear ye the Rod and who hath appointed it.

April 1st. I bled myself this afternoon in the left foot and took a great quantity of blood. On sunday in the evening of the 16 of December after I was found in the Stone pit I caused John Haigh to bleed me in the left arm in Bed and to take a large quantity of blood. On Monday the 17th of December I caused him to bleed me again in the left arm, and to take as much blood as he had done the evening before. On Wednesday the 19th of December I caused him to bleed me in the right arm and to take as much blood as he had done before. When Dr Thompson came to see me on the 21st of Decr and I told him that I had been bled 3 times, he shook his head, and said I had bled too much, and it would weaken me. I told him it was by my own order, and it had done me good.

4. Windy some rain. A prodigious strong wind & much rain in the afternoon. I was at Dan Thorps and reckoned with Mr Hardy for 2 years that is 2^s 1½^d for both & 4^d for the Clark. I was at the Club at John Booths' I received 6^d for forfitures of John Booth for being absent from the Club in January. Mr Eden, Wm Shackleton and Joshua Wilson paid me every one of them 1/- for the magazine & Mr Harrop had paid me 1/- before. I only want of Mr Morehouse & Mr Battye this is the first club I have been at since I was hurt.

5. Mrs Kaye sent the Boy over this night to invite me to come to Butterly to visit the maid and sent a horse for me to ride on, but it is so very cold I durst not go.

6. I was at Butterly to visit Mrs Kaye's maid. Mrs Kaye was very obliging to me and gave me 2 glasses of Claret wine. Honley Fair.

Ap^l 7. Rain Hail & Snow. Mr Eden preached from John 8.34.

10. I was at Stony Bank in the afternoon Mr Morehouse paid me 1/- for the magazines.

11. John Booth of Kirkburton buried this day.

13. I was at Yewtree[7] to visit Wid^w Tatterson's son Thomas who is distracted. I bled him.

14. Esther Sunday. Mr Eden preached from John 15.13, in the forenoon and from Rom 12.18 in the afternoon. The Sacrament. I was at Chapel. I have not been there for 18 weeks before. I paid Mr Eden at Newmill £2 10s. 0d.

16. A very cold eastwind. I was at the Yewtree to visit Thomas Tatterson. I bled him. I called at the mill to visit James Battys' wife. They had been at the vicar Mr Royston[8] for Thomas Tatterson and told him that I had bled him and given him a purge &

---

[7] Yew Tree, a homestead in Kirkburton.
[8] Mr Rishton was the Vicar of Almondbury.

ordered him a very low diet, and he said I had ordered for him as well as could be, he could have ordered no better if he had been there. he was glad they had sent for me for they could not have sent for a better, he said that I knew well enough how to manage him, by bleeding and purging, and he had some experience of such cases, and would assist the best he could, and he hoped that we both together could do him service and he would be better.

21. Cold wind Mr Aldred preached from Ps 50.22. much rain in the morning.

23. I was at Stony Bank, I bled Mr Morehouse.

27. Holmfirth Fair.

28. Mr Shaw preached from Michah: 6.9.

30. I was at Joshua Cuttells & paid him 1/- for the Rate money.

May 5. Mr Eden preached from Rom 12.18. I was at Chapel in the afternoon.

May 8. Joseph Hollingworth of Hades Ing. drowned himself this morning in the Mytholm bridge Dam, he was laid upon his face & scarce covered with Water & had his Hat upon his head. Burton Court. Mrs Tinker came back to Holm.

10. The Coronor's Inquest went upon Joseph Hollinworth yesterday & I hear he was buried yesternight at Burton.

11. Thunder lightening & rain. a fine growing day.

12. Mr Eden preached from Rom: 12.18. I was at chapel in the afternoon. I was at Stony Bank after service to visit Mr Morehouse's son Thomas.

16. a rainy day. I was at Newmill to visit George Morehouse's daughter at Ben Greens I got my dinner with Mr Eden. I was at Stony Bank.

17. Great storms of Hail & rain.

19. Mr Eden preached from Psalm 118.6.

21. Benjamin Stacks of Woolraw died on the 17th was buried on the 19th inst.

22. Timothy Swift should have sent hither yesterday morning at 8 of the Clock and did not and the Boy called here soon this morning and said he was very ill and would not let them come yesterday morning and said he could not speak this morning and had sat up all night and he had a Bottle and was going to Holmfirth for some wine, he promised me . . . to send for some medicines yesterday and for any thing I could see was in as hopeful a way as most in a pleurisy but he would not let them come & said nothing did him good. I was sent for again to Timothy Swift and went this night to visit him Wm Holden had been at Mr Royston's of Almondbury for him and he asked who they had employed & he said they had employed me and he said they could not have employed a better, they had done very well, he thought I was a very good man. He

said he would advise me to bleed him again, and to give him a
(purge?) and lay a Blister between his Shoulders.

23. I hear this morning that Timothy Swift is dead.

25. Timothy Swift of Ebson house was buried this day.

26. I was not at chapel. Mr Eden preached from Luke 15.32.

27. Samuel Dixon buried this day.

31ˢᵗ. Rainy day. Mr Crosland was come to Wᵐ Shackleton's to
receive his Rents, and went to him for £6 which he oweth me, but
his rents came in ill and I got nothing. I staid a while with him
& Mr Wood, Mr Harrop, Mr Holdsworth and Wᵐ Shackleton.

June 2. Mr Shaw preached from Heb: 2.3.

7. I hear that Mr Daniel Dyson of Crosland died at Mr Marret's
at the Horns at Huddersfield yesterday at the Club and the Company knew nothing of it till he was expiring.
Almondbury people had a Club on the same day that we have
ours at Holmfirth and some of Honley and Huddersfield and Mr
Harrop and several others are members of that Club, and he (Mr
Dyson) died suddenly among them.

8. I hear that old John Shaw of Swinden⁹ is dead. I hear the
Clark of Cumberworth was buried yesterday after a short illness.
Mr Buck came & staid a good while.

9. Mr Buck preached from 1. Samˡ 3.18.   Trinity Sunday.

11. Some flaques of snow upon the moors.

13. There was a terrible storm of hail & rain yesterday in the
afternoon when it thundered he(avily) at Stockwood hill, Thurstonland, & Almondbury and several other places, extraordinary large
long sharp pointed hail, a very sore long tempest windy & some
rain.

16. I was at chapel in afternoon. Mr Eden preached from
Matt: 12.41.42.

18. I was at George Wood's with a note for Mr Charles Killing-
beck of Sheafhouse, Jonathan Wood says that he is dead & buried.
I bought a pair of Gloves at Sinderhills at 1ˢ 1ᵈ. I was weighed
there and weighed 11 stone and 1 lb—15 lbs to the Stone. I was
weighed at Banks woodmill several years since and weighed 11 stone
14 lbs so that I weighed 13 lbs more then than now.

19. In the afternoon I was at Stony Bank and gave Mr Morehouse
a Bill for 16ˢ 8ᵈ besides visiting 60 times he would have me set down
what I would have for visiting him & I set down a guinea, and he
gave me £1 18s. 0d. Hot day.

22. Mr Kenworthy & Mr Harrop fell out at Wᵐ Shackletons.

23. Mr Shaw preached from Phil. 3.20.

24. Much rain last night.

25. I heard yesterday that Martha Jackson that is Widow Lister,
who was married since Mr Jackson left Totties to Mr Wᵐ Cowill of

⁹ Swinden is five miles north of Gisburn.

Leeds is dead & buried, they say she was buried on Saturday the 15th.

28. A very great shower. I was at James Battyes of Mill to visit him. Mr Holdsworth was there and desired me to call with him at Mr Thompsons' and Mr Holdsworth & me and Mr Harrop send 2^d a piece for ale.

30. Mr Eden preached from Matt 12.41.42. I was at chapel both forenoon & after. I have not been there both ends of the Day before since I was hurt.

July 2^d. I was at Copthurst[10] at Humphrey Kayes. I called at Hades, Mr Kenworthy was gone from Home.

4. Young Robert France was here and paid me £50 in part. I was at Elihu Hobsons, got home about 10. We sold 4 of the first volumes of *Tillotson's Sermons*. Mr Morehouse bought the first 3 volumes.

7. Mr Shaw preached from Phil. 3.20. I was not at chapel in the forenoon.

8. Wm Newton was here & I lent him £50 for which he gave me a note.

July 14th. Mr Eden preached from Matt. 12.41.42. I was not at chapel in the forenoon. After service I was at Ben Green's & paid Mr Eden £2 10s. od. There was Joseph Greaves, Thomas Firth of Shipley, Mr Tinker & Mrs Tinker of Car, Zedbar & Ebenezer Tinker and another man.

16. Cor. Bower of Wooldale got out of bed last night and shot the lock and got out, And they called up all the neighbourhood and sought him long, and at last found him in the wood near Mytham Bridge Dam commonly called Roger Wood and brought him home again. We began to mow. I hear that John Kenworthy was married to Dr Wilson's daughter Hannah this day.

19. James Bower of Townend brought us a load of Peats. very much rain.

20. Nathaniel Berry of Damhouse died this day.

21. Mr Eden preached from Matt. 12.41.42.

22. Nathaniel Berry buried this day. I was at Holmfirth and talked a long time with Danl Thorp and he told me that Mr Harrop swore and cursed most bitterly and said damn and double damn all the congregation many a time.

23. Thornhill Races yesterday. I hear Old Alice Heeley of Brockholes Scar is dead.

24. I have now finished the 63^d year of my life. I bless God who hath graciously preserved me and provided for me so long a time notwithstanding my great unworthyness. Lord I shall bless thee to continue to be gracious unto me protect and provide for me and make me . . . and better for the time to come.

[10] Copthurst is one and three quarter miles south of Holmfirth.

I hear that William Hill of Kirkburton hath drowned himself, he had listed for a Soldier sometime since, and they gave him his liberty for a while and they say that they was come to take him, and was pursuing him and hath drowned himself to avoid being taken for a soldier.

26.   I was sent for to Butterly to visit Mr Kaye who had a violent fit.   He was got out of the fit when I got thither, and they had sent for Dr Cookson.

28.   Much rain.   In the afternoon Mr Eden preached from Job 1.9.   Some heard it thunder, and there was terrible black clouds.

29.   Extremely sharp frost for the time of the year in the morning and very cold.   I was at Butterly and Mrs Kaye gave me 2/6 for visiting Mr Kaye on the 26th.   I hear that Mr Hawksworth of Nether Denby was buried on the 27th.   He sent a servant with a letter to me on the 11 of last march, desiring me to go & visit him but I was not able.

30.   We finished getting the last of our Hay this day.

Augt 1.   The Assizes at York this week.

2.   very hot in the afternoon a very great shower, much rain towards night.

3.   Wooldale Rushbearing, very hot afternoon.

4.   I was at Butterly this morning & bled the maid & came from thence to chapel and set up my mare at Moorcroft.   Mr Eden preached from Job 1.9.   In the afternoon I was on Wooldale Cliff with William Beiver, Daniel Rowbottom and my brother this night to view the place where I fell on the 13th of December last.   I fell directly down a rock full 6 yards, a wonder & mercy that I was not broken to pieces.

5.   I was at Carlcoats & called at Mr Empsons I was at Sofley to visit John Wadsworth's aunt.

7.   Thunder & exceeding much lightning yesterday.

10.   I met Mr Jackson in the Low in Holmfirth and he said he was very glad to see me so well recovered.   Mr Buck was at Burton and sent his service to me by John Kilner.   I hear that Wm Crosley's wife of Hag died suddenly this morning.

11.   Mr Eden preached.

13.   I was sent for to Butterly to visit Mr Kaye and got my dinner with them and walked in the Garden with him.   His hands tremble so much that he can scarce get a Glass to his head to drink.

14.   I saw some oats shorn in a close of Wm Newton's below Brig mill.

15.   Lydgate Rushbearing.

16.   A rainy day.

17.   Great showers of rain & hail.   Rush-bearing from Scholes, Oxlee[11] & from Austonley.

[11] Oxley in Hepworth.

18. Prodigious strong wind, very turbulent & rainy, a very blustering rainy day. I was not at chapel nor any of our Family It hath done great damage to corn.

Aug 19th. I was at Joseph Horsfall at Carlcoats to visit his maid. I called at Sofley at John Wadsworth's and at Maythorn. As I came through Newmill I met Mr Kaye and we called at Ben Green's & had two pints of Ale & he paid for them and we rode up to Scholes and upon the Scholes moor and there parted.

24. I was at Butterly to visit Mr Kaye and got my Dinner there.

25. Mr Eden preached from Ezek 18.2. The fathers have eaten sour grapes &c. A fine day very hot.

27. A strong wind. I was sent for to Butterley and rode upon Mr Kaye's horse to visit him I was there again at night.

28. I was at Huscroft near Deanhead¹² at Mr Wᵐ Denton's to visit Miss Woodhead. Mr Denton paid me 1ˢ 10ᵈ and Miss Woodhead paid me 2/- for what they had of me last year when they were at Austonley. As I went I called at James Garlicks of Meltom.

29. I was at Butterly to visit Mr Kaye. I was there again in the afternoon.

30. I was at Butterly again this morning.

31. I hear Mr Kaye died between 6 & 7 yesternight. I lost one of my Buckles yesterday morning at Butterly & Madam Kaye gave me a pair of buckles.

The Pretender's Son in Scotland. the Highlanders raising a Rebellion this month.¹³

Sepʳ 1ˢᵗ. Mr Shaw preached from Rev 2 part of the 7 & 10 verses. Mr Kaye buried this day in the 34 year of his age.

2. I called at Hades but Mr Kenworthy is gone to Wakefield Races.

Sepʳ 8. Mr Eden preached from Ezek: 18.2. I was not at chapel in the afternoon.

11. I was at Maythorn. I was at Charras there was nobody in the house but a woman. I left word that I wanted 9/- of John Smith. I was at John Swindens of Rhoyd, I called at Charles Askins who is removed from Ecklands to the Rhoyd. I was at James Papleys' of Flushouse. I went to William Booths who now liveth at the School above Bullhouse.

15. Honley Feast Sunday. Mr Eden preached from Hebr: 4.9. I was not at chapel in the afternoon. I hear the Grand Duke of Tuscany is elected Emperor of Germany¹⁴ for which there was

¹² Deanhead or Dainhead is a mile from Scammonden.
¹³ Charles landed in Scotland on July 23, 1745.
¹⁴ Francis I, Grand Duke of Tuscany, 1737, married the Empress Maria Theresa, the daughter of the Emperor Charles VI. On the death of Charles VII in 1745, Maria Theresa's husband was recognized as Emperor under the title of Francis I.

great rejoicing in this nation last week, Ringing of Bells, Firing of Guns &c.

16. Mr Bradley of Huddersfield died on the 14th & was buried this day. I hear that he began to be ill on the 13th & died the following day.

19. We got done our Shearing this day.

21. I was at Hepworth at Joel Morehouses.

22. Betty Littlewood of Dammos married to Jonathan Shaw of Greave this day Mr Alred of Morley preached from John 10.27. My sheep hear my voice & I know them & they follow me. I was not at chapel in the afternoon. I hear the Pretender was proclaimed at Edinburgh on the 17th I hear the rebels have taken Stirlin[15] a Strong place in Scotland not Edinburgh.

24. Thomas Littlewoods' Daughter who married to Jonothan Shaw of Greaves had a child born about 8 weeks before her marriage. very bad news, they say that Edinburgh is taken by the Rebels.[16] The Gentlemen of the County of York have a General Meeting at York this day. they reckon there would be a vast number of Gentlemen to consider what method to take to prevent the Rebels from Coming into Yorkshire.[17]

26. I hear they have blown up the City of Edinburgh from the Castle[18] if this be true it is likely most of the Rebels are destroyed. However things go on the people both of Leeds & Wakefield, they say, are in great consternation.[18a]   Bolton Races yesterday.

29. I hear Mr Croft got a fall from his Horse on the 21st as he was coming from Almondbury and hath broken some of his Ribs in his side so that he could not preach last Sunday and cannot preach this Sunday. Mr Eden preached from Matt: 7.12. we were not at chapel in the forenoon, there was a good congregation in the afternoon. there was no Service at Holmfirth. Mr Harrop went to Honley in the afternoon to preach for Mr Croft. James Batty of Mill was buried yesterday. Mr Dawson of Wakefield was buried on the 26th. Thunder, a very great thunderstorm in the afternoon.

Oct. 1st. I was at Ranaw at Joseph Greaves to visit his Daughter in the small Pox. I called at Thos Haigh's of Hazlehead but neither he nor his wife were at home. I hear the Rebels are still at Edinburgh.

3. I was at Dan Thorpe's at the Club. Mr Eden bought the 6 volumes of *Tillotson's Sermons* for Mr Morehouse. The Chief Con-

---

[15] Stirling was still in the hands of the Government.
[16] Edinburgh was taken by the Jacobites, but not the Castle, the governor of which was General Guest.
[17] The meeting was summoned by Dr. Herring, Archbishop of York. Upwards of £30,000 raised, with four companies of the "Yorkshire Blues."
[18] One of the many untrue rumours.
[18a] For the facts see C. Collyer, *Yorkshire and the Forty-five, Yorkshire Archaeological Journal*, 38, p. 71.

stable came to Collect money to raise men against the Rebels & I gave him 2/-.

6. Cold wind some rain this morning. Mr Shaw preached from Gal: 5.1. Stand fast therefore in the liberty wherewith Christ doth make you free and be not entangled again with the yoke of Bondage. He shewed wherein Christian liberty did consist, principally in a freedom from sin, from the Ceremonial Law, from the terror and condemnation of the law, from Ignorance & Superstition, from both religious & civil Slavery, and he showed that Popery was directly against liberty in all these cases, gave reasons why we should make a vigorous stand against popery and Slavery, and for liberty and made a suitable application. The whole discourse was pertinent to the present occasion, and designed to animate us to stand for King & Country against the Rebels.

8. Mr Croft preached on the 6th in the forenoon from Eccles 8.2. I council thee to keep the King's commandments, and that in regard of the oath of God, and in the afternoon from Prov. 24.21. My Son fear then the Lord & the King & meddle not with them that afe given to change. I saw him yesterday going about with Mr Armitage to collect money to raise forces against the Rebels and they would get a deal of money.

9. Burton Court.

12. I was at Ranaw to visit Joseph Greaves Family in the Small Pox. I called at John Greens of Smaw-Shaw.[19] I went to the Rhoyd to visit John Swinden's Daughter. I called at Josh Greens of Maythorn. Honley Fair.

13. Mr Eden preached from Matt: 7.12. I was not at Chapel in the forenoon.

15. I was at Hill to visit John Morton who is speechless. I called at Eli Pennys. I hear that John Morton died in the afternoon.

16. Old Margt Ellis Housekeeper to Thomas Cuthill of Bents buried this day. I was at Holmfirth and called at Jonas Eastwood's to read the Newspaper but they had none this week. I called at Widw Booth's and Mr Milnes of Flockton was there and we had 4 pints of Ale & he paid for 3.

17. Parliament is to meet this day.

18. Abundance of people are gone to Doncaster to see the Soldiers encamp'd there.[20] they say there are 12000 there.

[19] Small-shaw.

[20] In December 1745 the Doncaster Corporation sent to Marshal Wade to complain of the number of sick soldiers sent to the town for whom they were unable to provide. The troops quartered on the Wheatley Hills were not well received. The inhabitants of the town refused to have the soldiers quartered on them and objected even to admit them to their houses. The chief objection seems to have been that so many were foreign mercenaries. (Tomlinson, *Hist. of Doncaster*, 1887, p. 230.) The number of soldiers there seems to have been greatly exaggerated.

19. very great showers, a very tempestuous day, great flashes of lightening and great claps of thunder towards night and very great storms of hail. I paid Joseph Woodhead 4/- for a pair of shoes. Holmfirth Fair They say there are but 8000 soldiers at Doncaster & 700 at Leeds and how many there are at Manchester & other places I do not know.

20. Cold wind. Mr Eden preached from Luke 16.8.

23. I was at Stony Bank to visit Mrs Morehouse.

24. I was twice at Cross to visit Henry Hinchliff who had eaten a rasher to his breakfast and was as ill as if he had been poisoned. Two of his children had eaten a little and were very ill, but vomited soon and were some better. Henry was desperately ill and had much excruciating pain in his Belly. I gave him a deal of warm water and sweet oil, and he vomited soundly and after some time he was some better. The Baily feast begins this day.

25. I went to Ranaw to visit Joseph Greaves Family, as I went the mist was so thick that I mist my way and went to Carlcoats before I'knew where I was. I called at Mr Empsons. I went to Sofley and called at John Wadsworth's. I came back to Hazlehead and Thomas Haigh paid me 10/- I went to Rhoyd to visit John Swinden's Daughter. I mist my way as I came home and rode a great way and thought I had been at Oxlee but I was got back into Smaw-shaw Closes and was long before I got out. I got home about 8 of the clock.

27. Fine day. Mr Shaw preached from Rom: 10.2. "For I bear them record that they have a zeal of God but not accoring to Knowledge," all against Popery &c.

28. I was at Stackwood-hill at Wm Newtons, and gave him a Bill of £194 1s. 6d. and I gave him £6 which made it £200. I did not reckon the 1^s 6^d £180 was lent money & there was £14 1s. 6d interest. Wm Newton gave me a Hare.

29. Mr Hurst a Clergyman who lived at Flockton Hall and had no cure got out of Bed early on Sunday the 27th in the morning and drowned himself. I was at Holmfirth to visit Mrs Thompson and whilst I was there they came to tell us that Thomas Woodhead's son was fallen into the water at Lawrence Mill[21] and was got under the mill wheel and they could not get him out. Mr Harrop and I went to Thomas Woodhead's to visit his wife who was in extreme sorrow. We staid there until they brought the child dead home. Joshua Hall of Townend died yesterday.

30. We have no newspaper this week either from Leeds or Manchester, which is very strange. I called at Jonas Eastwoods but he had no papers come. I called at Mr Greenwoods of Totties, the Leeds newspaper was come to Huddersfield. and Mr Greenwood read it. Mrs Woofenden wife of Thomas Woofenden of Holmfirth

[21] At Holmfirth.

died on Wednesday the 2nd of this month at night in child-bed, and was buried on the 3rd She was the daughter of Mrs Tinker of Cross by a former Marriage.[22]

Nov. 1st. They have begun to keep Watch & Ward in Holmfirth this day. They had begun in Several places before. rain last night, a Dark misty day.

2. I was at John Booth's to read the Manchester Newspaper. I was at Moorcroft at John Morehouse's and wanted to know when I could have my money, he says he will give it me sometime before Christmas. John Wood of Sinder-hills hath brought an express from Preston in Lancashire that a Body of Rebels were going to fetch arms & Ammunition &c from a French ship at Montross[23] and the Earl of Loudon[24] fell upon them and hath taken 1400 of them which put the Pretender and the Rebels to the utmost confusion.

3. Misty day—Mr Eden preached from Matt. 23.8. be not called Rabbi for one is your master even Christ and all ye are Brethren. I lent Mr Eden the *Mercury* which gave an account of the trial of Derwentwater and the rest of the Lords which were tried and condemned with him.[25]

8. I was at Holmfirth to speak to Mr Crosland.

9. I hear one Smith a Tanner near Cannon Hall hath his House burnt down. And that John Hoyle of Whiston's haith (h)is mow on fire [sic].

10. A fine day. Mr Shaw preached from 2. Cor 1.10. "Who delivered us from so great a Death, and doth deliver, in whom we trust that he will yet deliver us."

11. Misty day. I was at Holme at Mrs Tinker's.

12. Dark misty day, small drisling rain. There are stories abroad that the Rebels are Come forward into England, but I know not the truth of them. The Rebels are come into Cumberland.[26]

15. Frost & Snow last night. There is a snow this morning.

16. The Pretender's declaration was burnt on November 5th before the Royal Exchange by the hands of the Common Hangman by order of the Right Honourable House of Lords and the Honourable House of Commons.

---

[22] Jessop calls her in another place Miss Earnshaw.

[23] A false rumour except that a ship or two brought arms and ammunition to Montrose.

[24] John, fourth Earl of Loudon, b. 1705. Governor of Virginia and Commander-in-chief of the Forces in America. Representative peer for Scotland 1734-82. He died in 1782.

[25] The reference is to the Impeachment of Lords Derwentwater, Widdrington, Nitherdale, Carnwath, Kenmure and Nairn which began on February 9th, 1716, after the former Jacobite rising.

[26] The Prince entered Carlisle on Nov. 17th.

17. Sharp frost extremely cold wind great Storms of snow and a good deal of snow fallen. We heard last week that the Rebels were in Cumberland marching towards Carlisle. we also heard that some of them were in Westmorland. Sharp frost, snow & sleet this morning. A great Snow.

19. Rainy day, much rain, the snow goes apace a flood.

20. We have no newspaper from Leeds or Manchester, neither are there any in Huddersfield. It is supposed the ill weather hindered them from coming. extremely cold. a very strong frost wind.

21. I was at Stony Bank. Mr Morehouse paid me 2/4 for the 6 volumes of *Tillotson's Sermons*. the Rebels are in Carlisle and we hear that General Wade is got thither with the Army and hath blocked them up.

22. very dark cold day, there is news from Penistone that there hath been an Action betwen General Wade and the Rebels at Carlisle and he hath slain 2000 of the Rebels and taken a great number of them Prisoners and the rest are fled away. And they were ringing the Bells at Barnsley this day for joy of the victory.[27]

23. We heard the worst news that can be this day, they say the Rebels are come forwards and hath sent to York to demand £40000 and will come thither and to Leeds and Wakefield. They are in a terrible fright at both places. There was nothing to do at Wakefield Market yesterday, but the great men were busy talking together, and were sending their best Effects away, and abundance of people are for leaving the Town and want to be boarded at a distance from the Town to escape the danger. Robert Middleton was here and says that Madam Kaye is gone to Heath but will come back soon to Butterly unless there comes better news & because she dare not stay there He is going to Holmfirth to see if he can get a woman boarded who hath a mind to come thither to be more secure. He wants me to draw a Bill for Madam Kaye. They say that the Rebels in Carlisle took the women and children and bound them hand and foot and chained them together and set them in the forefront of the Castle so that they could not shoot at them but they would kill their wives and children first and so took the castle.[28] they say that General Wade is going back to Newcastle.[29] A cold dark rainy day. Sleet in the evening.

---

[27] False rumours. Charles was pursuing his way by the western route and with diminished numbers. Wade went westwards as far as Hexham and then returned to Newcastle "as he found it impossible to subsist his army any further." (*Hist. MSS. Comm*, Various, VIII, p. 131.) The roads. too, were impassable.

[28] The kind of lie we learned to call " propaganda " in the two last wars. The garrison of Carlisle was small in number and consisted largely of old and infirm men.

[29] He had only advanced from Newcastle as far as Hexham.

24. Mr Shaw preached from Matt 23.8.9.10. in the afternoon from Rom: 13.1.2. Let every soul be subject to the higher powers &c I was not at chapel in the forenoon. Dark day. I hear the Rebels are at Kendale.

25. Sharp frost. I called at Mr Greenwoods of Totties, they say it was reported yesterday that the rebels were gotten to Otway[30] which is 7 miles from Leeds and they seem to reckon they are in Leeds this day.[31] The Clothiers are gone to fetch their cloth from Leeds and Halifax. They have sent them word to fetch it. Madam Kaye hath been at George Tinkers of Scholes and at John Batty's to bespeak beds for people who are coming out of Wakefield to Butterly unless there be better news today.

26. I was at Jonas Hobson's of Wooldale to hear what news they had brought from Leeds, when he went to Leeds to bring his pieces back yesterday. They say that they are recovered from their fright at Leeds and hear the rebels are gone Lancashire road, and so go to Preston. Frost broke, a close day.

27. A dark rainy day. I was at Miry Lane at W^m. Beever's with a 1 lb 20 ozs of lead to be cast into bullets. Part of the Rebels entered Lancaster on Sunday the 24th. It is probable they are at Preston by this time. We hear this morning that the Rebels have burnt Sawforth,[32] they had heard this news at Marsden and a great many people were gone to hear whether it was true or not.

28. Sharp frost.

29. They say that Mr Eden is getting Men, and several men have set their hands to a paper to go with him if there be occasion. It is reported this day that the Rebels are for leaving Lancashire and are for coming into Yorkshire and so come by Woodhead, and they are for pulling up Holm Causeway to hinder any of them from coming over Holm moss, and some say they have pulled it up. We hear that the Rebels are in Manchester. I hear this afternoon that the Rebels are in Stoppard[33] and have pulled down the Bridge and that they will be at Woodhead this night. A cold wind. I hear this night that the Rebels are in Manchester and that General Ligonier is at Stoppard which is but 5 miles from Manchester and that General Wade is coming from Newcastle towards them with expedition.[34] And it is hoped that the news we heard in the begin-

---

[30] Otley.

[31] The Stuart army did not march through Yorkshire at all, whatever some small parties may have done in scouting from the main body for arms and ammunition.

[32] Salford. It was not true.

[33] Stockport.

[34] All wild rumours. Ligonier was at Lichfield with the Duke of Cumberland as late as Dec. 1st. On Dec. 6 Wade was at Ferry Bridge marching south.

ning of the week that Admirol Vernon[35] had met with the French Fleet and destroyed a great part of them will prove true.   I hear this evening that General Wade's Dragoons went over Blackstonedge yesterday.   Wm Burn & Joshua Newton were here this morning and Wm Brought us some bullets.

30.   We heard soon this morning that a very great Mob was risen and plundering all before them, and was got to Marsden and would be in Huddersfield this day, and they sent from Huddersfield in the night to the Clothiers to fetch away their Pieces, and they are gone for them soon this morning.   They are in a terrible consternation in Huddersfield, Holmfirth, Wooldale, Scholes and all places hereabouts and are securing their best effects.   And in Holmfirth they are getting their Guns ready and Iron forks &c and they are coming into Holmfirth from every side with what weapons they can get.   Some of the Rebels comes into Manchester on the 28th inst.   And a great many of the Manchester people enlisted themselves for the Pretender.

I was sent for soon this morning to visit Daniel Thorp who is almost expiring.   I want £2 of him and he would not let me acquaint Dolly with it.   I spoke to him to let Jonas Eastwood draw a Note for it and set his hand to it, and he consented, and I called at Jonas Eastwood's & he wrote a note and said he would go and get it executed. I was at Holmfirth again at John Booths' and whilst I was there I heard that Dan Thorp was dead & that he died whilst I was there. I suppose it might be about 12 of the clock.   Mr Eden hath been at Holmfirth with a great company of Men and they were drinking at Holmfirth.   I was at Holmfirth again at night at Jonas Eastwoods and he gave me my note and had got Dan Thorp's hand to it before he died.

they say there is a foreign invasion[36] and that General Ligonier is recalled from toward Manchester, which I hope is not true.   If it be we have nobody to depend upon but General Wade[37] who they say now would be at Leeds this day.   They say that the Rebels or the Mob are in Saddleworth this day.   Cloudy for the most part rainy. The Rebel Saturday.

[35] Admiral Vernon had organized a system of intelligence by means of small ships, and he and Admiral Byng were keeping a keen look-out.   The succour sent by the French was insufficient and part of it was cut off. On 22nd Nov., Lord John Drummond landed at Montrose with about 800 men of the Royal Scottish Regiment in the French service, and a small portion of the Irish brigade.   The rest of the reinforcements were captured by the Government forces.   Of three privateers which set out together from Dunkirk, one of them, with part of Drummond's men, reached Scotland, the other two were taken, and a fourth was captured a few days later.
[36] There was no foreign invasion.
[37] Wade, for alleged reasons of ill-health, resigned at the beginning of January.

We have heard very uncertain different news some days past both of the Rebels and our own Forces, So that we could make nothing of it.

Decr 1st. A close day. Mr Buck preached from Psalm 112.7. "He shall not be afraid of evil tidings. His heart is fixed trusting in the Lord." I hear that the Rebels are at Manchester, Mottoram[38] and thereabouts, and that some of them were at Oldham and about 40 of them came to or near Saddleworth to get Horses, Guns &c which caused such uneasiness here yesterday.

It is not known what course they will take. Mr Buck and the Mistress and his Son came into this country to avoid the Rebels. They say Ligonier is at Lichfield and General Wade is about Ripon and his men very weak through cold and want of provisions and not fit for service. They say it is confirmed that our Naval forces have taken a French ship with abundance of French officers in it and one of them is supposed to be the Pretender's second son.[39] It is also reported that they have taken a great many Transports which it is hoped will prove true.

3. Sharp frost, close day. I hear that the Rebels have left Manchester and are gone towards Buxton.

Letters from Manchester to Woodhead yesternight. On Thursday 28th (of Nov) came into Manchester two of the Rebels, and beat up for the Pretender's service, and enlisted several persons on friday came in about 600, on Saturday comes in the Whole Army computed to be about 10,000 undisciplined Men,[40] and with them the Young Chevalier and several other persons of distinction. They have collected the Excise and took off all the Horses & Guns in the Country around. This Morning they beat to Arms and at 6 began to March. They have now left Manchester and are gone off Stoppard road, but whether they go Chester or Buxton road is not known.

It is certain that the Pretender came in on Friday about two in the afternoon. A Messenger came from Manchester to Woodhead and assures us that this morning the Rebels were divided into 3 Columns. One went Nutsford[41] road, another went Stoppard road and the third followed by not known which road. Dec 1. at 9. at night I hear this afternon that some of our forces have met with the Rebels and have Killed 500 of them.[42] Some say Ligonier's men, some say the Duke of Devonshire's men & some say the Earl

[38] Mottram.
[39] The Duke of York, afterwards the Cardinal of York. It was not he. It was Lord Kinnaird.
[40] On December 1st Charles was at Macclesfield. On Dec. 6th the retreat from Derby began. On Dec. 20 Charles left Carlisle. It took some little time for a rumour to spread. The Stuart army numbered not more than 5,000 men.
[41] Knutsford.
[42] Not true.

of Warrington's men at Warrington Bridge, and that the Rebels are fled into Manchester again.

3. I hear this morning that there was no truth in the report yesternight that 500 of the Rebels were slain and the rest fled into Manchester. They say that our Army and the Rebels are drawing nigh and that the Rebels say they will fight them, and they expect to hear of some action in a day or two. I hear again that Ligonier's army and the Rebels are drawing nigh and that Duke William[43] is come to Ligonier's Army, and that we shall hear of some Action soon. They are riding from every part of this country that way where the Armies lie, so that if there be a Battle we shall hear of it soon. It is thought our Army will meet with the Rebels about Maxfield[44] in Cheshire. They say that General Wade was in Leeds yesterday and it is expected they will come to Halifax this day. They say that the Ship which we have taken with a great many French Officers on board is brought to Deal, and that one Kelly who fled away the last rebellion and the late Earl of Derwentwater's Son are with them.[45] It is reported that several travelling Scotchmen are with the Rebels. The late Earl of Derwentwater hath no son living, it is Mr. Radcliff a relation of his who is taken. Dan Thorp buried this day. I was invited to the funeral.

4. We hear that yesterday was heard Cannon playing for a long time so that it is thought the Battle between General Ligonier and the Rebels is over. We are impatient to hear further advice. Some say that the Rebels are entered into a Town and Ligonier hath blocked them up, and that they offered to make their escape.[46] I was at Wm Shackleton's to read the Leeds Newspaper.

5. Fresh cloudy. The Ship which the Sheerness Privateer Captn Bully took was formerly called the *Soleil* but now the *Esperance*. There was Mr Radcliffe who calls himself the Earl of Derwentwater some French and Scotch officers, and it is thought the Pretender's second Son is amongst them. His middle fingers are grown together[47] They are conducting them to the Tower under a Strong

[43] William, Duke of Cumberland.
[44] Macclesfield.
[45] Charles Radcliffe, *de jure* fifth Earl of Derwentwater. Born 1693. Surrendered at Preston, Nov. 13, 1715, but escaped in December to France, where he became an officer in the French Army. He was taken prisoner on his way to England to join Prince Charles Edward. The ship was the *Esperance* and wis bringing supplies to Prince Charles. His son, Viscount Kinnaird was with him, and the captors observed some resemblance to the Chevalier's younger son, and imagined that they had captured James III and his son, the Duke of York. Kinnaird and four French officers were liberated on parole and returned to France. The father was beheaded on Tower Hill on December 8th, 1746.
[46] Mere rumours.
[47] See J. J. Foster, *The Stuarts*, 1707. Facing p. 242 is a reproduction of the portrait of the Cardinal in the possession of the Duke of Hamilton. It shows both hands clearly without any such deformity.

guard. There are flying reports this morning that there hath been an engagement, and the Rebels are defeated, others say that our Army is gone further back and that the Rebels are returning, others say that the Rebels have given them the slip. It is thought that the Rebels will go to Wales if they can get. they say they were got to a Town a little East Maxfield. Maxfield is about 20 miles distance from Holmfirth, and 13 miles from Manchester. I was at Wm Shackleton's to read the newspaper. I was at the Club at John Booth's. The Rebels have given our Army the Slip and got to Derby yesternight, and it is said will go forward towards London.

George Alred went towards Manchester and a Scotchman with him and left their Horses on this side Manchester and met with some Soldiers and drank with them there, and George rid behind a Rebel Officer to Manchester, and drank with them there, and then went into a room by themselves and drank a Health to King George and Confusion to the Rebels which they heard and came into the room and threatened to kill them, and when they left Manchester, took them both with them. The Scotchman watched for an opportunity and ran away and made his escape, and when he came away they were guarding George Alred on the way with drawn swords about him. Frost. cloudy.

Dec. 6th. A dark close day and Cold. Cornelius Bower's wife of Oxspring died on Wednesday 4th. She had been above 5 weeks ill of a Fever. Her sister George Moorhouse's wife of Lydgate is very ill of a Fever and I fear will not recover this is the 16th day. I now hear that the Rebel Army have left Maxfield, Leek in Stafford-shire, and Congleton and are gone to Darby and Asburn and that many desert from them and that Duke William & General Ligonier are going full march after them, and are within 5 miles of them. They say that the Rebels are vastly more cruel and inhuman since they left Preston and Manchester.[48] They say that Duke William and Ligonier have an army of 17000 men.

7. We hear that a party of our Men have surprised and taken the Rebel Carriages as they were about passing the River Trent. It hath been often affirmed that the Rebels leave abundance of Lice behind them where they come, and that Manchester is very full of Lice, and that a great many of the Rebel Army are such Lousy tatter'd nasty Creatures as never was seen. Cornelius Bowers' wife buried at Lydgate this day. A close dark day, sleet & cold.

8. We hear that the Rebels left Darby and are gotten to Ashburn and are returning, and that our forces are in full march after them. We hear again that part of the Rebels are coming back and have sent to Manchester to provide for them, and that they are arming in Stoppard & Manchester and are resolved not to receive them. They

---

[48] There was much more disregard of the prohibition against looting during the return march from Derby.

say that Ligonier is indisposed and that part of the Duke's forces
fell on the vanguard of the Rebels and pushed 600 of them into the
Trent and that another party of them fell upon the Rear and took
their Carriages from them, and that General Wade's horse are got
to Doncaster and the foot to Ferry Bridge.

they say that Several from Penistone went towards the Rebel Army
and lodged at some distance and some of the Rebels came in the
night and broke into the House and took their Horses, boots &c and
that great Jonathan Wadsworth the Shop keeper and another man
were gone after them to the Army to see if they could get their
Horses again.   We hear that the Rebels have shot a young Man,
but whether it was George Alred or not is not known.   We hear
nothing of Mr & Mrs Alreds being come back from seeking their son.
the Rebels had forced Mr Perkin, the Usher to the Parson at
Penistone School to be their Hostler and take care of their Horses.
Mr Eden preached from Gal: 6.3.4.5.   We hear that a great part
of the Rebel Army is blocked up in Darby.

they say there hath been a desperate plot discovered at London
to blow up White Hall, the Parliament House &c.[49]   A close, dark
day very cold.   Some snow towards evening.

9.   Another cold dark day.   Snowy.   There is some snow lies
upon the Moors.   I hear that between 3 and 4 thousand of the Rebels
are come back into Stoppard and Manchester.   I hear that they
have taken and imprisoned some of the Rebels at Darby.   I hear
that 2000 of Wade's Horse were in Doncaster on Friday to join
the Duke and were with him before this time, they say that a number
of the Rebels came by the Watch at a certain place and would not
stand, but one of the Watch shot after one of them and wounded
his Horse and he alighted and threw a little Book into the Wain rut
and outrun the Watch, but they found the book which gives an
account of all the Chiefs which are concerned in the Conspiracy both
in England and Scotland George Alred hath made his Escape and
got home yesterday at noon but it is not known where Mr & Mrs
Alred are.   They say George hath brought a fine Horse of the Rebels
with him.

10.   A close dark cold day a small drisling rain & sleet.   We hear
that they were bringing their Horses (Tuesday) into the Country
again for fear of the Rebels and that they begin to be uneasy in
Holmfirth again for fear of a visit from some party of the Rebels.
We also hear that the Rebels are blocked up in Derby but we know
not which is truth.   Some men came into Newmill to Ben Green's
yesternight with some Horses, and Jonas Eastwood the Constable,
John Booth &c are gone to Newmill to examine them.   I hear that
they have examined the Strangers at Newmill, and that they are
gone off towards Marsden.

[49] More rumours.

I hear that the Rebels are blocked up in Derby but that 400 Horse have got out of the town and made their escape. I hear that the Rebels are some of them got to Woodhead and some of them coming over Holm Causway. However this be they are in greater consternation in Holmfirth than they were on Saturday 30th of last month. I hear that the Rebels have had a Skirmish with the People at Ashton and have killed many of them, & that they have killed some of the Rebels. I hear that the Rebels called at a Man's House (a Shoe-maker) to take his Horse and all went away but one who was left to bring away the Horse, and the man shot after him, and after some time he dropt, and a Company of the Rebels turned again in the night & burnt his House and Laith,[50] Hay and Corn. All this is uncertain News. They say the neighbours all around rose with great shouts and the Rebels fled away. I hear that General Wades Men were encamped on Wakefield Outwoods and he hath sent some of them to Huddersfield this afternoon to give them notice of his coming, and they are very busy in making preparations for them, and expect them either tonight or tomorrow. We hear that the Rebels are gone away towards Wales they say that the Pretender hath made his escape and is gone. they say this evening that the men at Newmill are secured and have their hands tied upon their backs.[51]

11th. Sharp frost. Close dark day. A company of the Rebels are in Ashton[52] Abundance of people went to Woodhead to hear news. Jonothan Wood went thither for Loads but came home empty for no carriers were come. General Wade's men they say are in Huddersfield & Halifax, but they think the Rebels will go back to Scotland. I hear Mr & Mrs Alred are got home. The strangers at Newmill gave a good account of themselves and some of them were related to Mr Mathewman and were dismissed. We have no newspapers this week. Anthony Armitage sent his son for his Gun this day.

12. Sharp Frost & cold. I spoke with Mr Jackson this forenoon as he was going from Holmfirth towards Sinderhills. I hear the Rebels are about Preston, and are going back to Scotland. They say the Royal Hunters[53] and a great many of General Wade's Dragoons are in Huddersfield and the rest of the Army at Leeds and will be at Halifax this day. They say a great many people here-

---

[50] Laith, a northern word for barn.
[51] Wild stories going about.
[52] They had begun their retreat before this unless some had been left behind.
[53] This Royal Regiment of Hunters was a volunteer regiment formed in Yorkshire under General Oglethorpe for service during the '45 rebellion. It was presumably disbanded after the suppression of the rebellion. It has been called "the germ of the Yeomanry." (Etlinger's *James Edward Oglethorpe*, 1936, pp. 259-63.)

abouts are gone to Huddersfield to see the Soldiers. They say the Rebels are at Preston, and the Duke at Manchester. They say the Rebels left Manchester yesterday morning and the Duke came into Manchester in the afternoon A great many of Wade's Soldiers came through Almondbury yesterday to Huddersfield and went away betime this morning and was going up Paddock and received an Express and turned again and went through Huddersfield towards Halifax. A great many of the Soldiers staid in Almondbury last night, and Mr George Morehouse had 4 Troopers and 5 Horses. they say that the Rebels have used them in Manchester ten times worse this time than they had before.

The Schoolmaster of Newmill sent a letter about the Rebels dated the 4th at 9 in the morning, which was read in the Club on the 5th, and he hath sent no letter since and nothing is heard of him.

13. Sharp frost. A close misty dark day an extremely cold strong wind. The Coldest day we have had this winter, wind rain & sleet in the evening. I was at Lydgate to visit George Morehouses wife, called at Ben Green's & carried Mr Eden the 2nd volume of Burnet's History[54] &c which I had borrowed. I hear the Rebels are gone towards Preston they have used them ill at Manchester. have made them pay £2,500[55] to avoid military execution and besides have plundered and ruined several good Houses. They are as is thought hastening back to Scotland and our men pursuing after them. The Schoolmaster of Newmill came home yesternight. The Rebels say they are going back to Scotland but threaten to come again at the spring with a great Army and overrun all. They say the Pretender never came farther than Edinburgh but another goes with the Rebels who personates the Pretender.

14. A close dark rainy day. They say Duke William is in full march after the Rebels and it is hoped will come up with their Baggage this day. They say that Duke William hath overtaken the Rebels and destroyed most of them. I called at Wm Shackleton's to borrow a newspaper, but Mr Harrop had it. I went to Mr Thompsons for the newspaper and Mr Harrop came with me to Wm Shackleton's and spent 2d.

15. A close dark thick mist. Mr Eden preached from Gal: 6.3. 4.5. I hear the Rebels were caught at Preston and that the Royal Hunters and some of the light Horse were got before them and stop'd them,[56] and that young John Goddard came from Manchester yesterday as far as Marsden and came home this morning

[54] Burnet's *History of My Own Times.*

[55] Owing to the attacks of the mob at Manchester, Charles levied a fine of £5,000 on the town. There was considerable looting with some violence on their return journey.

[56] What really happened was that a body of Cumberland's men attacked the Stuart rearguard under Lord George Murray near Penrith but were driven off with the loss of a hundred men.

and says he heard a Letter read from Thomas Syddal to his wife which said there was nothing but death and confusion before them. We hear the Rebels demanded a Contribution of £30000 of the Town of Derby and that the Inhabitants paid down £16,000 and gave 2 Hostages for the payment of the remainder.

16. A close dark day cold wind and rain in the afternoon. It is just a year since this day since I was found in the Cliff and brought home in so sad a condition that my life was despaired of. There are flying reports that we have taken the Pretender and the Duke of Perth[57] they say also that the country people stop'd the Rebels at Rossington[58] and our forces have defeated them.

17. They say that the Royal Hunters stop'd the Rebels but the Rebels killed some say 13 and some say 30 of them and that they killed some of the Rebels & that the Rebels are in Preston and they expect an engagement either yesterday or today. Others say they have taken the Pretender. They say Jonothan Thornelly was at Milnsbridge yesterday in the evening and they say he reported that an express came thither that there had been an engagement and that a great many of the Rebels were killed. They say the Rebels are encamped past Preston and that 1300 have made their escape and are coming this way, they say the Rebels are not met with at Preston but at Garstang a good way off Preston. A close dark day rainy, but warmer.

18. A General Fast. The Rebels have given our Army the slip. They left Lancaster at 8 on Saturday the 14th at night and it is not doubted but they are at Carlisle by this time, and will go directly into Scotland there being no sufficient force to oppose them. It is feared there will be hard work to suppress them now. Duke William hath been disappointed in pursuing them. Though we are delivered from our fears here yet in the whole we are in a worse condition. They say the Rebels are such a Shabby lousy crew as was never seen, they stink abominably that nobody can come near them. Mr Shaw preached from Luke 13.3.5. Except ye repent ye shall likewise perish. after service my brother & I went to Ben Green's with Mr Shaw, Mr Scot, Mr Tho⁵ & Geo Morehouse and we spent 6ᵈ a piece.

The Rebels were in the utmost terror & confusion upon the approach of the Duke and fled with the utmost rapidity, we are in great fear

[57] James, third titular Duke of Perth, was not captured. He was wounded at Culloden and died on 13th May, 1746, on the French frigate in which he was escaping to France. He was attainted in 1746, but was already dead. The attainder took effect on his only brother, John, "the person taking upon himself the rank and style of Lord John Drummond." He became the fourth titular Duke, but all the Drummond estates were seized by the Crown. He died in 1747.

[58] Rossington is near Doncaster. At this time the Jacobite army was nearing the Border.

of a French invasion and are taking the utmost we can to prevent it.

19. The Rebels went to the town of Derby, & then returned. Maxfield, Manchester, Preston, Lancaster &c. have been visited twice by them, that is as they came southward [and] as they return Scotland is like to be the scene of Bloodshed. The Rebels have done incredible damage. A prodigious strong wind, rainy.

20. They say the Rebels could not pass the water at Carlisle and are met with and our men have killed several thousands of them and the rest are fled without arms and the country people will destroy them all. They say they have taken a Chest of Money from the Rebels. Cloudy, windy, Rain in the afternoon.

21. Cloudy, windy & rainy.

22nd. Mr Eden preached from Gal: 6.3.4.5. They had stop'd a Rebel at Lydgate & came to tell Mr Eden when Service was done in the forenoon, and Mr Morehouse & he went to examine him and sent for the Constable & they have taken him to Arthur Hudson's. I hear the Rebels were stop't in the North by some of Wade's Horse &c who were got before them, and they turned back into Kendal when the Duke came up with them and they fled into the woods. The say the Duke hath slain 5000 of them, but hath lost a great many men & horses & some officers, and is himself wounded with attacking them at such disadvantage in the wood. They say they have taken the Duke of Perth and have also taken the Pretender in womans' cloths. They say Townsend hath met with the French Squadron and hath destroyed most of them. They say Lord Louden hath had a sharp engagement with the Rebels in Scotland, Remained master of the field Baggage &c but lost a deal of men.[59]
Rain last night, windy, some rain towards night.

23. I was at Arthur Hudsons this morning to see the man they have had taken up, but he was gone, the Constable set out with him by 7 this morning towards the Justice. They say Mr Milnes & several Gentlemen out of Wakefield & Leeds are gone into the north towards the Duke's Army to be satisfied how affairs stand there, so that we shall have certain News.
Windy, very cold, Rainy morning.

24. The man which they took up at Newmill on Sunday the 22nd is Committed to the House of Correction at Wakefield by Capn Burton. I hear the Rebels are in Carlisle and our Men have surrounded them, which I suppose will prove true. There are flying reports I suppose without foundation that the Rebels were divided into two Companies, and our men attacked them and a great many of our Men were destroyed. I bought a cheese at 2½ per lb. A mighty strong wind cold rain, a very blustering day.

[59] Lord Loudoun on Dec. 3rd relieved Fort Augustus, threatened by the Frazers.

25. I hear the Rebels are blocked up in Carlisle and that our Admirals have destroyed a vast number of French ships.
Joseph Hinchliffe of Anondine buried this day, the Clark of Lydgate was here and I gave him 6ᵈ.
26. There was a snow shower last night, some frost this morning. I hear that the Ships which we have taken are Martinico Ships, very rich prizes. Henry Hinchliff gave me a Partridge because I would take nothing of him for restoring him when he was poisoned.
27. I hear the Rebels are in Carlisle & that the Duke hath taken a good deal of Prisoners and hath Hanged up 4,⁶⁰ and that the Pretender hath sent to the Duke for quarter but in vain. Mr Kenworthy's servant call'd here to invite me to Dinner but I did not come home until about one of the Clock and could not go. Frosty morning and clear day.
28. I hear the Rebels are in Carlisle & have sent to the Duke for quarter which will not be granted.
There was some snow last night.
29. Mr Shaw preached from Isaiah 26.9. I was not at chapel in the forenoon. Richᵈ Turner was at Mr James Haighs' near Halifax a cloth buyer on Thursday the 26ᵗʰ and brought a copy of an express which came thither, and as he came home met with a man and said he was Lord Malton's servant and had an express and had authority to take any Man's Horse and took the Man's horse from him by force, and went to Wakefield the day after, and the man & his Son came to Wooldale yesterday about the Horse and stayed all night somewhere and Richᵈ Turner is gone with them this morning and what end they will make of it, or what Richard hath done with the Horse is not known. I hear the Rebels were blocked up in Carlisle and that they sent four men to the Duke to treat with him, and he caused them to be hanged up. It is Admiral Townsend⁶¹ that hath taken and destroyed so many French ships.
The Bluecoats⁶² searched at Mr Scot's of Woodsomes last week (friday the 29ᵗʰ) upon suspicion that some Rebels were harboured there. Sharp frost, close day.
30. I was at Holmfirth at Josʰ Wilson's the Shopkeeper. He tells me that some time before the last Rebellion he was with one Bouker, Mr Thompson and Mr Kaye of Netherthong at Cavehull

⁶⁰ Charles left Carlisle on the 20th. It was invested by the Government troops on the 22nd. Charles had left a garrison there, hoping that he would soon return. The place surrendered on the 30th. Out of eighteen officers, Cumberland hanged nine.
⁶¹ On Oct 31, Nov. 1, Admiral Isaac Townsend had attacked a large convoy of French ships off Martinique and had taken, burnt, or destroyed over thirty ships. (See Admiral Richmond, *The Navy in the War of 1739-48*, II, pp. 228-9.)
⁶² The local levies, not the Royal Horse Guards.

well and they drank the Pretender's health; and he charged Dr Wilson his Brother not to keep company with them for if he did he would be hanged. He had told me this once before as I was going with him to the Club at James Englands of Honley. Snow last night, frost, close, snowy.

31. I hear that the Rebels were blocked up in Carlisle. I hear that some of them are escaped and I hear that they all are escaped & got into Scotland.

Frost, snowy & close.

Richard Turner I hear hath agreed about the Horse. Mr Armitage of Dudmanston[63] died this day.

Of the Rebellion in 1715. The Rebellion broke out under the Influence and direction of the Earl of Mar. The Duke of Argyle was sent down against him. The business was decided by the Battle of Sheriff-moor near Dunblain, fought November 13, 1715, the same day that General Foster & the English Jacobites surrendered at Preston.

By the Articles of the Union the Land Tax was adjusted in the following proportion viz that where England paid £1,997,763 8s. 4½d. Scotland should pay £48,000 and so in proportion. The Representation of Scotland was fixed at 16 Peers and 45 Commoners, which, though small in proportion to the English peers & Commoners, yet was high in Comparison of the Share born by Scotland in the Taxes.

When England paid 2 Millions by way of Land Tax Scotland was to pay but £48000, yet in return for bearing a fortieth part of the Expence they had the eleventh part of the Legislature given to them.

The Rebellion began in Scotland in August 1745.

1745-6

Jan^{ry} 2^d. Mr Armitage of Dudmanstone buried this day.

6. Josiah Rowbottom's wife died on the 3^d & buried this day.

7. John Cook of Scar buried this day.

11 (Saturday). They gave up keeping Watch & Ward in Holmfirth. They began on the 1st of November.

---

[63] Deadmanstone is between Huddersfield and Honley, not far from Castle Hill.

16. I was at Shaley[1] to se the Blue Coats Exercise.

17. General Hawley & General Huske had an Engagement with the Rebel Army near Falkirk in Scotland. Hamilton's Dragoons fled & lost us the Battle & seven pieces of Cannon, but it is said the Rebels have a great many more men killed than we.[2]

19. I hear Hannah Bray of Riding died this day.

20. Humphrey Kaye of Copthurst buried this day.

27. I was at Hades at Dinner. Snow in the morning.

28. A great snow fell last night. frost. cloudy. snow showers. There was a Battle between the King's forces under Lieutenant General Hawly and the Rebels on the 17 of this instant. The right Wing was thrown into Confusion by the running away again of the 2^d Regiment of Dragoons who ran away in the former battle of Preston Pans. The left wing of the King's Army under General Huske[3] broke and defeated the Right of the Rebels. It is said we have lost 200 men and the Rebels 7 or 800. Other letters say that we have lost above 300 & the Rebels 900. Others say that the Rebels lost 1000 and we not above 250 and that the Ld John Drummond and the Duke of Perth are mortally wounded.[4]

29. I hear this morning that Mr Maud & Mr Rawson came into Huddersfield yesterday from the North and report that the King's forces engaged the Rebels again on Friday the 24th and were worsted, that they attacked them again on Saturday the 25th and the advantages on both sides were nearly equal. They engaged again on sunday the 26th and gained a complete victory, killed the greatest part of the Rebels and took most of the rest prisoners.[5] Whitehall Jany 25th. His Royal Highness the Duke of Cumberland set out between twelve & one this morning for Scotland to command the Army there. Sharp frost, some little Snow. A very strong wind and exceedingly cold. It blows the snow hard about. Some lightening in the morning.

30. Frosty cold wind, some snow showers.

31. Sharp frost, cold wind.

Feby 2. Candlemas day. A remission of the frost. Mr Shaw preached from Rom: 14.17. It was commonly reported in Wakefield on friday the 31 of last month that the good news we heard on Wednesday the 29th from Huddersfield on the 28th was true but we cannot yet believe it. John Hay of Ridings is fourscore and eleven years old this day.

[1] Shelley, near Kirkburton.
[2] At the battle of Falkirk on January 17th, 300 English were killed and a hundred taken prisoners. The opposing army only admitted a loss of 40.
[3] On Sept. 25, 1745, the Duke of Newcastle wrote to the Mayor of Newcastle that he was sending down General Huske. He commanded the right wing which stood firm at Falkirk and the second line at Culloden.
[4] Lord John Drummond did not die for another two years yet.
[5] Quite untrue.

Feby 3. William Burn was here yesterday & brought the pistol and had paid 1/6 for mending the man hath made it very bright but hath done little or nothing at the lock Wm Burn took it again. Mr Kenworthy and Mr Winterbottom the Gauger tell me that General Blakeney[6] Governor of Stirling Castle hath slain a great many of the Rebels, some 3000, some 2000 and some 1500.

Old Esther Beever, Ben Beever's Mother of Carlcoats buried this day. Mr Bray of Hepworth his servant called here this night to tell me that his master would give me a Beagle if I had a mind to keep one.

4. Some frost, cloudy, cold. I hear all are false reports and that there hath been no action since the 17th of last month when our forces were worsted.

5. Sharp frost.

6. Snow last night, frost.

7. I hear that Joshua Wilson hath received a letter from Leeds which gives an account that most of the Rebels in Scotland are slain. Mr Kenworthy tells me the same news, and that our forces are in possession of Stirling, and also that General Blakeney sallied out of the Castle and killed a great many of them. They say the Battle was on Sunday last, on Candlemas day, wind & sleet.

8. I hear that the Duke offered to attack the Rebels at Stirling expecting they would stand a Battle but they fled upon his approach, and General Blakeney made a seasonable sally out of the Castle and cut off all Lord John Drummond's men but 40 and Ld Drummond himself is slain. The rest are fled & have left their baggage &c. Cold sleet and rain a very ill day.

9. Some frost, cold. Mr Eden preached from Luke 14.21.22.23.

24. Shrove Sunday.

10. Sharp frost, very cold wind. John Haigh of Carlcoats married.

11. Exceeding sharp frost, a very cold wind. I hear that a Bullet grazed upon the Duke of Cumberland's Shoulder in Scotland, and another bullet buz'd by his Ear. Joseph Swallow of Townhead I hear was married on Sunday the 9th. I hear Joseph Dearnley of Townend is begun to Brew for sale and also John Morehouse of Moorcroft.

[6] General Blakeney, the Hanoverian commander, who successfully defended Stirling Castle against the Stuart Army after they had possession of the city. Stirling itself was easily taken, but not the castle Charles began to invest it, but the siege was interrupted by the battle of Falkirk. It was impossible to continue it owing to the rapidly diminishing numbers of the Highland army. It was abandoned on Feb. 1st, and the next day the castle was occupied by the Duke of Cumberland. The story of the great slaughter by Blakeney is not true.

12. Exceding sharp frost, very cold wind.

13. Exceeding sharp frost, very cold wind. It hath been the sharpest frost for the 3 last nights that hath been all winter. I was at Newmill at the School & the Schoolmaster made me 4 pens. I called at Stony Bank and read the Leeds Newspaper. The Rebels fled at the approach of the Duke and got over the Forth at a place called the Frew.[7] General Blakeney hath slain above a thousand of them, and the King's forces are in pursuit of the rest. The Hessians, no doubt, are landed in Scotland.

14. Exceeding sharp frost, an extremely cold wind. I hear the blue coats are all turn'd off. If this be true the Gentlemen hope that the danger of the Rebellion is over.

15. We hope the Rebellion is almost at an end for the Gentlemen have discharged the Blues.

16. The Minister of Wharley[8] preached from Heb: 11.5. Neither my brother nor I was at chapel in the forenoon. wind & rain last night, a close rainy day.

18. I hear that the Rebels are dispersed into small parties and have thrown away their arms and the Souldiers are continually seizing some of them and plundering the Houses, and that the Duke is at Perth. I had three Trouts to my supper which my brother had caught.

19. The Rebels are dispersed and it is assured that not above 80 of them are in a Body. The Pretender and the Chief of the Rebels would fain get to Sea at Montross and make their escape to France.

20. A snowy day, Snow all day. The dispersion of the Rebels in Scotland has been as sudden as their first appearance but a better account may be given for it, for they met with nothing but discouragement. Frost & snow. There is a great snow fallen. Mr Walker of Hunchill house burnt down. There is great talk that Mr Croft is dis . . .

23. Frost. Mr Eden preached from Luke 14.21.22.23.24. It is currently reported that the pretender, the Duke of Perth &c are taken in a vessel at sea by our naval forces, we heard before they

[7] On 13th September, 1745, Charles and his army, on the way to Edinburgh, crossed the Forth at the Fords of Frew in spite of the caltrops thrown into it by the enemy. On Feb. 1st Cumberland reported that the rebels had blown up their powder. They had stored fifty barrels of gunpowder in the Church of St. Ninian. The explosion was perhaps an accident. (Hume Brown, *History of Scotland*, III, p.317.) They also left some of their artillery behind. The Highlanders wanted to go home for the winter, but there was such a disorderly rush over the Fords of Frew, that their enemies might be pardoned for thinking them in full flight—just after the battle of Falkirk, too.

[8] The minister of Warley (Halifax) at this time was William Graham, M.A., described as "a man of learning and ability." He died in 1763 and was then a Unitarian.

were endeavouring to get off in the Hazzard Sloop.[9]   It is certain the Rebels are quite dispersed and shifting for themselves.

A vast snow upon the Moors.   There was a very sharp frost last night.

24.   Frost last night.   Snow, sleet, & rain.   the frost broke in the afternoon.   I called at Wm Beevers for the Pistol which was come from the mending.

26.   Our forces are pursuing the Rebels as the weather will permit and sometimes seizing some of them.   The Duke of Cumberland no doubt hath left Scotland by this time and is going up to London. There is no truth in the report that the Pretender the Duke of Perth &c. were taken.

27.   General Blakeny hath slain about 1000 before Stirling Castle. The King's forces have taken 500 Rebels at once.   The French have taken Brussels.[10] Hail & Snow.   Penistone Fair.   John Crosland of Shipley buried this day.

March 1st.   Frost very cold, snow.   I hear old John Worthy of Wilberclough is buried this day.   Bought a cheese in Holmfirth at 2½^d per lb.   I hear that the Pretender and Lord John Drummond and about 500 Rebels are taken at Sea.   More snow towards night.

2.   Frosty morning, cold rain.   Mr Eden preached from Eccles: 12.14.   They say a Body of 4 or 5000 of the Rebels are got together at Aberdeen.

3.   Frosty morning.   I was at Oakes to visit Edwd Bradley's son, as I went Jonas Hobson of Mytham Bridge paid me 3^d.   They are for building a Mill at Mytham Bridge upon his farm, and I saw workmen digging the tail goat.[11]

4.   They say the *Hazzard* Sloop is got safe to Dunkirk with a company of the Rebels, and that several thousands of the Rebels are got together at Aberdeen.   I hear that the Rebels are gathered together again in Scotland, and that several thousands of French[12] are landed there.   A close day.

5.   John Morehouse of Moorcroft began to sell Ale on Monday

[9] The *Hazard* sloop was one of the few vessels which had been able to bring any assistance to the Prince.   On March 25th, 1746, however, as she was returning from France, she was captured by Lord Reay with 12,000 guineas on board.   Lord Cromartie with a band of men tried to recover this lost treasure from Government hands the day before Culloden, but was defeated and he himself and many of his men captured.   The French ships all along had difficulty in landing men and money because of the ubiquity of the English fleet.   The Prince was not trying to escape in the *Hazard* before Culloden and his men were not yet " dispersed and shifting for themselves ".

[10] The French had not taken Brussels yet.

[11] The tail gut or channel, gut, sluice, stream, a small artificial watercourse made in order that a portion of the upper water may flow down into the tail or lower stream immediately in front of the wheel.

[12] Throughout the whole rising the French helped only to the extent of between ten and twelve hundred men.

3ᵈ. I was at Scholes at John Battyes. I called at Totties at Mr Greenwoods and read the Leeds newspaper.[13]

6. The Rebels have left Aberdeen and for all their boasted numbers, are but few, and in poor condition, and the Duke of Cumberlands army was got to Aberdeen above a week since. It is thought about one hundred French may be landed in Scotland which was all that escaped being taken by Commander Knowles,[14] the Duke it is said will not leave Scotland so soon as was expected. Some little snow hail. Cold wind.

7. There is one Rockley a Quarter master taken amongst those 500 which Commodore Knowls took coming from France for Scotland, which gives some suspicion that it may prove young Mr Rockley that ran away from London with the King's money into France several years ago. Frosty morning Snow. the ground in the afternoon covered with snow.

8. Snow last night. There is a great snow fallen, a very cold wind.

9. Sharp frost, much snow and very cold. Mr Winterbottom tells me that the Rebels have [cut]Ld Loudon to pieces[15] and that 20,000 French are landed.[16]
Mr Eden preached from Eccles: 12.14.

10. York Assizes began this day. Sharp frost, snow all day there is a great snow fallen.

11. Fresh, cold, a clear snowy day. I hear there is very bad news, some say the Rebels have destroyed a great many of Lᵈ Louden's men, others say he hath retreated and made his Escape we hear no certain news but fear it is bad.

12. I hear that both French and Spaniards are landed in Scotland[17] and that they have joined the Rebels and taken Inverness where Lord Louden was, and some other places. Frosty morning, Snowy cold day.

15. I hear that two French ships were got to Scotland and 3 more coming, and that the Rebels are at Inverness having forced Lord

[13] The *Leeds Mercury*.
[14] In the general naval arrangements for defence against invaders, Captain Charles Knowles had a small squadron watching Dunkirk, Calais and Boulogne. On Feb 21st he captured two French ships, *Bourbon* and *Charité*, with 500 or 600 men on board. A third ship got away with about 100 men. (H. W. Richmond, *War of 1739-48*, II, p.189.)
[15] On Feb. 16th, Loudoun attempted a surprise attack on Charles Edward's army, but there was no surprise and Loudoun's men fled back to Inverness. On the 20th Charles Edward captured Inverness and the castle surrendered. During March Loudoun himself was driven from one place to another and was forced at last to take refuge in Skye.
[16] Not true.
[17] Only a few Frenchmen landed and certainly no Spaniards; the British Navy was too vigilant and it was because there were so few French reinforcements that the English Jacobites did not rise.

Louden to Retreat, and that the Duke of Cumberland is at Aberdeen.
I was at Hades at Mr Kenworthy's and borrowed the *Leeds Mercury*
which he had borrowed at Holmfirth.

16. A Fine Day. I was not at chapel. Mr Shaw preached from
Col: 3.12.13. I hear there hath been some action in Scotland and
that the Rebels have gotten the better.

19. There is an abundance of false Trators in Scotland both at
Montross, Aberdeen and Edinburgh and other places. The Duke is
at Aberdeen and the Rebels at Inverness and threaten that they
will fight the Duke.

20. I was at Holmfirth to reckon with Mr Hardy paid him 10ᵈ
and 2ᵈ for the Clark. The clark was for eggs this morning. Mr
Kenworthy was there and had a pay-day for Wood and I had some
Roast Beef & Drunk a while with him and paid nothing.

Mar 21. There is a great Meeting today at Burton. they have
begun to dig up the church yard to make a fine way through it to
the Church and this part of the Parish are against it and will go
this afternoon to oppose them. Eli Wilkinson a Carpenter who was
stubbing[18] a Yew near the steps between Lockwood and Huddersfield and a Boy that was with him were both killed with the fall of
it on tuesday the 18th. Eli Wilkinson served his apprenticeship with
Abraham Eastwood of Hag, and they say he lived at or near Linley,
and hath left a great many children.
A Boy at Miltom, Edward Bowes apprentice was shot dead on
Monday the 10th. I hear another Boy and he were exercising and
had a gun which had no powder in pan and thought it was not
charged, and it took fire and shot one of them into the Breast through
the Lungs and he died forthwith. Much rain last night. a close
warm rainy day. Mr Jackson hath been over from Fairfield this
week went back this day.

23. Mr Eden preached from Eccles 12.14. Several people went
to Burton on friday the 21st. Burton people did not meet them,
but they left a paper for them, subscribed by several, to let them
know that if they did not make up the breach they had made in
the church yard in a months time they would proceed against them
according to law upon which the following case was drawn up by
Mr Battye of Scholes for the opinion of Council. The original is
in my possession.

CASE. To witt the parish of Kirkburton in the West Riding of the
County of York consists of eight Townships, that is, Kirkburton,
Shelley, Shepley, Fulston, Thurstonland, Wooldale Hepworth and
Cartworth. This parish is supposed to be about 8 miles long and
four broad and by reason of the Woollen manufactory is exceedingly
populous. The dead of all these townships excepting some few
Quakers and Dissenters are buried at Kirkburton where the church-

[18] Stubbing is grubbing up by the roots.

yard is so full thronged with graves that the parish Sexton hath often publickly declared he scarcely knew where to put down his spade. About Christmas last five of the Churchwardens for five of the Townships without consulting the parishioners or giving any publick notice, agreed to pave a way with flag 40 yards long and near 2 wide through the midst of the graves and the very heart of the churchyard, this walk will contain 70 square yards. On hearing Earnshaw one of the Churchwardens and the Sexton had sunk this walk about 10 inches below the surface of the Church yard, and that in doing of which some indecencies were committed on the graves of some of the chief Inhabitants of the said Towns, on friday before good friday last went to the Churchyard and left with the parish clark the notice marked A which was on the Sunday following published. When the churchwardens gave notice for a Vestry meeting to be on good friday see paper marked B, a vestry meeting was then, see paper D, and the Churchwardens gave out that this is only a repair and as such they can do it by virtue of their office, but in fact it is otherwise for the ground which they desire to flag was as frequently buried in as any other part of the churchyard."

" I am of opinion that a Citation may be taken out at the suit of any Parishioner or number of Parishioners against the Church-wardens to answer articles for breaking open the graves in the Churchyard, and to show cause why an Inhibition should not be granted against them from paving or making any alteration in the churchyard without the Consent of the Parishioners, and I apprehend there can be no foundation for a prohibition to such a suit. The Vicar may give leave to pave it as it is his freehold, but the Churchwardens have no right to put the parishioners to that expence without their Consent. If all the Churchwardens concurred in giving the order they should all be made parties or as many of them as did, and the Sexton is proper to be left out of the Citation in order to make him a witness."

York. Ap¹ 24ʰᵗ: 1746.   W. STUBBS."

It ought to be observed that "pursuant to notice given" a vestry meeting was held at 4 o' the clock in the afternoon on the 28 of March 1746 at Kirkburton Church when the "undecent proceedings" of the Churchwardens were overruled by a very large majority. Previous to the foregoing meeting the following notices were posted up.[19]

" This is to give Notice to all Gentlemen, Ladies & others that a great many Lords & Gentlemen who were in full Chace after DECENCY the daughter of RELIGION last week, were so fortunate as to catch her in the Highlands: but not knowing what advantage they could reap from her, they called an Assembly of their own clans, who with one voice agreed to have her banished their Country and

[19] " On 29th March "—(written in pencil).

unanimously resolved to send her to her MOTHER. Upon this a strong Guard was to conduct her towards this place, where they thought she resided, but Alas! the guard being somewhat negligent She slip't from them o'th Stocks Moor and made her escape into the adjacent Woods. If any Gentleman or others can apprehend her & bring her safe to the D-v-l of H-w-th or Old Dn Hudibras of Holmfirth or either of their Squires, viz, Squires Sancho of Scholes or Squires Ralpho of H—es[20] shall received a thousandth part of a farthing for his pains.

N.B. He that is so happy as to find it is desired to bring it to the Vestry exactly at 4 o'th clock this afternoon."

Another public meeting of the Parishioners was called which was very numerously attended at which the following Declaration was signed by all the parties then present but two, namely by 127 persons containing many of the most respectable persons in the parish and only two persons in favour, neither of whom could write their names.

The declaration is as follows.

"We the Parishioners & Inhabitants of the Parish of Kirkburton whose names are hereunto subscribed being met in Vestry in the said church of Kirkburton on wednesday the 30th day of April 1746 betwixt 2 and 3 of th' clock in the afternoon pursuant to publick notice given last Sunday in the said Church in time of Divine Service to consider about paving or flagging a Causeway through the Churchyard of Kirkburton do hereby declare our dissent to and protest against the doing the same. Witness our hands this said 30 day of Ap[l] 1746."

March 24. I hear that the king of Sardinia hath gained a great Victory over the French, and hath taken a great many prisoners[21] Some rain & hail.

25. I hear that the forces in Scotland have slain 2000 of the Rebels. I hear also that the forces cannot come up with the Rebels, but that they are very strong. I heard yesterday that John Charlesworth of Hogley was dead suddenly. I hear this day that John Lee Blacksmith of Honley died suddenly. I hear of a truth that that Rockley which Commodore Knowles took coming from France is Robert Rockley son to Mr Rockley of Woodsome.

26. Forenoon very much rain & hail, in the afternoon I was at Carlcoats. The King of Sardinia hath taken between 7 & 8000 prisoners.

[20] The devil of Hepworth, appears to be Mr Bray, Squire Sancho of Scholes, Mr. Batty, Sir Ralpho of Hades, Mr. Kenworthy (who lived at Hades) and Don Hudibras of Holmfirth, whose identity seems uncertain, unless he is the Mr. Earnshaw before mentioned.

[21] The French had made an armistice with the King of Sardinia on Feb. 17th, but Charles Emanuel suddenly attacked them. Eleven French battalions were forced to surrender at Asti (March 8th).

The Duke of Cumberland intends leaving Aberdeen on Monday 17ᵗʰ and march towards the Rebels.   He hath been long hindered by the great Snow which fell on the 8ᵗʰ inst.   The recruits which the French sent into Scotland, do them very little Service for they are composed of Deserters, Criminals, and Vagabonds, infamous in their own Country and despised here.   Upwards of 100 Rebel Spies have been taken up at Aberdeen in Womens cloths.   Lord Seaford and Mr Mackintosh are with the Loyal party, and Lady Seaford and Mackintosh's wife are with the Rebels.

27.   They say that young Mr Rockley ran away on Sunday the 14ᵗʰ of February 1730-1.   So that he had been 15 years absent last valantines' day.

28.   There is a Vestry this day at Burton & abundance of people hereabouts are going to oppose such as are for making a way through the Church yard.   A very wet day, hail & rain.

29.   I called at George Tinker's and John Battys at Scholes. At the Vestry at Burton yesterday those that were for making the way thro' the church yard were but 8 and those which appeared against it were near an hundred, but 5 of the Churchwardens were for it and but 3 against it.   They had fixed a paper upon the church door to abuse Holmfirth people and particularly Mr Bray, Mr Kenworthy and Mr Batty and somebody in Holmfirth, for it mentioned the D-le of Hepworth & Don Hudibras and Sir Ralpho of Hades and Squire Sancho of Scholes.

Mar. 30.   Easter Sunday.   Mr Eden preached from John 6.54. Whoso eateth my flesh and drinketh my blod hath eternal life: and I will raise him up at the last day.   The Sacrament.   I collected 3ˢ 7ᵈ at the Sacrament and paid Mr Eden 1ˢ 9ᵈ for Bread and wine and 1ˢ 10ᵈ remained.   I hear little Joshua Haigh above Holmfirth, the Potter, fell into the water at Ousebridge and was drowned last night.

31.   Snow and rain very cold.

April 2ᵈ.   We had Thomas Littlewood to plough for us.   They ploughed a day work and a half and we paid them 6ˢ 9ᵈ.

3.   We sowed the day work and half and broke it in.

6.   Some little rain in the morning a great shower about noon. Mr Eden preached from Eccles: 1.   I paid Mr Eden £2 10s. od. quarterage as I returned home I heard a clap of thunder.

10.   A close rainy misty day, hail and some thunder.

11.   A close misty rainy day much rain last night and this forenoon.   I was at Middlecliff²² this afternoon at John Marsden's, to visit his maid, a very cold day.

13.   Frosty morning.   Mr Shaw preached from Heb: 12.17. I heard yesterday that Robert Jagger of Shawhead²³ is dead

²² Middlecliff, three miles west of Penistone.
²³ Shawhead, near Honley.

K

and buried lately and that William Jagger died some time since.

15. I was at Stackwoodhill to visit Dame Newton. I called at John Hollingworths to ask how John Bray does, who works at Stony Bank.

April 16. There is pretty good news the Rebels have raised the Siege of Fort William[24] which Cap^n Scot hath bravely defended. The Rebels are in great distress for want of money & provisions and are deserting daily. The Rebels taken at Carlisle were brought to the Sessions at Old Bailey answered to their names, and had notice given them to prepare for their Trials against next Sessions holden there. There is also pretty good news from abroad. Some snow upon the Moor this morning. Cloudy for the most part, some rain. The Duke fought the Rebels on Straghallen moor, was himself in the battle and in the pursuit and took a great many prisoners near Culloden House.

17. Sharp frost. Cloudy. Some hail sleet and snow. I was at Meltham at Mr Sagers[26] to visit his child. He was the Clergyman at Meltham (chapel) church. I called at Mr Armitage's at Thick-hollins.[27] I hear that the Duke of Cumberland hath killed several thousands of the Rebels and hath taken the rest prisoners But we know not the truth of it.

18. Sharp frost. I was at Thurstonland to visit Mr George Morehouse's daughter Mary. She went to Almondbury last week and fell into the fever which they have in the family. I called at Stack woodhill, Newmill, and at Jonas Hobson's of Wooldale. Mr Eden was here when I got home.

19. Sharp frost very cold. Some flaques of Snow. I was at May-thorn to visit Joshua Marsden & called at Joseph Green's. I called at Milshaw at John Wagstaff's. I was at Holmfirth at Arthur Hudsons, there is an Auction there, and I looked at the Books but bought none, rain last night.

April 20th. Much rain in the forenoon. windy blustering and there is some snow upon the Moors. an exceeding wet turbulent forenoon. Mr Eden preached in the afternoon from Job. 20.4.5. We were not at the Chapel in the afternoon, it was so very rainy.

22^d. Showers. Great showers towards night. I was at Shaw-head to visit Christopher Shaw's wife. I got my dinner at Wid^w Jaggers, and called at James Armitage's of Hall-Ing. I was at Brockholes to visit Anthony Hutchinson.

---

[24] Fort Augustus surrendered to Charles on March 5th, but Fort William held out against the Jacobites till the siege was abandoned on April 4th.

[26] Robert Sagar, Deacon, 1724; Priest, 1728, St. Asaph; Curate of Meltham, 1728. He married the widow Broadhead of Cradlin Holes. He died 1770.

[27] Mr. John Armitage of Thickhollins was one of the Grand Jury of York in 1716. He died Nov. 14th, 1747.

23. Some little rain. John Batty of Scholes is set off for York this day about Burton affair. The Duke hath left Aberdeen and is marching towards the Rebels. He passed the River Spey where 2000 Rebels were ready to hinder the passage but fled upon the approach of our forces. The foot waded to the middle the water was so deep. The Pretender was at Inverness and Elgin spiriting up his men to stand. The Duke was near them a good while since, so that there hath been some action before this time unless the Rebels run away.

24. I was at Lankside[28] to visit John Mait who is very ill. I called to visit John Smith's son and to visit old Eliz: Kaye aged 95 years. I called at Ben Charlesworth's and at Ranaw and bled Joseph Greave's daughter.
I hear there is very good news. The Duke hath killed and taken most of the Rebels[29] and they were ringing the Bells and making great rejoicing in Leeds yesterday, having received expresses of the Victory which was gained with a very inconsiderable loss on our side, and they are ringing Holmfirth Bell this day, and made a Bonfire and they were ringing the Bell and made a Bonfire at Honley Great rejoicings ringing of Bells &c. at Cawthorne, Penistone &c. A great Bonfire on the Sudill.

Ap¹ 25. warm. There was great rejoicing at York. They had the Pope, Pretender and a Child in a warming-pan and all windows which were not illuminated on Wednesday the 23ᵈ . . . Mr Crofts[30] would not let James Cocken give them the Key of the Chapel door but they went in at the Bell holes[31] to ring the Bell. I paid Josʰ Woodhead 2s. 8d. for a pair of shoes for Sister Martha.

26. Some little rain. Holmfirth Fair. I was there in the afternoon.

27. Mr Eden preached from Prov: 20.4.5. I was not at Chapel in the afternoon. Humphrey Brook of Honley wood bottom buried this day. Abundance of the Rebels are slain. The Pretender was not in the Battle but fled away,[32] but it is hoped he will be taken. Our men in general behaved bravely and in particular the Duke of Kingston's men are much commended. It is said the Battle was on Wednesday the 16ᵗʰ of this instant on Culloden Moor.

29. I hear that the Rebels are quite defeated and that above 2,000 of them are slain and above 2000 of them are taken prisoner.

30. Burton Court. There is a Vestry this day at Burton about the breach they have made in the Church Yard. Abundance of people will go to oppose them who are for making a way there.

[28] Langside, two and three quarter miles south-west of Penistone.
[29] Charles Edward lost about a thousand men killed and about a thousand taken prisoner.
[30] Mr. Crofts, the Rev. William Croft of Honley.
[31] The belfry.
[32] A slander.

Burton people never appeared and this part of the parish went in great numbers and had nobody to oppose them.

May 1ˢᵗ. I was at the Club at John Booth's I got home about 10. Mr Harrop was there and seemed to be disappointed.

2. The Battle on the 16 April was on a Moor, Straghallen Moor, near Inverness, near Culloden House. The Earl of Malton created Marquis of Rockingham in Northamptonshire. John Audley of Hall Ing buried this day. Joshua Marsden of Maythorn is dead.

3. I hear that the Pretender is taken. I hear that Mr Pollard, Clark to Sir John Kaye of Grange died yesterday. 200 Soldiers are come into Manchester sent down from London to bring up some of the disaffected to give an account of their conduct when the Pretender and the Rebels came into Manchester.

Huddersfield Fair day.[33]

4. Mr Buck preached from . . . 12.26. Great rejoicing in Manchester last Tuesday. They had the Pretender in Effigee on horse back, dressed in a plaid and a . . . burnt wig and a Scotch Bonnet on his head. The Souldiers went all up and down the Town with him attended with the Loyal party in the Town with Music and great vollies of Shot, and at last set fire to him. There was great rejoicing in Kirkburton yesternight. They had a Bonfire and a Picture of the Pretender which they shot at, and rang a frying Pan, I suppose this is upon the report that the Pretender is taken.

5. Hail, Showers. Last thursday night Mr Harrop, Mr Eden and Arthur Hudson & I spent 2ᵈ a piece, after I came away Mr Harrop talked against the Government and Mr Eden and Arthur Hudson . . . with him and he damn'd and cursed by . . . I hear on Friday the day after he was at Newmill with Mr Eden at night.

6. I hear that Mr Bradshaw of Manchester who had lands in Holmfirth is taken and was sent with some other Rebels at Newark with his Hands shackled. They were going with them up to London in a Cart or Waggon.

Holmfirth flesh day. I was at Holmfirth at John Booth's Mr Harrop was there and was very friendly with me. I hear that Lord Kilmarnock[34] who they say was taken prisoner by the Duke and engaged to take the Pretender after his flight to save his life and Estate took a company of our Men with him who are all cut off by the Rebels, through his treachery and that he is returned to the Pretender.[35] It was in the *Leeds Mercury* last week that James Bradshaw was taken.

7. The number of Rebels killed is 4000 in the field, and in the

[33] May 24, for lean horned cattle and horses. (Owen's *Book of Fairs*.)
[34] He was captured soon after the battle.
[35] The story of Kilmarnock's bargain to betray Charles in return for a pardon is quite untrue. He was beheaded on Aug. 18th, 1746. He repented of the bloodshed but died praying for King James. (Hume Brown says for King George, *Hist. Scot.*, III, p. 326.)

pursuit. I was at Mrs Thompsons to visit Mr Harrop. I hear that
Mr Morehouse and Mr Harrop fell out ill yesternight at John Booth's
after I was come away, and Mr Morehouse called him Rebel several
times.

11. Mr Eden preached from Luke 12.15. the latter part of the
verse For a man's life consisteth not in the abundance of the things
he possesseth.

14. They are hunting for the Rebels every day & scouring the
country. They are bringing a great number of Prisoners every day,
all the Gaols are full and they know not how to dispose of them.
Hot but an east wind and it is likely there was a frost this morning.
The battle wherein the Rebels were defeated was fought April 16,
1746 on Straghallen Moor near Culloden House.

17. Hot parching weather, frosty mornings.

18. I was at the Chapel in the forenoon and was called out before
Service began to Middlecliff to visit Joseph Mathewman. I called
at Burnside at Ben Potts. Mr Shaw preached from Eph: 5.1.
Cloudy. Thunder in the afternoon. Thunder & lightening and a
fine shower at night. Whitsunday.

20. We do not hear that the Pretender is taken.

21. Mrs Kaye came back to Butterly. On tuesday the 15ᵗʰ of
April there was a Battle at Golspie betwixt the Earl of Sutherland's
militia and the Earl of Cromarty. The Earl of Cromarty & his son
Lord McLeod 18 officers and 180 private men were made prisoners,
they were pursued to Dunrobin where they surrendered with about
£1200 in Cash.³⁶ It is assured that the pretender and several Chiefs
of the Rebels are lurking upon the Western Coast of Scotland to
escape by sea. There is advice that Antwerp is taken by the French.
John Goddard gave a Bond for £120 valid 9 April last.

23. An East wind continually a great drought.

25. Trinity Sunday. Mr Eden preached from Luke 12.15. A
great Shower of hail & rain in the afternoon, much rain at night.
I hear George Roebuck of Berrestial head³⁷ died this morning.

June 1. Cloudy. thunder & lightening & rain. Mr Eden
preached from . . . 7.21. I was not at Chapel in the afternoon.
There was no service at Holmfirth in the forenoon. Mr Harrop is
gone to Halifax.

2. Some small rain in the morning & windy was at Thurstonland

³⁶ What happened was this: On March 25th the *Hazard*, returning from
France with stores, amongst them 12,000 guineas, was captured by Lord
Reay. On the day before the battle of Culloden, an attempt was made
by Lord Cromartie to recapture the treasure. The result of the fight, in
which he was opposed by the Mackays, was that Lord Cromartie was taken
prisoner. His capture at Golspie made the defeat at Culloden more certain.
To make matters worse a French fleet with men and equipment was kept
off by the watchfulness of the navy.
³⁷ Berrestial Head, a hamlet of Hepworth.

called at Dame Moorhouses door but nobody was in the house but the Maid & I did not light.   There was no service at Holmfirth yesterday in the forenoon.   Mr Harrop they say was gone to Halifax. Mr Hardy preached at Holmfirth in the afternoon.   Mr Crofts preached yesterday in the forenoon, gave over soon and went to Halifax and Mr Sager preached at Honley in the afternoon.

3.   I was at Yatom but neither Mr nor Mrs Green were at Home.

4.   Much rain last night.   Mr Harrop preached at Huddersfield last Sunday, there is nothing in the story of Mr Crofts coming into trouble as was reported.   Mr Eden, Mr Tho[s] and Mr George More-house and myself had written to the Bishop about him,[38] and he got Mr Dan[l] Batty to speak to Mr Eden about it.

8.   Mr Shaw preached from Revel 22.12.   Mr Eden preached at Bullhouse and is going to see his Father and they say he will leave us soon to go to Elland.   There was no service at Holmfirth this forenoon.

9.   There is a great mob up in Lancashire who pretend to plunder the Papists and pull down their Houses and have done abundance of mischief.

[39] 1746.   July 3[d].   Mr Royston, (vicar of Almondbury) preached at Holmfirth last Sunday June 29th in the forenoon from John 6.67. Will ye also go away?   And he frequently asked, '' but whither? '' but he meant the Methodists.   he run down the Presbyterians.   He preached with unusual warmth and with great rancour.

[40] In the afternoon he preached from Eph : 4.3.   Endeavouring to keep the unity of the spirit in the bond of peace, he reckoned that they were run distracted in Holmfirth and said *The Independent Whig*[41] their darling author was a very pernicious Book—In a word he did not preach but . . . discourse was . . . malicious and uncharitable.

[42] John Kaye of Netherthong died 3 March 1744-5.

1745.   23 May.   I hear that Alexander Macaulay of Huddersfield died some since.   23.

Sarah Dixon buried on Sunday 27 May 1745.

Sawny Micolly[43] of Huddersfield.

20 July.   Nathaniel Bury of deanhouse buried 22.   died 20.

Aug. 30.   Mr Kaye of Butterly died aged 34 years.

[38] Probably about his alleged Jacobitism.
[39] On a scrap of paper pasted in.
[40] On the back of the same scrap of paper.
[41] *The Independent Whig*, a periodical edited by John Trenchard and T. Gordon, ran from Jan. 28, 1720 to Jan. 4, 1721.   It was republished by Thomas Gordon in 1732 in two volumes, with the title *The Independent Whig*, or a Defence of Primitive Christianity, and of our Ecclesiastical Establishment against the Exorbitant Claims and Encroachments of Fanatical and Disaffected Clergymen.
[42] On a sheet of paper pasted in after the end of the diary.
[43] Sawny Micolly is Alexander Macaulay (above).

24 April 1739. John Kaye of Netherthong married to Elizth Oxley.

29 Jan^{ry} 1742. I was at Netherthong to visit Abraham Woodhead he was dead when I got there.

Feb^{ry} 2. I was at the funeral of Abraham Woodhead of Netherthong buried at Almondbury Set up my horse at Mr George Morehouse & came home with Wid^w Morehouse of Thurstonland.

16. I was a Sofley to visit John Wordsworth's wife.

April 2^d. I was at Sofley to visit John Wordsworths daughter I called at Carlcoats at Mr Empsons.

May 1. George Beaumont of Netherthong died on Wednesday the 28 ult, buried this day. I sent my brother to the funeral in my stead.

RALPH WARD'S JOURNAL

1754-6

1754. A Jounal of some occurrances kept by Ra. Ward begun 6th Sep[t] 1754.

Sbr. 7. Sister Jackson came to Guisborough and stayed to the 28th when my servant John peirson set her home.

10. Fra Fox and self went over Hamilton to Sutton, the next day met Mr Collingwood of York and Miss Harvey with another young Lady to treat about the Sale of Sutton, but we could not agree. Mr Collingwood went for York in the afternoon, the Ladys to Thirsk in the Evening, but Mr Fox and I stayed Sutton that and the night before, Lodgeing at Ste: Stappletons, on Thursday Morning the 12th we went to Thirsk, stayed about an Houre, from thence Home bated at John Anderson's Stocksley.

12. John pease of Darlington and his Mother came from thence to my House. Stayed all night from thence went next morning for Whitby.

13. Mr yoward of york called upon me at Gisborough with whome had some conference about his purchase of my nephew Spencers part of Hutton Locers[1] Estate.

Mrs pennyman of Normanby and Mrs Finch came here in there Shaze, and reconed with me about Interest, they dined at Mr Jackson's.

16. I dined with the Justices at their Brewster Sessions, Mr Robinson, Mr Scottowe and Mr Beckwith.

Same evening Coz. John pease from Whitby came here about John Longstaf affairs, the 17th he went with me to Grange where parted the 18th. I dined at Steaths[2] with Mr Wardell at Mr Jefferson's, all went to Grange in the afternoon, and to Boulby in the Evening, the 19th having been at Boulby two nights I came home. 20th, nephew and niece Jefferson came to Gisborough and stayed until the 23rd when I went with him to Grange where met me Mr Charles Turner, Mr Nelson with two or 3 servants also 2 Mr Mewburns to se some fatt oxon they bid me 9[li] a piece for 8 but we could not bargain, I lay that night at Boulby. Same day the *Darling* loaded 42-10 allom. the 24th came home in the forenoon along with Mr Wardel on his way to Ellemor, at night I was with the Collectors of Excise of whom Received £130 for my Bill on Robert Core.

---

[1] Hutton Lowcross or Locras, a small township under Roseberry Topping.
[2] Staithes.

26ᵗʰ. went to the Cock and dined at the Clubb where was Sir Wm. Lowther³ Mr Turner, his two Bros. William and John and nephew Charles, Mr Lasscels, Mr Murgatroid, Mr Hide, Messrs John Jackson, William Jackson, William Bottom, Tho: proddy, a stranger one Fawcet a Lawyer and myself.

27. Mrs Chaloner arrived at Gisbrough from London setting out from thence on Wednesday the 25ᵗʰ. and got to Allerton the day after and to Gisbrough about noon the day following having been out upon the Journey less than a month. Mr Hide came to my House when we talkt over the Affair of building a bridge at Skelton Ellers, Sir William Lowther having agreed to giv 20ᵘ.

28. I wen to see a Tup at Widow Newburn's of Eston where stayed about 1½ hour, from thence I went to Normanby to see Mrs penyman, in my betwix parson Consetts house⁴ and hers my Horse takeing Fright threw me but thank God I got little harm. I did not light there. I was at home most of the time from 28ᵗʰ Sept. to the 4ᵗʰ of Oct. on which day I went to Grange along with John Aysley, he took measure for makeing Windows at the new house on Robinson's farm, that night I lay at Boulby, next day the 5ᵗʰ I came Home, in my way at Skelton I met Mr Wardel returning from Ellemore⁵ where he had been Since the 24ᵗʰ past.

Oct. 5. William Newburn sent me a Tup which I paid him for £2 17s.

The 7 at home from the 5ᵗʰ to the 10ᵗʰ when I went to Boulby was all night there, from whence came with Mr Wardel and Mr Jefferson to Grang next morning. So home at noon.

13. being Sunday Mr Thos. Spencer dying the 10ᵗʰ he was buried this day when I was a bearer.

14. Wm. White came to Gisbrough to by Seed Wheat, bought 15 bushels from Ridcar at 4/- for sowing Low Miklehow. Same day Mr Mathews paid me £100 from Mrs Lisle and John N of Saxby for Sheep £16 9s.

15. John Flownders and Wm. Tose came to Gisbrough and dined

³ The Rev. Sir William Lowther of Little Preston, rector of Swillington; son of Christopher Lowther; born 1707; married Anne, daughter of Rev. Charles Zouch, vicar of Sandal; died June 15th, 1788.
⁴ The Rev. William Consett, of Normanby House, which he built, married Elizabeth, daughter of William Pennyman, Esq., of Normanby, and died Hay 29th, 1762, aged 76 years. He was B.A. Trin. Coll., Camb.; Deacon, 1709; Priest, 1711, York, and Vicar of Ormsby, 1743.
⁵ Ellemore, called Elmore and Elemore Hall in eighteenth century—a house and land about two miles N.E. of the city of Durham. *The Diary of Thomas Gyll* notes, "June 5, 1751. Towards the end of last year George Baker, esq., finished the building of his house at Elmore Hall," and "1758. Jan. 6. Mrs Francis Burton, widow of Richard Burton, late of Elmore Hall was buried." (Surtees Soc., 118, pp. 197, 203.) Mr. Wardell himself had a house near Skinnington Bank.

with me and paid me the Ballance of an Account 42 : 8 : 0 Returned 15/6. the rest of the day at home.

16. Mrs Joana Consett came and dined at my House when we sent for Mr Hide who also dined and then granted her administration of her Son pennymans Effects. I and my servant Tho : presswick was Bound with her in £70 for her performance.

17. All day at home when ordered a Staddle[6] to be made in the Stackgarth to set Beans upon.

October 18. I went to Stockton in the morning along with Fra : Fox where I settled with Mr Maddeson a difference betwixt him and Mrs Joana Conset about his Bill out of which I paid hime £13 8s. and he abated £5. I was also at Mrs Dowthwaits but she was out a visiting So did but see Mrs Allan. I was at Mr Bells the Book seller and paid his Bill £8 : 13, who and Mr Maddeson came and Sit the Evening. next day the 19th we went to yarm Fair where I had many people met me about business and Bought 3 Steers for Wintering, about half after three we came from thence and got home abiut half after six.

20. being Sunday nothing remarkable.

21. begun Flaging the fore kitching by N. patton and lead all the Beans from Westland ground which was set upon the new Staddle and Covered in, though most of them was led the 19th.

22. Wm. Westland and Richard Walker haveing great difference about a large Sum the former ought the latter, was with me in the morning who was reconciled for the present. Afternoon I went to view 11 acre of Fogg[6a] and some pasterage by Chappel Bridge for which I bid 55/- but we did not settle it.

23. All day at home.

24. went with John Aysley to Grange about the windows which he put in that day. I went to Boulby and to Steaths where I dined and lay at Boulby.

25. I came Home in my way met the Skelton Doctor, got home about 2 o'clock, gave same day my Bill to Mr Fox at 20 days for £20 16s. 10d.

26. all day at Home also 27th, on that morning begun to rain with the Wind at N. and N,W. which continued most of that day and all night all next day and most of the night which occasioned a very great Flood Seldom a biger has been known in these parts.

28. at Home, Mr Hide sent me Mrs Consett's Letter of Administration for her Late Son pennyman Consett which sent her same day.

29. at Home. Wm. Lincoln reckned with me at Home.

30. at Home all day.

[6] Staddle, a frame on which to set plants to dry, or on which hay is placed in making a pike, the foundation of a stack.
[6a] Fogg. The second crop of hay. Still called Fogg in Westmorland and Cumberland.

31. Went to Boulby lay all that night at Steaths.

1st November.   in my way to Boulby went by Dale House Mill[7]
to view the Bridge how it was after the great flood, all about it
lookt well, but the flood there seemed not to have been so high by
3 or 4 ft. as that in June 1725, got home 1st November about noon,
next day, the 2nd, all day at Home.

3.   Sunday at Church twice, afternoon Mary Hedon a poor
Woman was buried.

John price came to work at my new building.   4th all day at Home,
had some conference with Mr preston about my Chancery Sute
with Mr Dent and also about John Sayrs affair.   Wm. Willis came
to my House which I settled an account about his Kelp[8] and Rent
to whom I paid £4 0 4 to Ballance.   Same day Oliver pressick
desired two masons which I consented for 2 days.

5.   Sent Thomas preswick to Bishps Auckland to Receive Cousin
Ann Dunn's Rent.   Fra: Fox went along with him so far as Stenton[9]
near Bishopton.   I was at home all day among my Workmen.   Jack
Arrowsmith came from Boulby and returned again after dinner, in
the evening attended the Excise from whom received £150 for my
Bill.

6.   all day at home.

the 7th went to Boulby which in the forenoon was very Rainy
with Wind at S excessive high, called at Grange and ordered a good
fire to dry me being very wet lay at Bouby all night, next day the

8th.   bid Wm. White go to Redcar and buy some seed wheat
for sowing upon fore field Barly Stubble, I came home same
day.

9th.   At Home all day, afternoon one Coats came along with
Mr Fox to my House who is a Tenant to Nephew Thomas Spencer to
enquire about his farm at Stenton[10] in County Durham he being
under some uncertainty whether or no he was to stay upon it.   I
advised him to be easie for Mr Spencer would not turn him out
without just occasion.   Same day at night a House at Scugdale[11]
near Whorlton was Robbed and the Family ill used by four Thieves
who took away £20.

10th Sunday.   John price and his son came here to Work, John's
Wife and Daughter also, a child came with them, the 3 latter and
John lay at pulman's and the Son at my House.

[7] Dale House Mill, close to Staithes.
[8] Kelp is obtained from the combustion of seaweeds.   These are dried
in the sun and burnt in shallow pits, a ton of Kelp (the ash) being
obtained from 20 tons of seaweed.   It is of value for the iodine it contains.
It was not very largely used in the Cleveland district at this period.
[9] Stenton, Great Stainton and Little Stainton are close to Bishopton.
The latter is meant.
[10] Stainton.
[11] A small secluded valley, south-east of Whorlton.

11. all day at Home.

12th went to Boulby where they begun to slaughter beasts the 11th.

13th. Mr Wardel got there in the evening out Bishoprick where he had been since 19th Oct.

14th Thomas Knaggs and John Nickleson met me at Boulby the former paid me for Hides and the Latter for Cattle and Sheep. Mr Jefferson dined with us at Boulby that day, and the next, 15th, all day at Boulby, next day the 16th John p came there to carry Tongues &c to Gisbrough where I went with him, got home by noon, the 17th went to Church fore and afternoon. 18th faire day at Gisbrough. Mr preston dined with me, Robert Burdon paid me 2 years Interest for £100 and wanted to borrow £150 more for his Daughters portion. I promised to lend him that sum.

Nov. 19th. All day at Home.

the 20th Went to Boulby called upon Mr Lascels at Skelton who followed me to Grang where met us Mr Wardel and there walked about an hour or more and then Went to Boulby where dined upon Beef stakes. after 4 we set out and parted at Skelton, self and servant got home about 7 at Night.

21st all day at Home.

22nd. Mr Fox and I went to Liverton[12] to speak with one Mr Beuley of York come there to divide a Common pasture. Wee appeared there in behalf of Nephew Richard Spencer who haveing a Freehold farme at that place and a Right to about 13 Acre of the said Common, after viewing the same along with Mr Beuley and settling the Affaire we went to Luke Ripleys the Tenant and dined there, from thence to Lofthouse, I called at Miss Mores but she was not at home. Mr Fox left me there and went for Gisbrough and I went to Grang from thence to Boulby, from thence to Steaths, where I met with Mr Wardel and the Skelton Docktor at Mr Jeffersons, and stayed there about 2 hours, when we 3 came away together the Doctor to Skelton and Mr Wardel and I to Boulby where I lay the night, next morning the 23rd we both came to Gisbrough, where we dined and he went for Bishobrig,[13] Richard Reah came same day to speak to me about taking armstrong Farm but we could not agree he returned home at night.

24th. 9ber. Sunday all day at Home.

On 25th. At Home Mr Jackson and Mr preston dined with me the latter paid me 24ll 10s 0d the remainder of Jo: Sayers money. I gave him 1ll 1s for his Trouble. John Clark of Lofthouse with whom I settled with to make up £30, he owes me £100 upon the

[12] Liverton, a village and ancient chapelry south of Lofthouse.
[13] The Bishoprick, as it was then generally spelt, i.e., the Diocese of Durham.

mortgage of Moorsom Tyth[14] under Lease from the Archbishop of York.

26ᵗʰ. All day at home, a severe frost, Will White brought three lean oxen to winter at Gisbrough, and took away 4 oxen and a Cow for feeding at Grange.

27. all day at home, a severe frost. T. Young paid his last may-day Rent, much snow fell last night.

28ᵗʰ. Sore frost all day and pretty much snow. Mr Wardel out Bishoprick came here in the evening and lay all night. I was taken ill of the Gravel on my left side went to bed at 7, but forced by an excess of pain to get up and order a vomit of Camamil which soon gave me ease.

29ᵗʰ. A great frost. Mr Wardel went to Boulby from whence he came the 23ʳᵈ Inst, myself at home where have been since the last mentioned day, in the night on the 29ᵗʰ had another severe fitt of the gravel being forced to get up about 2 next morning, but in 3 or 4 hours was much better, great frost.

30th. frost continues, all day at Home.

1754. 1ˢᵗ. All day (being Sunday) at home. Frost holds yet with more snow in the morning.

2ⁿᵈ. Some abatement of the frost, Wind high out the West but fair, thaw continues, more snow about the houses gone. gave Mr Jackson a bill on Mr Core for £300 of which he paid me 270 the . . . and his note, Mrs Consett sent me £13 8 I paid Mr Maddison at Stockton in October last.

1754. Dec. 3ʳᵈ. All day at home. Thaw continued.

4ᵗʰ. Went to Boulby with Servant John p, where I stayed, that and next day open weather. Wind at N. West.

6ᵗʰ. I came Home in my way called at Grang and saw 36 Bushels of Bean measured that Will White brought the day before from Whitby and then weighed half a bushel of it, which was 18 and ½ by my bushel, there I made out only 33 bushels. Same day a severe frost, Wind West.

7ᵗʰ. Frost continued. A shower snow the night before. Same day Mrs Mathews called at my House to Aquaint me about Ann Cornfurth and her Son William's affairs. She and he with some of her Family being very ill.

the 8ᵗʰ. Was month Sunday[15] Great rain part of the day.

10ᵗʰ. Fine day at night. Went to Excise and received £150 for my bill on Mr Core.

11ᵗʰ. I went to Boulby, with servant T.p.

12ᵗʰ. all day there, at night a violent Wind at So.E. and much rain.

---

[14] Great Moorsholm, a collection of houses near Skelton.

[15] The " month Sunday " occurs several times in this diary. It probably means that the Holy Communion was still administered here on the second Sunday (generally the second) in the month.

13th. A pay at Boulby with John Jefferson and Mr Sanderson dined with us. I received the case about his following the Idle Trad(ition?) of keeping a pack of Dogs and Hunting. Weather pretty good.

14th. Came home called at Grange and paid my men there all but George Langstaff the Carpenter. A strong wind all forenoon at West but dry weather.

15th. Much rain. Wind at S. Evening clear weather.

17th. Sent Mr Scottow £100 in part of my note to him for £1200, in the evening came Richard Reah, my Tenant at Ayslaby and his wive's brother, Richard Corker, near Stranton in Co. Durham, a Batchelor. To the latter I let my Farm at Ayslaby at present possessed by William Armstrong, for which he is to pay me £140 p.a. exclusive of the Hall and gardens, save the Barn and fould garth there which he is to have, and I am to allow him 40/- p.ann. for Manner he to pay all taxes except Land tax and quit rent, to have a Lease for 21 years to be if he pleases at Liberty at 3 years end. dry Clear Skie in the evening inclined to frost.

18th. Open Weather Wind South, fair all day, John price came here about noon. Richard Reah and his brother went away at same time.

19th. All day at home.

20th. Went to Grange where reckoned with George Langstaff and paid him to the last of November 1754 £8: 13 4: also Will White for one years Interest for 100, due. 22nd October last, then went to Boulby where reckned with Thomas Trattles about his kelp and Rents due March last, paid Mr Wardell in cash and paid years Rent £82 for which he gave me a Bill on Robert Core at 30 days paid £82.

21. Returned to Grang where viewed the Mason work and Thomas pressick met me there with whome came home in the evening sent for Mr Wm. Lor Bottom to whom I paid in part for Deals and Timber 22. 3: also settled with John price and paid his Bill £8. 2. 7¼. A severe frost all day.

1754. 22nd 10ber. fine Calm Weather, was at Church forenoon, and the Evening. Sent my Servants Thomas presswick and John pearson with £6 about the town to distribute among 110 poor people.

23rd. fresh calm Weather, in the morning Robert Aplebee of pate Hall came, also Robert Armstrong, the latter paid me his Father Wm. Armstrong last March Rent vizt. 57. These two with Mr preston and Mr Robert sugget dined with me to the Latter I paid £44 17s. to make up what he then owed me £1000, he gave me his Bond for 130. Mr Wm. Jackson paid me £30, remainder of the last Bill he had from me, also £200 for two Bills I gave him upon Robert Core one for £118, the other from Mr. Wardell to me for

L

£82. Joshua Stockton paid me a years Rent due May day last £2: 10. Lent Mrs Jane Stead £8 on her note to pay me again in a few days, paid Mr Bottom the remainder of his Bill for Timber, and 2^{li} odd money. had some conference with Mr Hide and Mr Lasscels about Skelton Ellers Bridges, they promised to assist in getting them forward.

24. at Home all day.

25. Christmas Day at home.

26. Dined at Mr Jackson's with Mr Garmisway and his Son in Law with Mr Jackson of Lackinby, stayed till about 7 in the evening. Nephew Ralph Jackson came here same day.

27. at Home.

28 & 29th. at Home.

30th. Mr Mathews paid me £23: 17: for a Land Bill. he dined with me when gave him a Bill on Mr Core £113: 7: 4 for which he gave me his note but no money Henry Steel desired to borrow £40 also Gregory Rowland of Wapeley[16] desired to borrow £30 the former offered a Mortgage, the latter is to have the money if his Father John Rowland will be Bound with him. Same day Mr preston came and showed me my case and opinion thereon about my peate affairs.

31st. Ralph Jackson went away but intended to lie at Yarm the night, the School Dame came when was entered 8 children into the Charity School and others their time was expired. Ralph Jackson did not go away till next morning.

1755

Jan. 1st. All day at home, but at Church the forenoon. Open Weather Wind at E.

2nd. at home, about Noon Mr Wardle came here and stayed all night.

3rd. about 9 in the morning he went away. Wind N.E. frequent showers of rain.

4th. at Home with John Sillaburn the Joyner was told that he need not come to work again till sent for.

5th. twice at Church, in the Afternon called at Mr Hides where stayed an Hour and Half when showed him Sir Wm. Lowther's letter about Skelton Ellers Bridge and gave him a paper I'd drawn up about it.

---

[16] Whapley, Waupley, to-day generally spelt Wapley.

6th. Sent for Robert corney and spoke to him about 6 years Rent he is in arrears with Mrs Chaloner for his Farm. I have engaged for £30 lent him, also sent for Widow Hudson to speak to her about her husbands will, same day dined with Mr Skottow and Mr Beckwith at Cock[1] when they held their Highway Sessions, where also dined Chris Jackson, Michael Smith, george Snowdon, a stranger and Mr Lawton.

Jan. 6th. Robert Dalton came and we agreed that he should give up his house and Farme at Lady day and may next when he promised to pay me my rent Honestly and when he did so, promised to be kind to him.

7. at home, very thick fogge wether, wind at E. & N.E.

the 8th. at home. Fine day. Wind at West. John pease from Darlington came here with his brothem Wm. and stayed all night. next day

9th. went for Whitby, when I set out for Boulby with servant T.p. met Mr Wardel at Skelton when sent T.p. back and Mr Wardell and I went forward to Boulby, called at Grang stayed about an hour. Fine open wether Wind at N.W.

10th. John Jefferson came and dined with us, after diner John Gallon came and paid me for an extra ox he had got last February, and Thomas Allen paid me £4. 15. 9. heed reckoned for beef and I paid him his Bill for Losses &c 1 : 2 : 3½. Mr Wardell set me to Grange in my way home where T.p. was come to meet me, got to Gisbrough about 2 in afternoon.

12. all day at Home being in a Sunday John pease and brother dind here and went for Darlington same day.

13th. was up street spoke with Mr Jackson about cash for Bills, but he had none to spare but I paid Mr Mathews 2 of Mr Wardell's Bills on Mr Core to give money for them the 26th inst. Saw Mr preston and parson Consett. Fine weather but very Cold. William Rogers my Tenant dined with me, Robert Thomas stayed with me near two Hours in the Evening.

14th. Much snow fell with Wind at N.W. in the Evening a Clap of Thunder with lightning and a shower of Haile.

15th. much snow, all day at home.

16th. I went for Boulby with my man T.p.[2] overtook company at Skelton and sent T.p. back again home. called at Grange, and so to Boulby and same day paid M[r] Wardell £200 for two Bills given me by M[r] Core. A most severe frost. Wind S and exceeding Cold.

the 17th. great frost. Wind S. Jno Jefferson dined with us at Boulby.

18th. the *Darling* lay on in the morning to take in 46 Tons of

[1] The Cock inn.
[2] Thomas Presswick.

Allom[3] for London. I came from Boulby 9 in the morning. Mr Wardells boy set me to Grange Gate to whome I gave 2/6 as a new year gift, at Grange Tho: presswick came to me with whome I came home, open Weather, fine Rideing. not very cold. Wind S. got here about noon.

the 19th. at home Wind So. Weather very Windy, Some drisling Rain.

the 20th at Home. Wind So. Weather, dark windy day frequent drisling Rain with Some heavy Showers. M[r] Mathews paid me £213. 12. 7, in part of £313. 12. 7 for Bills, remainder unpaid £100, paid me them at Mr Hides where I was with Mr Hide, Mr Prody, Mr Lasscels, Mr Smith Mr Danby and William Watson to consult about building two Bridges at Skelton Ellers, where we concluded to begin a Subscription for Carrying Same into Execution, in comeing home I met in the Market-place Mr Robert Walker the Butcher of Shields who promised to come and Sit the Evening with me which he did Staying till 9 a'clock. he wanted to buy some of my oxon but told him most of the best was promised. he intended the next day for Whitby.

Jana 21. I went in the morning to Ormsby along with John Aysley and servant T.p. there being a public sale there of Household goods where I bought 4 Fire ranges with fender, poker, Shovel & Tongs to each and 2 brushes to them all, also a dum Water,[4] Reading desk, with a little table and Candle stick all of mahoggany also 6 Chares for all which I paid 13: 8: 6, put up my Horse at M[r] Robinson's where I dined, he being then very ill in the Gout, his Tenant Mr Watson was there with him, ill in the same distemper. all day fine Weather Wind So. got home in same Company before 5 in the evening, when went to the Sitting of Excise and received of the Collector £150, for which gave a Bill on Robert Core, Stayed till nine at Night.

the 22nd. all day at home William Armstrong and Son Robert came about noon and both dined here, the former promised hereafter to *behave* well and leave his Farm in a Husbandly manner and all things else relateing thereto on which I promised if he did So

---

[3] The alum works at Belman Bank near Guisbrough were the oldest in the country and were begun by Sir Thomas Chaloner, some time previous to 1600. Alum works at Lofthouse and Boulby claimed to have begun in 1615. At first the alum fetched very high prices, but these had dropped considerably at this date. About a mile to the east of Guisbrough were the Alum House and the works belonging to the Chaloners. Sir Thomas Chaloner is said, perhaps with doubtful authority, to have smuggled Italian workmen out of the papal dominions in order to teach his people how to work alum. Fuller says that the first workers came from Rochelle. The manufacture continued in the district till the early years of Victoria. The Alum works at Egton claimed to be older than those at Belmangate.

[4] Dumb waiter, a piece of furniture with revolving shelves, enabling the users to dispense with a human waiter.

to be very kind to him and better then he can expect. Francis Fox who was married same day to John Danby sister came, with whom had some conference about the Sale of Sutton &c. Fine Weather all day the wind moderate at S.E.

23rd. all day at home.

24th. Went for Boulby. Tho: presswick Set me to Grange. A most severe Frost but calm the Aire at S. an ox was killed at Boulby for Jno. Jefferson, save a quarter for myself. M[r] Jefferson dined with us.

25th. John peirson came there for the quarter Beefs in the morning with Mr Wardell and my Self set out for Gisbrough called at Grange but did not light, got to Gisbrough about noon where he dined and went for Bishopric that night. Severe frost Wind at S but moderate.

Sunday 26. hard frost. Wind S and moderate. Mr Lascels made Service Mr Hide being at Yarm but came home at Noon they were both at Church but the former did service.

27. hard frost Wind N.E. very thick in the morning with some pewlings of Snow, up Street I called at M[r] preston's at J Husbands & M[r] Hides where saw Mr Nelson. Thomas Wharton came & paid his last Mar[t5] Rent. John Gallon came here, they both Dined with me. Richard Thomson of Redcar came & told me he hoped to pay me £20 he owes me in a little time. Dr Charles Bisset[6] of Skelton came & desired a Bill for 10[li] which I gave him upon Mr Core at 28 days. stayed an Houre when also gave him 15/- for Inocculateing a poor Child at Skelton.

28. at home. Mr Robert Walker called here in his return from Whitby and took a bate, & set forward for Sheilds, he prest me to sell him my best ox but I declined it. Wind at N.E. a moderate frost & fine Weather.

29th. went to Whitby Servant T.p. was with me, called at Boulby, got to Whitby about 2 in the afternoon A sore cold day, wind at E with frequent Shower of Snow.

30. all day at Whitby where John Jefferson came, did business with Sundry people. Sent for M[r] Taylor who is M[r] Cholmley's Clark and Agent about his Mills with whom I treated about some dam[a7] floor for my Sheep.

31[t]. Set out in the morning along with John Jefferson & Servant

[5] Martinmas.

[6] Dr. Charles Bissett lived in Guisborough for many years. He was the author of *Theory and Construction of Fortifications, 1751, A Treatise on Scurvy, 1753. An Essay on the Medical Constitution of Great Britain, 1762*. He was educated as a physician at Edinburgh University, and took his M.D. at St. Andrew's. He was an Army surgeon in Jamaica, a lieutenant and engineer in the Army in Flanders till 1748. For a time he preached at Skelton in Cleveland, and he died at Knayton, near Thirsk, in 1791.

[7] Dammar is gum used for making pitch and tar and for caulking ships, here a kind of asphalt floor is meant.

T.p. A Sore day with much Snow, wind at N. T.p. left us in Mickleby Fields & went over the Moor when Mr Jefferson & I went for Steaths where I dined & went to Boulby where I lay that night, next day the 1ᵗ February called at Grang, in my way home met T.p. with him came home. the Weather abated but Wind at No.

2nd. being Sunday at Church forenoon, frequent Showers of Snow moderate frost.

Febʳ 3. Mr Foster came here last night and left me a paper his Mrs had received from Mr Bows giving an Account of a further Imposition carrying on before parliament to increase the duty upon turn picks⁹ in the Coal way. I went with Mr Hide to Mr Chaloner with whom consulted about the thing in order to oppose it. Mr Wᵐ Sutton being in Town same day I went to him at the Cock and sit with the Company till 9 at night where was Mr Sutton, Mr Beckwith, Mr Hide, Mr Jackson, Mr proddy when I gave Mr Sutton a Copy of said paper and desired he would make further enquiry about it, he then paid me 20ˡⁱ for a year's Interest p. £500 due the 29ᵗʰ past and then lent Mr Beckwith on his note £16 to pay again the 17ᵗʰ July Inst.

4ᵗʰ. went to Boulby with T.p. where lay all night.

5ᵗʰ. Sent 2 oxon for John Gallon and Richard Andrew Slaughtered at Boulby day before Mr Milburn of Lyth called at Boulby to treat about my Wareh¹⁰ at Sandsend I set him £150 for the purchase. 2 Butchers out the Moor came, with whom I went to Grange to see the Sheep, one of them offered 37/6 a peice for few of them. came home same day, modderate Weather. frost Something abated.

6. all day at home. about noon Mr Wardel returned out of Cᵒ of Durham where he's been since the 25ᵗʰ January, he dined here and went for Boulby about 2 the same day.

7ᵗʰ. all day at home. Wind S.E. a frost at Night Severe.

8ᵗʰ. very severe.

9ᵗʰ. mᵒ Sunday. A Frost Wind N.W.

10ᵗʰ. went to Boulby on which day a large ox was killed there. weight 110 stone, also another about 74 stone, both for Mr Jefferson.

11ᵗʰ. met George Mewburn at Grange. Mr Wardel with me. sold the former 20 Wethers to be 2ˡⁱ 1ˢ 0ᵈ a piece to take 5. A Week till gone. Wind N. A frost.

12ᵗʰ. went to Allerton a hard frost. got there about 3. Mr Crosfield came & Sit the Evening with me Mr Hodshon paid me 16ˡⁱ for Interest. Saw Mr Careless that night.

the 13ᵗʰ. Was in the beast market but few Cattle in it, also few Sheep & those very ordinary. Mr peter Conset paid me £34 for Interest. Saw John Langdale & Duke Fogge, who and one Robson

⁹ Turnpikes.
¹⁰ Warehouse.

a Tenant at Dindsdale dined with me. A Frost. Wind N. Set out about 11 found much snow fallen the night before, good rideing but frost. got home ½ after 4 in the evening. Tho: p was with me.

14ᵗʰ. a very hard frost. Wind N sit home all day, at night met Sundry neighbours at Franklain's who had a tripe Feast that (*sic*) Inwards from Boulby, Mr Hide, Mr Lasscels, Mr Thompson out Bishopric. Mr Bottom, Mr Jackson, Mr Fox, John Husband, John Aysley, Mr Danby, Mr Foster & myself Mr proddy came after 9 at night. when I came away & left 5/- p. my Shot.

the 15ᵗʰ at Home. Wind S and a brave thaw. Mr Madden writ me a Letter along with Mr Wm Sleigh of Stockton his Clerk who brought me Mr Sleigh's Bond for £200 by whome I sent that sum. Same day had A good deal to do about Oliver pressick to whom had lent £300, he having sold his ship to Jacob Bottom, but could not confirm the bargain till I gave him 5 bills of sale I had in my Custody for the said £300. Writ to Mr Sutton about the Allom affair, also to Mr Wardell to be here on munday next by his boy who brought here from Boulby A piece of Beef to be sent to Ellemore by the newsman, the ox was Killed at Boulby the 10ᵗʰ.

the 16ᵗʰ. at home Wind S. and thaw afternoon. Rain and very much in the night following, at Church forenoon.

17. Mr Wardell came here in the forenoon, dined and went that night for Stockton, was up Street spoke with Chief Jackson, also Mr preston, John Nicholson paid me 26ˡⁱ 11s. returned 5/- again being for two oxen & 7 sheep.

18ᵗʰ. Mr Readhead came & desired I would lend him £150, which I agreed to on his & his Father Milburn's Bond to be Executed the 24ᵗʰ Inst. Mr Wardell returned from Stockton, dined here, and went for Boulby.

1755. 19ᵗʰ Febr. Jacob Bottom and his Sister Havelock desired to lend them on their Joynt notes £60 payable on demand wherewith I served them.

20ᵗʰ. went to Boulby at Grange met Mr Wardel, George Mewburn, & John Nickleson. George chused out 20 Weathers before sold him & sent 5 away when sold J. Nickelson 10 of the Worst at 31/- each he took two away. I sent one by cart to Boulby where he was killed.

the 21. Sent a quarter to Whitby, a loyn to Mr Jefferson, a legg to Mr Wardel A quarter to Mr More's & a qr home.

22ⁿᵈ. T.p met me at B, with whome I came home that night. I was taken with a fitt of the gout in my left great toe, the pain was not severe but continued.

23. at home all day.

24ᵗʰ. at home, at noon Mr Baker came & dined went for Boulby, that morning lent Mr Readhead and Father Milburn 150ˡⁱ.

25th. at home all day.

the 26th. the same Frequent Showers of Snow but moderate Winds much at S.E.

27. at home.

28. at home, Mr Wardel & Mr Baker came from Boulby, dined and went for Stockton or Yarm that night.

March 1^t. at Home, one Sidebottom, a Rider to a Distiller of London came & Shewed me a list of Contributers for putting posts upon the Moors from home to Whitby and from thence to Scarborough for the direction of Travelers. I gave him 2 guinys as a Contribution thereto.

2^d. at home Mr Jackson & Mr Longbottom came to see me.

3rd. at home, Mr Priston dined with me as did John Price. my Gout abates but am very Costive & dry this morning I lost a tooth in bedd by a grate of another against it, which gave me great pain.

4th at home. Sent Tho: preswick to Excise with my Bill upon Mr Core for £150 for which I Received the money.

5. at home my gout begun to pain me afresh on the outside my left Ancle, Maurice Lincoln came & reckoned with me about Tallow &c. Ballance due to me £43. 3. 6. he gave me a note payable on demand for 40 and promised to pay 3. 3. 6 very shortly. John Aysley came to see me.

6th Snow most of the day. Wind at E..

7. Snow most of the day. Wind at N.E. my Gout continues but not painful but my left legg and foot being Wrapt in flanel I cannot Stirr out of Doors besides the ground is covered with Snow.

8th. last night & this morning much Snow. Wind at N.E. with frost. Sent T. presswick to Stockesley with a letter to leave with Mr Scottowe & another for Mr Mathews about remitting £300 which Sum I intend to send Geo: Jackson who has got the place of Chief Clerk in the navy Office Conferred upon him and awaits that sum he has engaged to pay for his comeing into it, now being in possession thereof as hee's been for a Week or 10 days past.

9th. morning Sunday Snowy bad weather. Wind at N^o E.

10. ground covered with Snow but gone at Night. Wind N.E. Mr preston called & Stayed near an Hour as did Mr Mewburn to Enquire about the sale of Sutton. Also Mr Mathews came & desired I woud lend him & Mr Hewlet £300 on their Joynt Bond. I paid the money to Mr Mathews and took his note but am to have the Bond Saterday next the 15th Inst.

the 11th. Ground covered with Snow, Wind N & Stormy. Mr Hide & John Benneson the Mason called here the last night to treat about the Bridges building at Skelton Ellers and appointed monday the 24th of this month to confir together thereon. the said 11 Mr Edmund pressick called here & stayed near 2 hours, paid me 3 halfyears' Interest for £500 due the 9ᵗʰ Inst. Snowy morning. Ground covered but calm.

12. much snow in the morning. Wind N and Boisterous. Francis Fox dined with me today. Mr Errington called to see me. Will Dalton came to know what he might do about Staying in his House which we in some measure settled and that he should sell his Horses & Hay to pay his Rent that will be due at May Day.

13. Moderate Weather inclined to Frost. Wind N.

14. Severe Frost. Wind West. sent John Peirson this morning to Boulby with 7ˡⁱ to William Stevenson for the men.

15. great frost, Wind S, but came thence before noon. Mr Edmund pressick call here on his return home with whom had some Conference about the Allom Affair. Tho. pressick was at Stockesley today, was witness to a Bond from Mr Mathews & Howlet for £300.

16. Wind S. Skie dark & thick but moderate weather. Wm White from Grange came here to let me know how all was there.

17ᵗʰ. Wind S. moderate weather & faire. many people called upon me today. Mr Sleigh of Stockton, Mr preston, Chief Jackson, Nicholas patton, Wm Hobkirk & divers others.

18ᵗʰ. at home moderate weather Wind S.

19ᵗʰ. my Gout being very Easie I got on my Boots and went with Mr Hide, Mr Lo: Bottom to view Skelton Ellers where the Bridges is to be erected when Mr proddy, Mr Smith, Mr Danby, peter Con & William Watson met us, where we stayed above 2 Hours Expecting John Benneson the Mason but he did not come. So we parted. Mr Hide & I went to Skelton to dine with Mr Lassels where came to us, from Hunting Mr proddy, Mr Smith, Mr Isaac Scarth, Mr Lo. Bottom along with Mr Lasscels from the Field and all dined there with Mr Castle¹¹ the parson. Mr Hide and I left the company about 5, and came Home to geather. Same day sent Tho pressick to Stockton with 100ˡⁱ to Mr Maddison to be lent John Jordeson Claxton & His Son which with 100ˡⁱ he ought me before on bond which I lent Jnᵒ and they both Joyned in another bond of this days' date for £200. Weather Calme & modderate. Wind S.E. quite easie in my Gout.

20ᵗʰ. at Home.

21ᵗ. went to Boulby Tho. pressicks with me to Grang when returned stayed there 2 Hours. W. White went with me to Boulby. Viewed the Hedges now in Scouring where they were lowsing Allom.

22. went to pitts Hill. Tho: p. with me haveing come from G. that morning. Call at Grang stayed 2 Houres there to wate on Mr More but he did not come, from thence came Home where met Mr Wardel out Bishoprick he having been there since the 28ᵗʰ Febr in all 23 days.

¹¹ J. W. Ord, *Hist. of Cleveland*, calls him Castley. He was Vicar of Skelton and was buried there May 30th, 1760.

Mar. 23ᵈ. Sunday, all day at home. fine moderate Weather, as it has been for a week or more. Wind mostly S.

24ᵗʰ. fine day Wind S, dined with me Mr Const. Skottow to whom paid £200 for his Father: he beieng ill in an Eye & could not come himself, also dined Mr preston, John Harman. John Nickleson paid me 15ˡⁱ 5ˢ for 10 sheep, also George Mewburn called here with the two latter appointed to meet at Grang to buy 29 Wethers on Thirsday next. John Bennison called & left with me his plan for build two Bridges at Skelton Ellers. Mrs Chars Gardner¹² & John Wilson came and divided abundance of Grafts and Trees I had from Collo[nel] Gansels in order to Graft & plant.

25. moderate weather Wind S. afternoon took a Ride out with John Hamond to view lang Hall¹³ ground, when it came on Rain & Continued some Hours. Wind high at night.

26. at Home.

27. went with George Mewburn & John Hammon to Grang where met us John Nickleson to whom sold 29 Wethers, that is 9 Apiece at 35/- each. Mr Wardel came to us there with whom I went to Boulby and lay all night there.

the 28ᵗʰ. we went to Grang & stayd a Hour or two. So to Boulby again that evening. Danyel Chilton came out of Whitby in order to lye, or next morning to take 50 Tons of Allom, but the wind came too far Westerly & prevented him. John Jefferson came up early in the morning of the 29ᵗʰ when Alixʳ pullman came to meet me, in our Way home called at Grang, got home about 1 at noon.

30ᵗʰ. Sunday at Church forenoon.

31. Mr Scottow & Mr preston came about 11 Oclock. with the former I settled some accounts and I paid him £219. 5. 2 In Ballance, also Mr preston paid 31. 7 from Mr peirse for Interest which with 30 : 13 Oliver presswick is to pay for a Bill I had from Mr peirse is for one years Interest for all he owes me, then also Mr John Ward of Billingam & his Son came here and paid me £100 he had of mine upon Bond & all Interest due thereon, they all dined here and went away afternoon.

Aprill 1. Henry Mewburn & his Brother William called here in the morning in their way to Grange to See my Oxon, returned about 2 in the afternoon & dined. I sold them my great ox Fox and other two, the former at 25ˡⁱ & the latter two at 26ˡⁱ both, to take them away on munday the 21ˢᵗ.

April 2ᵈ. I went to Stockton Dined at Mr Maddesons, was at Mrs Dowthwaits where I see her Father Mr Allan and her Daughter, the former though turnd of 90 yet even at that age, appears much older. called at Bells the bookbinder. Mr Wardell came in the morning and finding Mr More at Stockton, he, Mr Sutton, Mr Wardell &

¹² Mrs. Chaloner's gardener.
¹³ On the eastern side of Guisborough.

myself had a meeting to Consult about the Allom Affair, but could not settle anything. Mr More left us and went that evening to Yarm, after he went away, Mr Sleigh, Mr Wilson the Collector, Mr Sutton and Mr Maddeson with Mr Wardell and Alderman Brown stayed with me till 11 at night.

the 3rd Mr Wardell, my Self & Servant went to Yarm where we had another meeting with Mr More upon the same Subject but to little purpose. Francis Fox came there about William Armstrong and a Tenant of Eate Spencers. I met them at Henry Coares where after Some Debate they partly agreed. Mr Wardell being engaged could not come Home with me I set out about ½ after 3 & got home ½ after 6.

Aprill 1755. Soon after Mr Wardell & Mr Fox came the former lay here all night, there was much rain fell in comeing home with wind at West & S.West, next day the 4th about noon we both went to Boulby called at Grange but Will White was at Whitby for Seed Barly out of Norfolk.

the 5th. Mr Jefferson came to us early in the morning & dined with us, after Mr Snowdon of Durham the Wood valuer came to us, where I left them about 1 a clock. Tho. p. came there to meet me. Same day Will White was Sent with money for East Side Kelp-men[14] I got home near 4 afternoon.

the 6th. being Sunday at Church forenoon had been much rain in the night before. Wind N.E. blowd hard.

7th. Mr Lawson called upon me about Mr Buxton's purchase of Sutton. I gave Mr Lawson the Bishop's Last Lease, also Thomas Spencer's Letter of attorney to me, home with him, dry day, blowed fresh, the Wind at NW. Mr Preston called upon me and left the Survey of peak Farm also Will White came here from Grange and brought 2 she young Lambs to be brought up here.

8th. all day at home, after noon Some Rain but not much, Wind West. Mr Foster called here with the Land tax papers for me to sign as Commissioner. Mr Beckwith & Mr Skottow haveing done so before.

9th. I went up to quarry where a mason & 4 labourers was Working. after I gave directions went to top of High Cliff Nabb, from thence down Kathergate to Chapel Bridge & So to pinchingthorp to view my House there, from thence home. A fine day Wind at West but very cloudy.

10th. I went to Boulby where lay that night, next morning the 11th Mr Wardel & I went & breakfasted at Steath with Mr & Mrs Jefferson where was Miss pease, we stay'd till 10 & so returned to

[14] Kelp was much used in the manufacture of sodium carbonate and iodine. It occurs as a dark grey mass, the most valuable being from drift weed. From it are obtained sodium chloride and carbonate and iodine. Formerly used in the manufacture of soap and glass.

Boulby, where dineing, I set out for Gisbrough about 2 but meeting with Mr More in Rocliff who desired I woud go to Lofthouse with him, there being a Sale to be of as much Allom as to raise £1300, accordingly I went but Sent for Mr Wardell who came to us at Grange from whence we all went to Lofthouse, but I did not alight at Mr Mores but kept on Horsback in the Street till Mr Howlet and Mr Mathews came, who at last came, we then all went to William Johnson's where the company was vizt Mr More, Mr Hakeny & his nephew Hakeny, Mr Brough the Collector, Mr yeoman with Mr Hancock, Mr Spark & Mr Matthews 3 attorneys & Benjamin Chip the Cryer, it was put up 50 Ton in a Lott, the first Lott was Sold for ¼12. 12. 6. p. Ton, the 2^d 50 Tons at £12 : 10 : 0 p Ton & 8 tons more at Same price all bought by Mr Brough & Mr yeoman in Concert, but no body bid anything but Mr Brough & Mr Howlet. there was pretty much company beside those menconed about. I stayd till after 6 & come home with Tho preswick & got there about 9.

the 12th. I went with Francis Fox to Stokesley. Mr Jackson going there we all went together, my business was to meet Mr Buxton of new building to Settle the Sale of Sutton he and I haveing agreed for the Same by Letter. Mr Lawson came to us, and drew an Article betwixt us, the price to be £2818, to pay the money 1^t of June at London. Mr Buxton, Mr Fox & I dined togeather at the Black Swan kept by Mr Anderson. Mr Forster of Yarme & Mr Sanderson of Steaths with an other unknown dined with us, came out about 3 & got home near 6, in our way had pretty much rain. Mr Buxton went for New building before us, who had no doubt a very bad night, the Wind being at West and rained much.

The 13th. month Sunday at Home. Mr Wardell's Boy came here with post Letters. Dry wether most of the day. Wind high at W.

14. All day at home. William Armstrong came here with his son the Glaizer and offered me his Rent which I refused, upon which many words & great difference Ensued but we could not agree. So parted when he told me he would not Suffer any to come there to plow. saw Mr Lawson, Mr Mathews & Mr preston the latter paid me Doctor Wanlas Interest, divers other people was with me. Spoke with Mr Lee & James Jackson about my house at pinchingthorp. William Rogers came here & paid me his last Mart Rent Stayed all night.

15th. went with me to grange from thence sent Will White with him to Boulby for Clarkes old Mare which I gave him. he had 1 : 11 : 6 offered for her as he came through Skelton. She is about 30 year old. Mr Wardell was at Grange when I got there with whome about 12 or 1 a'clock I went with him to Mr Mores where we dined and had much conference about the Allom affair, but I think to little purpose, from thence went went to Boulby where lay all night.

the 16. In the morning I went to Grange where met Tho: pressick who I sent to Mr Wardell with A letter from Mr Core that came by yesterday's post that the *Darling* was got to London. from thence came home where got about 12 at noon when Mr Wardell & I went from Grange to Boulby.

the 15th. We found John Jefferson his Wife and Miss pease who stayd about an hour & went away about 7 in the evening haveing notice that Mr Boulby was come to Steaths.

17th. I went with Will Hobkirk to pinchingthorpe about noon to view Judson's House in order to build a Chimney as it is the House Smooks past enduring, from thence went to James Jackson's & viewed the miry Close in order to take off the Springs which renders most of it a bogg, from thence went through Belts ground & by yarm lane Home.

18th. all day at Home in the Evening came Mr Wardel & lay all night.

19th. he went in the morning with Tho: pressick to Stokesley to speak with Messrs Howlet & Mathews about the Allom affair, he came home alone by noon & dined here when I agreed with him for my Farm at Boulby for £145 p. annum clear Rent exclusive of all other payments. he to enter at old may day next.

the 11th. he went away about 4 along with Will White who brought here 3 fatt oxen to go to Sunderland on munday next. Henry Mewburn of that place having Bought them of me at £51.

20. Sunday all day at home at Church forenoon.

21t. a man come night before & lay here when came here Duke Fogge for hay seed, he also lay here next morning the said 21. they both went away the former with 3 oxen for Sunderland & the latter with his Hay Seeds for Brumpton. Servant Jackd5 Set the oxen to Upsel. Same day Mr Lawson brought Sutton Deeds, Mr Howlet & Mathews came to Conferr about the Allom affair but settled nothing, in the Evening came Mr Wardel on his way to Ellemor but only lighted to take a dram & went that night for Stockton. Same day went up Street and bought Sundry goods belonging late Mr Thos Spencer, his Grandson being here to Sell them off. I bought what cost me £6. 5.

22nd. at home. Robert Dalton came & settled with me about his Rent that will be due at old may day next the same being 15: 13. Whereof his Brother John is to give me A note for it and pay at Xmis next. Date Danby is to pay me £1. 17. 3 & Robert himself at old may day next 15/9. much thunder & Rain but brok up. A fine day Wind at W.

23. at home. Date Danby came here & gave me his note for 1li 17s 3d, in part for Robert Dalton's Debt.

24. Several Neighbours that have ground near the South back

15 John Pearson.

lane met some with horses & Carts & others only themselves, when
was led a large quantity of Mason Rubbish out of my garth into
the back lane from lincoln pond to Worman Hole.   I attended the
workemen from 7 in the morning till after 5 at night, with great
pain in my back & feet.   Same day John Hawmon paid me for
Sheep £16.1.6, one of which dieing after he bote them I received
only 12/6 for him, that being part of the money.   much rain the
night before.   Wind at W. warm calm wether fine Spring.

25th.   Tho. preswick went to Bp Auckland being their Race Week
to Receive there Nancy Dincer's last Mar^t Rent & did so.   Same day
I went to Boulby where I found the heap Gantree wall fallen down.
lay all night there, on which fell very much rain but Tho: p: gave
Account of much more being in Bpbrig.

26th.   I came home as did Tho: p: and brought the Rent.

27.   Sunday at home being a rainy day did not go to Church.

28.   met Mr Robinson, Mr Skottow & Mr Beckwith at Cock, when
we all took the Oath of Abjuracon and Signed Warrants for the
L[an]d-tax, appointed the 2^d June for Appeal day.   John price
came here to work, much reain & Cold.   Wind at N.

29th.   Fare^{15a} day at this place much Cattle Sold.   Signed above
40 S^{r}tifficates, was at Mr Hides who came & dined with me as did
John Rowntree who paid me A yrs Interest for £100 due 8th Inst.
Mr Murgatroid sent by his Servant a Receipt for last Lady Day Tyth
rent per Lofthouse which I sent him.   Mr panty Lasscels came to
us after dinner, and stayed an hour or more.   Appointed to meet
here again on the 1st June in Case.   John Benneson came here
tomorrow about Skelton Ellers Bridges.   frequent Snow Showers.
Fine afternoon but Cold with Wind at No.   Mr Wm Chaloner 10
years Old in August next.   Went with two servants to attend him
for Eton School beyond London he called at my door to bid farewell.
John Robert Dalton came & Settled with me about a debt the latter
ows me.   John porrit came & signed our Agreement on taking
Daltons Farm.

30.   all day at home.   A Severe Frost last night frequent pewlings
of Snow, but a pretty fine day.   Wind N at night S. about 8 in
the evening Mr Wardel came here in his way to Boulby haveing
been from thence Since the 18th Instant.

May 1.   I Took on to Work as a Mason one Myers who said he
formerly was Imployed by me as Such at Grange 10 or 12 years
ago.   Went with Mr Wardel to Boulby, called at Grange.

2^d.   Mr Jefferson came to us at Boulby, from whence he Mr
Wardel & Self went to Grang where Soon after came Mr Oldfield,
we all Stayed there Some Hours dureing which it Snowed & Rained
very much without abatement so that my Servant Jack & I came
for Gisbr^o & the other three went for Boulby.   the like Weather

^{15a} Fair.

continued all the Way home, the Waters was very great, it fell dry Snow upon the moors which next morning the 3ᵈ was Covered over. Sister Jackson came here the 1ᵗ. Tho: preswick went that day to meet her at yarm Myres the Mason only wrought one day when turned him off. Wᵐ White brought Chaloner Mare here to go to Marton to Mr Walkers Horse there called Baboon Alsk: pulman carryd her there same day in order to be leaped by him, which he did & brought her home.

4ᵗʰ. Sunday all day at home. Weather bad & Cold frost Wind N°.

5ᵗʰ. Wᵐ Mewburn brought me a piece of my great ox Fox's beef about 18ˡⁱ from Sunderland where he was Killed. his 4 quarters weighed 120ˢᵗᵒ 10ˡⁱ. Tallow 21ˢᵗᵒ 7ˡⁱ. Hide 9ˢᵗᵒ 1ˡⁱ. Mr Lawson called here about Sutton Affair with Mʳ Buxton. Wᵐ Mewburn Dined here. Mʳ Mathews was enquireing of me if could help Mʳ Yoward with £2000 upon Mortgage of Hutton Lo(cers) but settled nothing. Signed many Sirtifficates. Jnᵒ Jackson the younger of Lackinby was here till near 10 at night.

1755. 6ᵗʰ May. came Mʳ Baker, Mʳ John Dixon & Sir Blakeston Conyers with 3 Servᵗˢ also Mʳ Wardel from Boulby all about 4 or 5 in the evening & lay at my House, next morning thay went for Boulby about 10.

the 7ᵗʰ. Mʳ Wardel had 25 Sheep and 2 oxon came here with A man & Boy, Jack lay all night, & went for Boulby next day.

8ᵗʰ. Went to yarm Fair, drank tea at Mʳ Burtons' where was one Mʳ Hall Lord of Eglescliff. Spok with Mʳ Killinggal, Mʳ Thoˢ peace, with Richard Reah & Bro: Corker with whome went in the Afternoon part of the Way to Ayslaby, but returned before got there & came home.

9ᵗʰ. all day at home.

10ᵗʰ. also at home..

11ᵗʰ. munth Sunday was blooded. Mʳ proddy took 15, or 16 ounces of Blood from my Right arme very thick & dark Collour, with little Cerum in it, before bleeding was very bad in my lungs with great Stuffing there, but better after & had a pretty good night. Same day came Jack Arrowsmith & brought A Letter from his Master who by A fall got a Strane in his Arme.

12ᵗʰ. Mʳ Lawson paid me £300 for Mʳ Buxton for which I gave him bill on Mʳ Core at 28 days Mʳ Matthews called upon me with whom made an appointment to meet him & Mʳ Howlet at Littlebeck allom work new begun to make Allom, met Mʳ Hide Mʳ Lassels with others at Cock where came John Benneson the Mason with whom agreed for his building two bridges at Skelton Ellers for which he is to have £120, but to make abatement for some days. the Country has promised to lead Stones.

the 13th came Mr Wardel & Will White who went to Brusby[16] to buy some Sheep of Geo. Snowdon these the former bought 20 but the other could not agree about other 20. thay returned about 6 or 7 in the Evening, thay did not put up their Horses but I got ready & went with them that night to Boulby, where we got about 10.

14th. we all three went to view Littlebeck Allom Works called to See Mr Mark Noble at Ayslaby but did not light at the Works. we met Mr Howlet & Mathews where came to us Mr More, we stayed here three or 4 hours & returned to Boultby near 9. Mr More parted with us upon Borrowby Moor.

15th. Mr Wardell went to view some Stock in order to buy it, vizt 6 Oxon 20 Ews & 40 Lambs with 2 waggons 2 Coops, & 7 Horses & Mares for all which he is to give me £137. I returned to Boulby where came to us Mr Jefferson, his wife & Ra: Jackson who stayed 3 or 4 Hours and after wee went (he on foot) to Grang & there made fully the bargains for the sundrys above, from whence I took Will White with me to near Skelton when he returned and I came home alone.

17th. Mr William Turner & Mr Hide called upon me, the latter stayed little but the former about half an Hour, his business was to talk with me about Mr More's Allom Works, who was to meet him & Mr Wm Sleigh at the Cock today in order to take the Works for Mr Sleigh's Son in law Mr Hoar. Jack Arrowsmith brought one of the mares his Mast^r bought of me he being to go with her to Marton to get her horst with Mr Walker's Babboon & returned same day with effect. Same day Cozin Martin Dunn came here.

18. Sunday at Church with Sister and Mr Dunn the forenoon, afternoon Mr Dunn & myself, Mr Wardell & Will White called here in their way to Darlington. John price came here to work. Dry weather. Cold with the wind at N°.

19th. Mr Dunn owing me 50^{li} with Int^r 60: 11: 4 which I made up £100 and took his bond for it dated this day. he went away about 10 in the morning. Will White came from Darlington about 10 at night & brought 8 beasts from Darlington 4 for Mr Wardell & 4 for me bought there.

20. Went with them all to Boulby, in the afternoon, parson Consett & his Nephew came & stay an hour when they gave notice of intending to pay me in 100^{li}, in part of what Mrs Conset owes me, appointed munday the 2^d June.

21^t May 1755. went to Ayslaby & took John price with me when viewed Wm Armstrong's Farm quited by him the 12th Instant & found Richard Corker the New Tenant in possession he haveing about 20 plows at Work in plowing his Fallow. Armstrong would not Admitt him to do it before the 12th Instant. Stayed & dined

---

[16] Busby, a little to the south of Stokesley.

there, Armstrong paid me at the Alehouse this may day Rent £57. we had some words in anger but parted Seeming Friends got home near 4 in the evening.

22ᵈ. in the morning I was taken with A pain in my Right foot which proved the Gout of which was better & worse, but not confined, moderate calme Weather, Wind for many days mostly dry but Nᵒ & Nᵒ E.

23ᵈ. John Jefferson from Steaths came here with whom Settled divers accounts when he paid me to Balance £67. 18. 6. he Stayd all night.

24ᵗʰ. he went away about 4 in the afternoon Soon after came Mʳ Wardell out Bishoprick but last from Stokesley. he Stayed very little but posted after Mʳ Jefferson to overtake him, Mʳ Wardell haveing been abroad Since the 18ᵗʰ, vizᵗ 7 days.

25ᵗʰ. Sunday all day at home Still in the Gout, often better & Worse. Recᵈ of Ailce Beadnell 1. 4ˢ Interest for £120 due the 20ᵗʰ July 1753.

26. Sister Jackson went away for home. A man came here the 24ᵗʰ to accompany her, She haveing been from home Since the 1ᵗ Instant. John Clark, Lofthouse Came here to borrow of me £18 which I lent him on his note, it was to rennew the Bishops Lease for Some Tyths. John price came here last night to Work. Mʳ Hide & Mʳ Errington calld in, the former to enquire how I did. the latter to Acquaint me with the Sitting of Excise Commissioners Lent John Aysley 20ˡⁱ to pay the 9ᵗʰ of next month also lent Richard Clark to pay same time £20, very bad in the Gout in my Right foot.

27. One Mʳ Sedgewick a Chemist of Newcastle called here to discourse me about Kelp but determined nothing. 3 Carts came from the lime today. no amends in the Gout, being very unable to get down & up Stairs.

28ᵗʰ. Received from Excise for my bill on Core £100. this day is the Worst I've had in this fitt.

29ᵗʰ. 4 Carts with my Own went to Hargil pitts belonging Martin Dunn where they loaded Coals & returned the 31ᵗ. my gout bad but Something better.

30. All day at home my Gout mending. Sent Tho pressick to Boulby where did not see Mr Wardell he being to dine at Steaths. T.p. brought me Word that the Sloop was to load Allom in the morning.

31ᵗ. calm Weather, with rainy afternoon. John Benneson called here in his way to Skelton Ellers where preparations is makeing to build a new bridg over upleatham Wath.

June 1ᵗ. Mʳ Wardel & Will White came here about noon, dined & returned about 5 in the evening I was not at Church being lame yet in the Gout.

2ᵈ. Thomas Warton Paid me his last may day Rent also Ricᵈ

Clark 200ˡˡ I lent him, paid Geo Snowdon for 20 Weather Sheep 2 years old 25ˡˡ 19ˢ. Recᵈ from Mʳˢ Joane Concesett £100, in part principle She owes me which has reduced her Debt to £2900. the Appeal day being this day Mʳ Beckwith & Mʳ Robinson could not attend it being lame, & Mʳ Skottow being alone could not act so was forced to go to the Cock in a Shaze to act there as a Commissioner of the Land tax. returned about 3. I paid Mr Hide & Mʳ Lasscell what I promised towards Building 2 Bridges at Skelton Ellers 10ˡⁱ 10ˢ 0ᵈ. Spoke with Mʳ Mathews about Mʳ yoward Affair.

3ᵈ June 1755. all day at home got some ease in my Gout pains.

4ᵗʰ. all day at home am much better in my gout, very dry fine Weather.

5ᵗʰ. I went to Boulby T.p Set me to Grange, when I came at Boulby Mʳ Wardell was gone to Steaths where I went and Stayed till 7. or 8 o Clock & then returned to Boulby where I lay. next day the 6ᵗʰ, afternoon, Mʳ Wardell Set me to Skelton where we lighted at an Alehouse & drank 2 potts Bumbo¹⁷ & he returned & I came Home.

7ᵗʰ. all day at Home.

8ᵗʰ. Cozen John pease & Son John came here from Whitby, they both paid me money for Interest due April last, the latter went for Darlington after Dinner but the former Stayed all night.

9ᵗʰ. Cozen pease went away for Whitby, being much better in my Gout I walkt up to market. I see mʳ preston, came to my House Wᵐ Mewburn of whome I desired money for the last oxon his Brother Bought which he is to bring me next fryday. Weather very Close & Calm Air at N°.

10ᵗʰ went to Bouldby with Jack Arrowsmith who I met in the street he coming with post Letters from Boulby & returned with me, called at Grang where all the Tiles was puld of the Sheepe house and begun to Cover the Same with Thatch, lay that night at Boulby where I carryed £80 in Silver & 40 half ginnys recᵈ of Mʳ Wardel for the same £101. next day the 11ᵗʰ was at pitt Hill from thence went to dine at Steaths, where we Stay till 4, came to Boulby & lay there. next morning, the 12ᵗʰ went to pitt Hill with Mʳ Wardel where we parted, on my way home called at Grange, got home alone near one, about 4 came there Brother George Jackson his son, Captain Wilson his Wife and their Sister Esther Jackson; next morning the 13ᵗʰ the two former and my Self Rid up Belman Bank to top the moor and Came by hycliff¹⁸ down to Hutton lane & so home where they all dined & took Horse about 11 in their return to Richmond, the day before Wᵐ Mewburn paid me £41 in part for 3 Oxon Sold his Brother.

14ᵗʰ. all day at home. in the evening I Sent for John porrit to

¹⁷ Bumbo, cold rum punch.
¹⁸ Highcliff.

talk to him about altering the Beck. we had above an hours discourse about it, he Seemed to be full of the project & to favour the thing.

15. being Sunday was twice at Church dined at Mrs Chaloners with Mr Hide only there, when we discoursed about the beck which She was determined to alter & Suffer no Clows[18a] to be upon it, when no other determination could be agreed upon She Sent her Gardner down in the Evening to Conferr further upon the Subject but it being after Eight was Just going to Bed, So did not See him but desired he would come next morning.

16th. the Gardner came with whom I went down & up the beck to Consider about the Scouring of it, but determined nothing. late in the evening M^rs chaloner came her Self with m^r proddy & the Gardner but what they Considered of I know not, had Some Conference with m^r Matthews about Mr Yowards affair but Settled nothing. Spoke with Mr Lawson also Mr Spark. Mr Clark of Lofthouse came down to my House about my Advanceing money upon a Bishops Lease of Moorsom Tyths, With whom agreed to make up what he now owes me £100, when he went to M^r preston & brought him down to me who took directions from us to draw an Assignment to me of Said Lease for my Security and to meet again next munday to Execute. M^r preston Spoke to me for 150 or £200 for one of his Clyants, but could not be certain of the Sum nor when wanted but would let me Know in a little time.

17. all day at home. Rec^d Some Deeds from Mr Mathews about M^r yowards affair which I Read over and Returned them again Same day by the post boy who brought them. Mr Jackson's Son came with one Carter of Allerton & desired my Interest to let the latter have the Carryage of our Letters from & to Allerton I told them I should agree to anything the rest of my Neighbours did, & Since as thay told me that Stokesley had given him a promise for theirs, so its likely we shall all come into the same measures.

the 18th. went to Grang & Boulby where I lay.

19th. in the morning went to the Rock from thence to Grange to take Some recknings from thence to Steaths where came John Pease & his Wife. Mr Jefferson, being not well we all dined there, about 5 we parted thay to Whitby & I to Boulby where the men came to see their reckonings in order for a pay the next day.

20. there was A pay when Rec^d A prety deal of money for Rents & Beef. there dined with us Mr Oldfield & Mr Jefferson. after dinner came Mr Sanderson. I left them about 6 & came home with T.p who met me there.

21. at home Mrs Chaloners Gardner came to see me in the fore-

---

[18a] A Clow is an instrument like a dung fork, with the prongs bent at right angles.

noon to acquaint me with his M^rs resolution to pull up our Clows, as did also Mr Foster upon the Same occasion. John Aysley came and put up the Weather Glass in the little new Room Window, the same I bought at London in September 1749. John Wilson near Gisbro desired I would lend him 5^li to pay again the 1^t of August next or before, which Sum I lent him.

22^d. Sunday, at Church forenoon.

23. Mr Foster came to acquaint me with the resolution of his Mrs about the beck. Mr John Clark of Lofthouse came with Mr preston to execute an Assignment of the Bishops Lease for the Tythes of Moorsom, the Same to be in mortgage for £100 I lent him. Thomas preswick paid me £250 in part of £300 his Brother Oliver owed me. Mr preston dined with me. James Mewburn with his Brother William came early in the morning and paid me £9 in Ballance for three oxon formerly bought, and then bought other 4 oxon to be £60 to take them away the 7th July.

24. at home. Thomas pressick brought me £40 from Maurice Lincoln which he owed me upon his note.

25. I went to Boulby about 12. T.p. set me to Skinnington Beck, called at Grange where met Mr Wardel Just arrived from Ellemore, last from Coatham, where met him Mr Sutton and Mr Moore. Same Evening about 9 a clock a young Woman Servant to Robert Cuthebert of Boulby going to bathe in the Sea haveing Seldom Seen the sea before, and being a Stranger to the Cliffs and not Knowing the way down and nobody with her unhappily fell over the Cliff not far from the Water pond in the Holes and was Killed, her parents lived within Danby near the Church whose name is Toes. she was found 26, next morning by the Ginnmen[19] then going to work at geting up Coals upon which Mr Richardson, the Coroner was Sent to at Kirkleatham also a messinger to her Father to acquaint him therewith. when I went to Mr Beckwith[19a] at Handel Abby[20] along w^ith her master Robt Cuthbert to desire his advice how to proceed in Case Mr Richardson Should be abroad. I stay'd there near two hours when Mr Beckwirth came with me to Lofthouse we called at Mr Mores with whome had Some Conference but did not

[19] At the end of the seventeenth century coal was raised to the surface by the "cog and rung gin", which was really a windlass worked by horses walking in a circle. This was superseded by the "Whim gin", the ropes of which passed over pulleys fixed over the pit mouth and were wound round a large drum which revolved horizontally at a distance. The gin continued in use in the smaller collieries till well into the nineteenth century. The gin men, of course, worked these gins. There is an example from Rothwell Colliery now in the Halifax museum. The wooden drum measures 12 feet in diameter.

[19a] Roger Beckwith, J.P., B.A., Peterhouse, Cambridge.

[20] Handale Abbey, about a mile and a half from Lofthouse, founded in 1133 for Benedictine nuns. No traces of the old buildings are now to be seen.

light, Mr Beckwith Set me to Wilton Mill Bank top and returned, when I came home to Gisbro.

27th. at home all day.

28th. at home.

29. Sunday at Church forenoon Mr Wardell Same day Sent his Boy desireing me to let him have by the lad £100 which I sent him the day before vizt the 28, I sent Tho: preswick to Boulby to be informed how thay got the Affair Settled about the unfortunate girle, he brought me word that Mr Richardson the Coroner came there as also the Girl's parents and got all orderly done.

30. I paid Mr Jackson £300 in Cash & gave him a Bill upon Mr Core for £100, being togeather £400: the Same I paid him for 8 Bills drawn upon me by M^r Ra: yoward of York, all dated the 28th of may last, but as none of the Bills was Indorsed, I gave them again to Mr Jackson, who promised to return them to London to have them Indorsed, so he gave me A Rec^t for £400 till the Bills be returned again Indorsed. I paid M^r preston his Bill 3:08:0: also Jn° Aysley for what he paid me at Newcastle (haveing been there last week) for Cider & Rum £2 18. 5. was twice up Street today. was at Mr Hides Spoke with Mr Lawson, also John Benneson about the Bridges.

July the 1^t. all day at home, Servant pearson & Robert Dalton brought each a load Coals, weather very variable with wind at N. frequent Rain.

2nd. at Home.

3^d. I went to Boulby, called at Grange where came two of Mr Baker's Tenants with Mr Wardel to view the place. in the Eveing we all went to Boulby where I lay.

4th. went to the Works & Stay'd Some time. Mr Wardel had the best Ox he bought of me ill in the Read water & other Alements which rendered him in great Danger he had Divers medicines given him to no effect.

5th. I called at Grange in my Way home where reckned with John Ellerby his partner Wallis & Will White from whom Rec^d 40^li, in part of the Ballance betwixt him & me, after came Home, where Wm Mewburn & 3 quakers, two of them from London that are Cow keepers there With Whom had some discourse about the distemper among Cattle &c.

6th. Sunday at Church forenoon. Mr Wardell's boy came here who told me that the ox was very ill & Supposed to be pudding link't.

7th. at home all day Mr Mathews dined with me to whom paid 1460^li. which with 10 bills M^r Ra: yoward had drawn upon me, all for £540, made up £2000, that Sum I have lent Mr Yoward upon his Bond & A mortgage of his Estate at Hutton in this parish, the Deeds of Security bears date the 21^t June last.

8. after dineing I went to Boulby called at the Bridg in building,

T.p went with me to Grang from whence he returned, said 8ᵗʰ July
went to Boulby & lay all night there.   next day the 9ᵗʰ Mr Wardell
& I Rid out into the fields & came to Allom House to Dinner where
was Mʳ Jefferson who dined with us, after dinner the former went
with me.   on my way home we calld at Richard Steavenson in
Brotton but he was not at home, but we Sent for Will Child &
drank two pints of ale, from thence we went to Skelton where drank
A pot of Bombo find he returnd.   I then went to Skelton Castle to
Se Mʳ Hall which I did, also Mʳ Lasscels, but I did not light.   the
former Arrivd the day before from his Travels in France & Italy
where he has been nere five years.

10ᵗʰ all day at home.

11ᵗʰ.   Mʳ Foster & Richard Steavenson of Brotton came to me
about a Child the latter had Fathered upon him, the Woman
belonged Mask²¹ parish, after I went up Street called at Mʳ Jacksons
who Gave Receipts upon 8 bills Mr yoward had drawn upon me
payable to him the said yowards nephew at London, after called at
John Husbands' Shop but he was not within, after went to Mr Hides
where Stayed an Hour, from thence home & dined, where was Mʳ
Wardells' Boy come for his letters, about 3 or 4 in the Afternoon I
went to Mʳ Skottows of Ayton to Confer with him about Richard
Steavensons Affairs, but to little purpose, Stayed there an Hour
or two & Came Home.

the 12ᵗʰ.   at home till near 12 a Clock, when Rid to Skelton
where dined with Mʳ Hall his Lady, Mʳ Hide, Mʳ Lasscels, & Jo:
Hall the Son then about 13 year old, came Home about 7 or near 8
Alone with Mʳ Hide.

13.   at home month Sunday in the evening Mʳ Wardell came here
& lay all night, next morning at 4 Set out wᶦᵗʰ him for Darlington,
in our Way he call'd at Yarm when I went forward to Ayslaby,
where I lighted at John prices but he being at yarm came Soon after
with Richard Corker and soon after them came Mʳ Wardel.   we
Stayed little after but went forward for Darlington but in our way
thether we Viewed John Rowntree & Widow Bamlets Farms, also
Mark Atkinson & Thomas Broughs Farms, also my own Farm
called Stoddo Neighbouring upon them the four Farms aforesaid
was as per advertisement to be Sold to the Highest bidders.   next
day the 15ᵗʰ at Darlington Mʳ Wardell & I dined at Wᵐ Fawcet's
my Stoddo Tenant.

the 14ᵗʰ.   that evening we went to Darlington where we lay that
night, next day the 15ᵗʰ I went to John peases & to peter Thornhils
where brought brass Rings & Crooks to the value of 1ˡⁱ 8ˢ 0 Mʳ Baker
met us the 14ᵗʰ in the Evening & lay there but did not Stay Saile of
the Farmes, but went home, Mʳ Bland was there he neither Stayed
the Sale but went away.   Mr Robson, an Attorney of Darlington,

²¹ Marske.

had the Conduct of the Sale which came on about 2 in the afternoon, when Mr Allan the Attorney bought Rowntree & Bamlets' Farmes, in one Lott for Mr Killingal & was to give for them . . . and Mr Hore of Stockton bought Atkinson & Broughs Farms to give for them . . . Mr Hore Mr Wardel & myself Set out for Stockton where we got that evening & went into the Company of Mr Sleigh, Mr Watson, Mr Hore Mr Sutton & Mr Brown with whom Sit up till 11, next morning the 16th Mr Wardell & I set out for Stokesley in our way we viewed Mr Wilson's Farm at Tanton^{22} for Mr Davinson of Stokesley, who intends to bid for the Said farm at the Sale of it, which is to be the 2^d of Augt next at Stokesley, we Stayed very little at Mr Davinson's there being then at his House Sir Wm Foulis^{23} & his Family. Mr Wardell went & dined at Mr Howlets, but I came Home in my way met with a great Shower of rain which forced me to put up at my little House at pinchingthorp where Stayed an Hour from thence Home, where Mr Wardell came Soon after and after eating Something went to Mr Jacksons to Whom he gave a Bill for £200 & went for Boulby that night.

17th. about 4 in the afternoon went to Skelton Ellers where the Bridge there in building over up leatham Wath^{24} the Arch being then near closed. I stayd near three Hours till it was done, young Mr Skottow coming by in his way home Stop't till I was ready to go along with him when we both came to Gisbro togeather and he Stayed at my House near 2 Hours & went home about 9 in the evening, about noon Mr John preston came here w^{ith} his Father's Letter to Borrow of me £200, the same being for Mr Vane of Long Newton which Sum I sent up per the former who is to get the Latter's Bond for it and bring me on munday next M^r preston dined here.

18th. all day at home.

19th. at Home.

20th. Sunday at Church forenoon, about 4 Mr Wardel calld here in his way to Darlington where he was going to be at the Sale of a further part of Dinsdale Estate on tuesday next, he purposed to lay at yarme tonight.

21. begun to mow Calvert Close, 4 mowers. Mr Robinson sent me £12 for A years Interest due in may last for £300. was up Street when paid John Husband his bill for goods from Burrowbridge 3^{li} 2^s. 3^d, also Settled A year's account for Rent &c with Mr Foster and paid him a Bill of 8:18:6. Spok Mr Mathews about M^r yoward affairs. Mr Thos peirce of Worsel^{25} & Mr Preston dined with me,

^{22} Tanton near Stokesley.
^{23} Sir William Foulis, bart., of Ingleby Manor, succeeded to the title Oct. 1741 on the death of his father. In 1721 he married Mildred, eldest daughter of Henry Dawnay, Viscount Downe. He died in 1756 and was buried at Ingleby.
^{24} Wath means a wading place or ford.
^{25} Worsal, a village a little to the south of Yarm.

the latter brought me Mr Lyonal Veans[26] Bond for £200 Sent last week by M^r prestons Son.

22^d. at home in afternoon went to Skelton Ellers where stayed an Houre & Home.

23. about noon Mr Baker & Mr Wardel came & Dined, thay both went up Street & Stayd but little, I went with them to Boulby, called at Mr Halls, stayd near an Houre calld at Grang but did not light, lay at Boulby the night.

24th. Mr Baker & I brakfasted at Steaths with M^r & Mrs Jefferson & two Miss Reads. Mr Baker & Mrs Jefferson, both a foot, & my Self came & dined at Boulby, afternon went along w^{ith} Mr Wardell to Rock on Horseback, Stayed a little, from thence to Grang Rid down to Breamises, viewe a Hay pike then in makeing, also the Garden, Went into the House where drank 3 bottles of Gooseberry wine & went to Boulby where Mr Jefferson left us. I lay the night at Boulby.

25. Mr Baker on foot & I on Horseback went & dined at Steaths from wence I returned alone, went up Hill where met Mr Wardell, there came to us Mr Moor's Clerk Snowdon about a paper to be sent to Mr Core at London concerning Mr Faikey's mens Wages, after which we went to Skinington from thence up the West Hill and down to Cattersty[27] to view Some Kelp belonging one King where wee met him but only viewd part of the Kelp the Rest being under the Cliff and the tide In So we could not come at it. So went to Brotton, calld at Richard Stevensons but not at home Spoke with Wm Child with whom left Monsr Le Stosses book[27a] about Shoeing Horses. drank two tankard of Bombo, but I did not light of Horse. Dr Bisset came to us with whome went to Skelton & came home, called at Skelton Ellers where saw John Bennesan, there Mr Jackson came to me with whome came to Gisbro.

1755. July 26. at Home all day, went to Cock to see Mr Davinson of Stokesley who wanted to speak with me but he was gone night before.

27. Sunday at home, was not at Church.

[26] Lionel Vane.

[27] Cattersty Sands, just west of Skiningrove.

[27a] The reference is probably to: *The Compleat Horseman, or Perfect Farrier.* Two Parts. Part I discovering the surest Marks of the Goodness, Beauty, Faults and Imperfections of Horses. The best Method of Breeding and Backing of Colts, making their Mouths: buying, dieting and otherwise ordering of Horses. The Art of Shooing with the various sorts of Shoes, adapted to the various Defects of Bad Feet and the Preservation of Good. The Art of Riding and Managing the Great Horse, etc. Part II containing the Signs and Causes of their Diseases with the true Method of Curing them. Written in French by the Sieur de Solleysel, Querry to the present King of France. . . . Done into English by Sir William Hope with the addition of several Excellent Receipts by our Best Farriers. Second edn. 1706. (First edition in 1697.)

28. was up Street twice, called Mr Jacksons. Spok with M^r preston, John Aysley &c. Len: Vollum paid me for 18 st of beef 2^{li} 2^s. Mrs Consetts' son paid me 54: 7: 6 for 6 months Interest for £2900 due the 11 July. Mr Baker and Mr Wardell called here in their way to Dinsdale and dined. went away about 3. John Nickleson the Butcher paid me in the evening 17^{li}: 10^s in part of what he owes me for Sheep and Lambs. Rowland of Waupley came here and desired me to lend him £20 upon his and Robert Fosters bond, Which I told him he should have on Munday next.

29th. all day at Home the Same being A post day. Received a letter from Nephew T Spencer that Bro. John Ward was at the writeing of it most dangerously ill and in great perrol of Death.

30. about noon came Mr Wardell and dined, with whom I went to Grang where they were Stacking hay, lay all night at Boulby. Next morning the 31^t after going with Mr Wardell to the Rock, also to view beasts in the pastures, I left him and went to Grange where mowing was at Work in near Roger Close and Haymakers in the lower. Stayed two or three hours and came home.

Augt 1. at Home. John Wilson paid me £5 he had upon his note which I lent him the 21st June last: John Benneson calld here about Skelton Ellers Bridge as did also Mr Wardell on his way to Stokesley to attend the sale of Mr Wilsons farm at Tannton, but he only lighted but did not stay to eat or drink.

2nd. Went out about 4 in the morning with Servant T.p for yarm where Received Sundry Rents also the remainder of Hubback's Bond with Interest vizt 52: 13: 6, when Richard Cocker signed his lease for his Farm at Ayslaby. Saw Mr Wardell there also Mr Hore, the former came from Boulby about noon dined at Gisbro on his way. I set out of yarm about 4 & got well home, Wm Cass came along with me.

3. at Church fore noon, Mr Wardels Boy came here in the Afternoon, much rain following night. Wind N.E.

4. was up Street, Spok with parson Conset, Mr Lawson, Mr Mathews, M^r preston &c. Mr Wardell calld & dined here in his way to attend the further Sale of Dinsdale Estate at Darlington, went hence near 6 in the Evening in Company with Mr Spark & parson Hobkirk. Gregory Rowland of Wapelay & Robert Foster of Marton parish gave me their Joynt Bond for £20. John Thomas paid me 24/- for 1 year's Interest per £30 due the 10th past.

5th. abundance of Rain last night with very thick Fog. Wind at N.E.

6. all day at Home much more raine last night. Wind at N.

7. about noon came young Edward pease and Robt Allan from Darlington to See our Wool at Grang, & Boulby, thay dined & I went with them thither after viewing the wool went down to Allom House where was two persons & Mr Jefferson, Stayd about an Houre

& Returned to Gisbro With the Wool buyers, where we got about 8 at night after Suping.   About 9, Mr Wardel came there Last from Stokesley, Sit up till 11 & all went to Bed.

8th. we could not Bargain for the Wool, M^r pease only bid 9/- per Stone & Mr Wardel offered it 9/3.   So they went away Mr Wardel dined & went away about one for Boulby.

9th.   Mr Wardell had a Bull Calf of 8 months old brought here from Durham, after bateing here about 2 Hours, the man that brought him went with him for Boulby.

10th. month Sunday, at home. Mr Wardells boy came here for Letters.

11.   at Home but went up Street.

12th.   at Home.

13th.   dined at home.   at Noon went to Boulby T.p Set me to Skinnington Bridg called at Grang, I went to Boulby where was the *Darling* ashore Delivering Coals.   She went off & lay by all night & came on again next morning.

14th.   and took in 60: Tons of Allom Mr Jefferson his Wife & two Miss Reeds came on Board & went of with the Ship & went on Shore at Steath about 9 that evening.

15th.   I went & breakfasted at Steaths, after set Mr Jefferson to Hinderwell in his way to Whitby we both call'd to Se Mr Tod he being very ill who Seemd to be in great Danger.   I came to Boulby & dined there, when in my way Home Mr Wardell Set me to Skelton but call'd at Grang & Stayed there about 2 Hours, got home about 6 in the Evening.

17th.   at Home all day.

18.   I was up Street.   Mr Lawson came down & took all papers & Deeds belonging Sutton for Mr Buxton, Mr Fox was present when delivered them to Mr Lawson, I saw Mr Jackson & promisd him A Bill for £150, also Mr Hide, with whom had some Conference respecting Mrs Chaloners affaire about the beck, call'd at M^r preston's but his Son was only here.   Asked Mr Mathews to dine with me which he did along with Mr Fox when in Some measure Settled Mr Thomas Spencer's affair respecting his Estate under Lease from the Crown. along with M^r yoward about Hutton Estate, Richard Thompson of Ridcar paid me 2 years Interest for £20 due 20th Septr next 1^{li} 12^s.

19th.   John pease Junior of Darlington came here and Dined. after went to Whitby.   Mr Wm Jackson came & paid me £120 in part for my Bill on Robert Core at 30 days for £150, afternoon went up Street, stayd Some Time at Mr Jackson's, who Shewed me his House, Chambers &c, went & Stay'd Some time at John Husbands Shop intending to Waite upon Mrs Chaloner, but she had Company, Skelton Family being there, about 6 I went to Cock expecting the Collector of Excise, where Stayed till after 10 with

Mr Errington & Mr Baldock, the latter haveing lately marryed Mrs Stead who kept the House there, the Collector of Excise did not come.

20th. went to Mrs Chaloner's about the beck, but She was gone out, was at the Sitting of Excise where Rec'd £100 for my Bill on Robert Core Dined at Mr Jacksons along with Mr Hall his Brother Major Hall Mr Hide, his Son, proddy, & young Mr Jackson, before we parted Mrs Chaloner Sent for me, when I came there in talking about the beck She insisted of my Clow being taken away & was Instant for the doing it, So I ordered it to be puld up the next day. I went from her to Mr Jacksons again where notice was given me that young Cozen pease, his Mother & Sister, was come from Whitby. So I left the Company after 7 & came Home, where I found Cozen peases, next morning the 21^t they went for Darlington, Same day begun Walling from opposet the Stable Door toward the Old peartree with Stone by N. patton. Also Fishuck the plasterer begun with Sealing the low Clozet.

22^d. at home all day.

23^d. at Home till one in the Afternoon when I went with Mr Maddeson of Stockton & his Son for Skelton, in our way thither Mrs Chaloner with Mr Hide in her Coach and 6, overtook us in her Coach & 6, going to Skelton on this Side the Ellers, where young Mr Maddeson went for Maske and left us but wee the rest went to Skelton & Dined at Mr Halls where was Mrs Chaloner Mr Hide. M^r O proddy, Maj^r Hall, Mr Jackson, Mr Maddeson, Mr Hall, his Lady & Self all dined togeather about 4 or 5. Mr More came & dined, near eight Mr Maddeson, Mr Jackson, M^r proddy & Self came Home togeather, the Coach Setting on before us got Home near 9.

24th. Sunday at Church forenoon, at Home in my return from thence found Mr Wardell who dined here to whome paid £100. he went away about 6 for Boulby. Weather Soft & Rainy Wind N.

25. all day at home attending the masons.

26. at home forenoon about 1 went for Boulby T.p along with me lay at Boulby that night, next morning Mr Wardel came home with me where we dined and both went to Stockesley, that afternoon Stayed at Mr Davinsons about 3 houres from thence he Thos Weatheril & his Son Walker went with us to Tanton near which place Mr Wardell & I left them and went for Stockton that night where we arrived about 8 at night Sit up till nine & went to bed. next morning the 28th I went to see Mrs Douthwait where I breakfasted with her & her Daughter Mr Allan being then at Darlington at his Mothers Funeral. I saw Mrs Lisle there with whome had some Conference about her removal from thence to Stockesley, I calld at M^r maddesons also at Bells the Bookseller, Saw Mr Sleigh, about 10 Mr Baker^r M Jo. Dixon & one Mr Pexell Forster came to meet us, & took Mr Baker & me Sworn to our answers to Mr Tempests' Bill

against us as partners to Biddick Colliery.²⁷ᵇ I then Executed a Deed of Asignment of my Farm at Boulby to Mʳ Baker & he gave me a Bond of £5000 for Performance of Covenants. Tho. presswick haveing been at Ayslaby met me at Stockton & brought Wᵐ Armstrong along with him, with whom I Settle Some things in difference with him. about 4 in the Afternoon we parted & I came home that night, Mʳ Wardell & the rest went for Ellemore & Durham.

29. at home.

30ᵗʰ. at home.

31. Sunday at Church forenoon.

September 1ˢᵗ. John pease from Whitby came here and being a Rainy day he Stayed all night. Mʳ Sutton came to Se me & Stayed drinking a little Ale & went to the Cock in order to Stay all night. John Nickolson came in the Evening & Supt with me when paid me £9. 2 in part for goods & the next morning he bought 2 Spᵈ Heifers and 2 Cows the former he is to give 19ˡⁱ: 10ˢ and the later £13. 10 in all £33.

2ⁿᵈ. Mʳ pease went for Darlington near 7 in the morning, much Rain with the Wind high & at N.

3. about noon went for Boulby where lay all night, in my way called at Grange where John Nickolson came to me with whome & Will White I went to the park. I there sold the former 2 Steers for £13. 15. next morning 4ᵗʰ I went to Steaths where I found Niece Jefferson in bed not well but had been worse. during my Stay there Mʳ prody came to her where I brekfasted & dined, about 12 came from thence, call'd at Allom House from thence to the Rock & So to Grange, but it rained much, Stayed there to 4 & came for Gisbro, in my Way had much Rain & was Sore Wet.

5. all day at home, Sundry Showers but the night following And next morning the 6ᵗʰ a deal of Rain, no harvest yet got in & much Hay out, all day at home Wind most quarters but fair weather after 9 or 10 a'Clock Sent 4 beasts to Grange & brought back 3 large oxon for Fogg.

7ᵗʰ. being Sunday at Church forenoon, all day at home, good Weather Wind NW.

8ᵗʰ. up street twice, Mʳ Mathews called here about Mʳ yowards affair, Saw Mʳ Chiefe Jackson, was at Mʳ preston's office with Mʳ M. Smith, when Signed A notice to meet Commissioners for the devision of Mask & Ridcar Fields on Thursday the 25ᵗʰ of this month at Mask Hall about 10 in the Morning, also Richard Lincoln met me at Mʳ prestons with Some Wrightings to be Shewn Mʳ P, in order to Secure £50 he wanted to Borrow of me but what he produced was not Sufficient So we did not agree.

9ᵗʰ. much rain in the morning, wind at N. all day at home.

10ᵗʰ. at home about 6. this Evening Mʳ Wᵐ Proddy was buried,

²⁷ᵇ Biddick is north-east of Chester-le-Street, Co. Durham.

I was a Bearer there with Mʳ Jackson Mʳ Miller, Mʳ Bottom, Mʳ Fox, Mʳ Danby & John Husband, much Rain in the night Wind at N.

11ᵗʰ. Mʳ Wardell came here about noon haveing been in Bishoprig about 14 days, he dined here & I went to Boulby with him that afternoon, we called at Grang, where they were Sheering Barly in Sweetland field, having Cut all the Bigg[28] in Inghead[29] & the Wheat in Low micklehow. Same day my men Carryed a Basket of pears to Steaths from Gisbro. Mʳ Jefferson came to Boulby & Stayed the Evening with us.

12ᵗʰ. went up to pitt hill with Mʳ Wardell, from thence to Grang where thay begun cuting Wheat in forefield about noon, haveing the Same day Cut all the Barley in Sweetland, from there I came home. in the Evening Bro: Jackson came here & wanted to Borrow £100 of me, which I lent him, & he went away next day about 11.

13ᵗʰ. all day at Home.

14ᵗʰ. month Sunday at home.

15ᵗʰ. at Home.

16ᵗʰ. unrooft my new House in order to new Tile the same by John Fishook the plasterer, also begun Leading Stones with 3 Carts.

17ᵗʰ. got the House tiled in again, Signed Sundry Sᵗtifficates today. in the Afternoon Mʳ Nelson & Mʳ Atkinson of Kirk Leatham came to desire my Workman Fishook the next day, only to put up a Fain[30] at the Hospetal, they Stayed the Drinking A Bottle Wine. fine Weather for 3 days which has scarce happened togeather for 3 months past. Wind off Land.

18ᵗʰ. Dined wⁱᵗʰ Mʳ Hurstler, Mʳ Robinson & Mʳ Skottowe at Cock it being Brewster Sessions. I left them near 3 and went for Boulby. Same night called at Grange where Low Micklehow and forefield both Wheat also Spring Head in Bigg, & Sweetland in Barly was all got in. next day begun shereing Oates in East upton pasture, at night John pease his Wife & their Son John all came to my House & Stayed all night, as thay came from Darlington. they went for Whitby next morning.

19ᵗʰ. Came from Boulby Stay'd at Grange about 2 hours by the Sheerers got home after 1.

20. being Latter Lady faire[31] was twice in the Beast market. Mʳ peirce & his Son with Mʳ preston dined here. Wᵐ Willis came

[28] The Scottish *bere* or *bigg* (*Hordeum vulgare*) is the cultivated species of barley, and grows as far north as 70 degrees of latitude. It is distinguished from the other kinds of barley by having its grains in four rows.

[29] Inghead is the name of a field.

[30] Vane.

[31] Latter Lady Fair. A fair was originally kept here, it would seem, on the Feast of the Annunciation (March 25) and on the Nativity of Our Lady (Sept. 8). The second was the Latter Lady Fair, though it seems to have moved away somewhat from the original date.

& paid his years Rent due Martinmas next, two Miss Reeds from
Steaths called here in their way to yarm in A Shase, went away
after 4, Signed Sundry Sirtificates to Day. Wind Strongly at East
but dry Weather. Wm Marshall p^d 4^li for 1 years Interest 100^li due
this day.

21.   being Sundy, frequent Showers of Rain. Wind N.E. very
strong, was not at Church, young John pease in his way from
Whitby dined here & went from hence for Darlington near 2,
along with Mr Spark, who called upon me about business from
Mr Hall.

22^d.   had been faire in the night but very thick Skie with wind
at E.   Dr Cha. Bisset came here to desire a Bill for 6^li : 6^s which I
gave him upon Mr Core at 20 days.

23^d.   about 12 I went to Boulby, called at Grange, where Stayed
about an Hour, in Skelton Ellers met Mr Hall, beyond Skelton overtook Wm Brown who went with me to Grang to view that place,
lay at Boulby.   Wind at E, about 12 oClock Mr Wardell & M^r
Jefferson Set me to Grange.

on 24th, called at pitt Hill in our Way Stay^d about an Hour at
Grang from thence I came Home met Mr Hall in Tokets lane, John
price came Here to work.

25.   about 9 went to Marsk along with Mr Danby to meet the
Commissioners about a Division of Marske & Ridcar Fields, where
was M^r Ra: Robinson, Mr Thos Rasibeck, Mr Fra: Richardson, M^r
John Jackson of Old Hall, Mr Isaac Skarth, Mr Wm Richardson of
Ayton & my Self being 7 in all as Commissioners.   Mr John preston
as Solliciter, his Son, Mr Richardson of Darlington, & Anthony
Foster as Surveyors with many freeholders Rid about the two Township Fields & came to the Hall about two & dined.   Stayed till 4
& parted, came home with Mr Danby but appointed another meeting on munday the 29 at 10 in the morning.

26.   at home all day got the new House pointed out per Fishook,
high Wind at S.   at noon came on Rain which continued that
afternoon & all night.   Wind abated.

27th.   very Calm but much rain & very thick fogg.

28.   Sunday at Church forenoon pretty fair all day Mr Wardells
Boy came here to whome gave two Letters that Came by post for
his Master.   high wind at S.

29.   John Aysley & John price put up the Guns, Swords, & other
arms in the new low Clozet.   about 9 I went with Mr Danby to
Mask where we met the Commissioners and Sit close to business till
1, when dined, Stayed till 4 & come Home with Mr Danby, appointed
to meet again on tuesday the 14th of october at Same place.

30.   Mr Hore of Stockton came here about 10.   after dineing I
went wth him to Boulby but the *Darling* being on to take in Allom
he did not See Mr Wardell that night, about 4 he & I went to Steaths

in order for his laying there all night, but M[r] Jefferson being on board the Allom Ship got not home till next day.

The 1st October. Mr Wardell and I went from Boulby in the morning to Steaths but Mr Hore was in Bed. After breakfast we all went to Boulby, from thence to pitt Hill, from thence to the fould in Newfoundland, where Mr Wardell left us & Mr Hoar and I went to Grange where we Stayed about two Hours, my people being then leading otes cut of upton East pasture field. from Grange we Set out, he for Kirkleatham & I for Guisbro, but I set him to Saltburn Where we parted. there I saw Mr Castle & his son Forster to whom I spoke but did not light, got home near 6. great wind at W.

2. At Home.

3[d]. at home Excessive high Wind at W.

4. at Home. A very fine day, moderate Wind at W[t].

5th. fine Weather mostly from S.W. to N.W[t]. Mr Wardell call'd here in his way to Bishoprick, dined and went for Stockton about 3.

6th. went up Street. Spoke with John Jackson. O. Hall went to Mr Hides where Mr Nelson came to us. I stayed near 2 Hours, when William Mewburn came home with me & paid me £42, in part for the 4 oxon, with whome drunk a pint of white wine. Anthony Foster came to me from Mr Lee who offers to buy Nephew Spencer's Hutton Farm. I appointed him to call on me on munday next, when would give him an Answer. John Boys brought me a Bottle of Woond water and I gave him a Bottle Ginn.

1755. October 7th. at Home fine Weather the wind at W.

8th. at Home good weather & calme. Wind at West. what there was. this evening about 6 Mrs Honor Chaloner[32] on the 92 or 93[d] year of her Age, who died at York the 2[d] Instant in the night, was brought to Gisbro to be interr'd. She was directly taken out the Hers that brought her & Carryed into the Church.

9th. Tho: preswick Set out this morning for Bishop Auckland, upon my Business and to go to Thirsk upon his own, at home my Self all day, fair Weather. Wind at W. and N.W.

10th. fair but Cold. Wind N toward night, at home all day.

11th. very Cold and frequent Showers with Wind at N, paved the new dung hill place.

12th. month Sunday, a very great Shower of Snow in the morning and frequent Showers, Rain all day. Wind high & at N[o].

13th. frosty morning. Wind S. but little of it. Mr Crow of

---

[32] Mrs. Honora Chaloner. William Chaloner of Guisborough married Honora, eldest daughter of Sir David Foulis, Bart., of Ingleby Manor. This is the lady here referred to. Their son, Edward, who married Ann, daughter of Sir William Bowes of Streatlam, died in 1737, and was succeeded by his son, William Chaloner of Guisborough, who married Mary, daughter of James Finney, Esq., of Finny Lane in Staffordshire.

Stockton called upon me with Mr Maddeson's Letter desireing to Borrow £900 upon Houses in Stockton to be paid about Martinmis next, but being low in Cash at this time I durst not promise but referrd my Answer to him till Sunday evening next, when I hoped to be at Stockton. in the Evening came a messenger on foot from Durham with a letter from Durham from one Mr Goddard and another from Mr Dunn with a bundel of Deeds to peruse of an Estate of 36ʰ a year, the letter proposed to Mortgage to me for £400 being Copy hold tenure.   I writ back to Mr Dunn and appointed to meet him at Stokesley on Saturday next the 18ᵗʰ Instant. up Street today, Spoke Mr Jackson, Mr preston and divers others, of the 2 former proposed to Borrow £500. for 6 months certain.   Mr preston gave me encouragement, but the former was out of Cash.   fine day, much like frost in the evening.[33]

Oct. 1755.   13.   all day at home as before last night came A purpose Messinger from Durham with two Letters from Mʳ Edward Goddard an Attorney and Cozen Martin Dun about Lending him £400, the Messinger brought 16 Deeds and papers relateing to the Security.   I returned an Answer to Mʳ Dunn appointing him to meet me at Stokesley the 18ᵗʰ, the messenger lay at my House Last night and went away this morning, the 14, about 9 A Clock.   I went with Mʳ Danby to Marsk where I met the other 6 Commissioners about the Division there. after doing business therein dined & Stayd till 4 & parted.

15ᵗʰ.   about noon I went for Boulby.   Tho: preswick Set me to Skinnington Bridge very Rainy day Wᵈ at Nᵒ. called at Grange where ordered Wᵐ White to go the next day to Dabhom for 20 bu: Seed wheat to come from Mʳ peirse in A Boat Sent there to take in otes.   lay at Boulby that night.

next morning the 16ᵗʰ.   I went to Steaths & breakfasted at Mʳ Jeffersons of whom I asked to Borrow £500 for 6 months certain at 4ʰ: 10ˢ p. Cᵗ, which he told me I might have at Martinmis next, from thence I went to the Rock & then to Grange where Stayed but little.   Seting out for Gisbro, on my way met Wᵐ White comeing with an other man & 4 Horses without the wheat the Boat not comeing to Dabhome. before I got home was overtaken by Mʳ Hall his Bro. Major Hall, with an other Gentleman & 2 Servants going to Dine with Mʳ Jackson at Gisbro, at the Weding Feast of his Son with Chiefe Jacksons Daughter, the marrige being some days before. I got home about 2.

17ᵗʰ.   all day at Home when patton the mason Set two ranges in the ground Clozet and that above it.

18ᵗʰ.   I went to Stokesley where met me Mʳ Martin Dunn at Mʳ prestons' when settled the affair about £400 I am to advance him as

---

[33] Here follow entries for the 14th, 15th and 16th of the month.   They are crossed off and rewritten on the next page.

Soon as Deeds can be prepared for that purpose. I returned home where I got about 5 a Clock.

19. Sunday at home the forenoon, about 1 Set out for Stockton where got near 4, came to me in the Evening Mr Sleigh, Mr Sutton Mr Brown Mr Crow & Mr Maddeson, all whome Sitt with me till nigh 11. Settled with Mr Crow & Mr Maddeson (after the rest was gone) my lending the former £900 to be paid 10th Nov^m at Stockton upon proper Security.

20. I went for yarm being fair day there where got about 7. met with Mr Wardell who had been from Boulby Since the 5th Inclusive, in all 18 days. Mr Beckwith near Doncaster called to See me at Yarm. Spoke with Bryan Harrison to whome offered the Sale of Nephew Tho: Spencers Estate at little Stainton in the C° Durham but he haveing laid out his money in the purchase of an other, was not for buying any more, did my business with Sundrys. Set out near 2 with Mr Smith of pinchinthorp and my man T:p. got home about 5.

21. at home.

22^d. At home, about 3 or 4 in the Afternoon came to my Door Nephew Wm Gansel in a Chase & 4 Horses, the former his own, but the latter Hired from Allerton he had no Companion but his Servant Thos, thay set out from Doneland on munday last the 20th.

the 23^d. Mr Gansel his Servt & my Self set out about 7 in the morning for Boulby but near Skelton he found himself not well & got a drink of Water at Skelton, but before we got to top of Brotton Hill he became very bad not being able to ride any longer, but got of Horseback to walk on foot, when he was So weak that he could not walk alone but as he was Supported by his Servant & me, and was obliged to Sitt down frequently, at last after a great Struggle we got to Wardells House on this side Skinington bank where we got him to Bed in his Close I then dispatched a messinger to Grange & an other to Skelton, with my request to M^r & Mrs Hall to Send their Shaze in order to Carry Mr Gansel back to Gisbro, in about an Hour ½ Mr Jefferson & Mr Wardell came to us from Grang where they were come to meet us, in About 1½ hour more the Shaze came and we got him into it. Setting out near 2. for Gisbro where we arrived near 5 and he then was better but desired he might go to Bedd which he did. next morning friday the 24th he was much better when Mr Jefferson & Mr Wardell came here from Steaths & Boulby the latter went to dine at Cock with Mr Sutton & Mr More at an Appointed meeting there about the Allome Affair. Mr Gansell, Mr Jefferson & my self dined togeather at my House when A Letter came Inclosed in the newspapers directed for Mr Gansel with an order to hasten back with all expedition on Account of the Government Affairs, So he gave directions to Allerton postman for 4 Chase Horses to be here from thence at 7 next morning the 25th about

N

which time they came. So about 9 Mr Gansel & his Servant got into the Chase and went away for Allerton. Mr Wardell came here from Stokesley where he went last night. he dined with Mr Jefferson & me and thay both went that evening for Steaths and Boulby. Wm Armstrong came here the 24th above and paid me 16: 13: 4 onstand for his Corn when gave him ten ginnys for which he was very thankfull. very varyable bad Weather with frequent showers of Rain. Wind N^o.

26th. Sunday at Church forenoon, much rain the night following.

27. Spok with Mr preston & Mr Mathews, the latter came to my House, gave him Some Grapes & peaches. Spoke Mr Hide.

28th. at Home.

29th. at Home but dined at Mr Wm Jackson with Mr Robinson, parson Conset, his son the parson, late Capt Consetts' Son.[34] Mr Watson the Brewer, Mr Jackson and his Son new marryed to Mr Jackson's Daughter of Lackenby, who & miss yeoman was at Table. Stayed till after 3, and parted.

30th. met the Commissioners at Mask, went there with Mr Danby. in our way met Mr Scarth, Mr John Jackson, William Richinson, Commissioners, Mr Smith, Mr Miller & William Watson, when we viewd Barley moor in order to Set out Mr Millers' part he claimed thereon. When wee'd done went down to Mask and had a long debate about the affair which we at last got Settled, appointing Mr Miller ten acre next his own ground on the north thereof and South Side Burley Moor Hill near upleatham, he to make East and west fence & Sir William Lowther that on the north upon the Side of the Hill. came home with Mr Miller & Mr Danby, where got near 5, all the Commissioners was there.

31. about noon went along with John Arrowsmith and one of Webster ladds to Grang, thay comeing to Gisbro with 10 lambs which Mr Wardell had sold to one near yarm Who sent for them the next day. I stayed Grang not an Hour but went to Boulby where was John Langstaff with Mr Wardel. he stayed after about an hour. I lay there that night.

Nevt morning 1^t of Nov^m. I went to Steaths & there breakfasted at Mr Jeffersons. the Fishing Boats returning from Yarmouth a day or two before, from whence I came about 10 & went to pitt hill along with Wardell where was about an Hour, from thence I went to Grang where stayed near 2 hours. from thence came home alone.

---

[34] The Rev. William Consett, who died in 1762, had a son, the Rev. William Pennyman Consett, who died at Guisborough 1800, aged 76. Matthew Consett, Captain R.N., brother of the elder William, married Joanna, daughter of William Pennyman, Esq., of Normanby, died in 1748, leaving a son, Matthew Consett, born 1732. Matthew became a captain in the North York militia and author of *A Tour Through Sweden, Swedish Lapland, Finland and Denmark*, published in 1789.

2^d. Rain most of the day. Wind S.W. at Home all day & not at Church.

3^d. Was up Street. Spok Mr Preston who told me that the Commissioners for dividing Mask & Redcar fields was near a Conclusion and that they had appointed Wednesday the 12th of this month to make a full end. also Spoke Mr Matthews about their agreement at Whitby the 30th past among the Allom makers, and Signed an Agreement about it. Same day gave Mr proddy a ginny for his attendance upon Mr Gansel when here. William Bowser paid me a year Interest for £100 due the 6th of this month. William Rogers paid me 7^{li}: 10^s for his last Lady-day Rent. Thomas Mawer and James Jackson in difference, both came Seperately and afterwards togeather and Joyntly desired I would make an end betwixt them which I agreed to do if in my power.

4th. In the morning I went to Eston where called at Nicholas patton's and lighted there a little, where was Mr Mathews Setting affairs respecting a marryage between Nicholas' Daughter and John Jackson of Lackinbys son which is Supposed to be soon Accomplished. from thence I went to William Mewburn to Se a Steer, where stayd about an Houre & then went to dine at Mrs Joanna Consetts^{35} at Normanby which I did with her Self, Son and Mrs Finch & got home near 5.

5th. at home all day, fine Weather.

6th. had been much rain last night with a great Storm. Wind N^o. Mr Jefferson came from Steaths about noon along with my man J. pearson. I sent there for some Bisket & Read Herringe, the former brought me £460 with Mr Wardells Bill on Robert Core to William Jackson, who paid money for it, the same being to make up £500, which Mr Jefferson lent me on my note, payable at 6 months. he stayed all night.

7th. A Severe Frost otherwise A fine day. Wind N, but faire all day. Mr Jefferson with Mr Fox dined here. the former went away near 3 along with Mr Wardell's Boy that came for post letters. Wind N^o but not great. At home all day.

8th. sent Thomas preswick to Stockton with £791. 8. o in part of £900 lent to Mr George Crow there, my note for £100 and 8^{li}: 12^s o^d in Mr Maddeson's hands was to make it up. he returned same night, great frost and much Snow. Wind N^o, at home all day.

9mo. Sunday, Snow in the night before with frost, at home all day. Mr Wardell's boy was here.

10. Thomas Knaggs paid me £26. 5. o in part for Hides. I paid Mr Fox 1 years' Bread 2^{li}. 12^s to 2 November. this years all the same from said time for one year following. David Button paid me 6 months Rent for his Mother due Michaelmas last 1^{li}: 15^s: o^d. Mr

^{35} The widow of Matthew Consett, R.N., and mother of Matthew the younger.

preston & Thomas Knaggs dined with me.   I went to William
Corneys where I met James Jackson & Thomas Mawer with each
their friends and Mr Matthew Jackson's attorney, where after much
debate made up a difference that was depending betwixt them for
more than 9 years, about some Beast-gates which I made an end of.
Assigning each to pay 13/- for Law charges & Mawer to pay Jackson
15/-, which was there done accordingly, and a final end made.

11ᵗʰ   At home all day Mr Wardells Boy was here for Letters.
John price came here & dined, went away in the afternoon.   William
Mewburn came here to Acquaint me about Some Steers and dined.

12.   I went to Marsk & met 5 Commissioners with Mr preston &
2 Surveyors, but little business was done.   Mr Robinson was not
there, the others Stayd all night.   I came home with Mr Danby
about 4 in the Evening.   Severe frosts the two days before, much
Rain last night tho a frost this morning, about noon much rain
& cold with Wind at N & N.W.

13ᵗʰ.   About noon I went with Aysley to Grange, when there it
begun to Rain where Stayd till evening, but before I got Boulby
was miserably wet, where Stayed all night.

14ᵗʰ.   I went to Grange where we put up a new pump in the
Well by the House and covered in said Well.   about 3 Set out from
thence with John pearson my Servant for Gisbro where Arrived
near 5, exceeding wett having rained most of the way.   with Wind
at Nᵒ.   Same day 2 Ships was put on Shore on Humbersty Sand
near Mr More's Allom House, said to be the *Midum*ʳ³⁶ and the *Cod*
smack.

15.   at home all day.   Dr Waugh came to see me but Stayd little,
at Night a Cruel Rain.   Wind at S.

16.   Sunday at Church forenoon, at night much rain.

17.   Gisbro Fair, was up in the Beast market when Mr Hall with
parson Lasscels and his Brother Captain came by.   thay called
at the Cock where I went & Spoke to them, they came to my House
and had their Horses brought them, but Stayed very little, took
Horse & went away for Durham.   Mr Hall intend to go from thence
for London & to Bath.   Mr Chief Jackson, Mr Mathers & Wᵐ Mewburn dined with me.   Spoke with Danyel Ling.   John Nicholson
paid me £35 in part for goods, John Wilson £10 for money Lent.
John young 1: 0: 6 for his last may day Rent much rain in the
night.

18ᵗʰ.   at Home all day, fair Weather, wind at N.W.

19ᵗʰ Novᵐ 1755.   all day at home, much Rain last night.

20ᵗʰ.   I went to Grange.   Tho: presswick Set me there, where
met Robt Beadnel, Husband of Alice late Wife of Miles Mewburn,
with whome I went to Lofthouse, where he discharged John Ling
their Tenant there to A little farm of 7ˡˡ A year, to go off at May

³⁶ This is all the clue he gives to the name of the ship.

day next, I went to Se Mr More with whome Stayed near 2 Hours and took of him A little Bank at end of Brea Mires, & to give him 7/6 a year for it from May day next, had much discourse with him about Allom affairs. from him I went to Grange where Stayed 2 or 3 hours about the pump fixing, from thence went to Boulby in the Evening where I found Mr John Jefferson & Mr Wardel the Latter Just Arrived out Bishoprick where he went the 12th Instant being absent 8 days. Mr Jefferson went home about 8 at night.

21^t. I went to pitt Hill with Mr Wardell, from thence to Grang where Stayed very little but came for Gisbro along with Will. White & his Nephew White, arrived at home about 12, thay dined here & Set out near 1. for Darlington, martinmis day fair being there the next day, intending to buy Some oxon there.

22. Will White came from Darlington in the Evening but bought no Beasts, he went to Grang that night, my Self at home all day.

23^d. Sunday forenoon at Church, at home the remainder of the day.

24. I was up Street. Saw M^r preston, had Some Conference with him about Martin Dunn's affair had the Votes from Mr Mathews the first time, from whom am to have them every Week So long as the parlim^t Sitts. Mr Wardel came here today from Boulby he and Mr Hide dined with me.

25th. A Sore Rain last night and most of this day, wind at S.E & NE. much Snow the following night.

26. at home, much bad Weath^r wind N. John Hawman paid his last Mar^t[37] Rent.

27. at home.

28. at home, frost & Snow but thaw in the Afternoon.

29. pretty much Snow last night, Sent J pearson to Grang, Boulby & Staths, at home all day.

30th. being Sunday at Church fore noon, Mr Wardells Boy came here for Letters, by Whome Received 49 gins[38] from his Master, & by him Sent £53 pounds in Silver for it.

December 1. was up Street Spok Mr Lawson, Mr Matthews, from the latter Received Some Deeds in Mr Yowards affair, also M^r preston, who came & dined with me, before we had Done Mr Murgatroid came Who had dined, to Whom I paid £7. 18: for a years Tyth Rent due next Lady day. Rec^d of James Jackson his last Michaelmas Rent £3: 10. also from Mr Skottowe £40 being the remainder of one half years Interest due 26th Aprill last past. As M^r preston brought the money I returned a Receit by him. Scarce 24 hours for Some weeks have been free from Rain, Snow & frost with the Wind from all quarters. So that it has been a miserable Season even for many months.

[37] Martinmas.
[38] Guineas.

1755. Dec^m 2^d. at home.

3^d. this morning was found in the pasture the black Horse (I formerly bought of one Burrel in the County of Durham) with his far fore Legg brok in a most miserable manner above the Knee as there was other two Horses with him its Supposed one of them had done it by A Stroke. I ordered him to be Killd which was done accordingly. at Home all day.

4th. I went for Boulby about 10. with T. presswick, call'd at Grang where Stayed about an houre, at Boulby there was a fitter at Boulby, a Sunderland Fitter, and an other Stranger who was going away as I got there, where I lay that night.

5th. Mr Jefferson came to us that morning & I Stayed till after eleven haveing Sent Will White to view Some oxon at Tho: Hills, but he did not buy any, as Soon as he returned went for Grange where Stayed about an hour & Set out for home & met T.p. on the Way with Whome came to Gisbro about Sun Sett.

6th. at Home forenoon, but went & dined at Mr Hides being Invited, but none was there but him & his Wife. Came home about 5. where was comed Duke Fogge[39] to pay his last May day Rent, Robert Dalton came & paid me 17/6 & 15/9, had much Wrangling with him about 7 days leading Stores, which he thought himself wronged in but could not Settle it.

7th. was Sunday, at Church forenoon. Mr Wardells Boy was here for Letters.

8th. was up Street, Spok Mr Mathews & M^r prestons Son, himself not being here, also young parson Consett at M^r prestons Chamber, was at Mr Jackson's shop, took up 2 Sheet almenacks for Mr Wardell, paid for them 8^d.

9th. at Home but in the Evening went to the Excise where Received £150 for my Bill upon Mr Core on Works account.

10th. sent Thomas preswick to Stockton with £101: 8: 8. for Mr George Crow & £4: 1: 0 for Mr Maddeson. to the latter I writ with two different Accounts about the money. T.p. came home about 5.

11. Jane Whitby paid her last Martinmis Rent 8/-. Mr Emd[40] presswick came here and paid me 10^ll for 6 months Interest for £500 due 6th September last. Mr Wardel came here about noon, but went to dine at Cock along with Mr Sutton, Mr More, Mr Heath, Mr Mathews, Mr Edmund pressick all met there towards Settling the Allom affair, but this meeting was to little purpose. Mr Wardell went to Boulby Along with Mr Moore.

12. at home all day, little remarkable.

13. Datus Danby came here this morning, after much Conference about his ill behaviour I lent him a ginny to pay me again at

---

[39] Among the first names (they can hardly be called Christian names) in this volume are *Chief* Jackson, *Duke* Fogg, and *Datus* Danby.
[40] Edmund.

Chrismis, also Mr Mark Etherington came & desired to Borrow 15^{li} till next May day which I lent him upon his note.

14th. munth Sunday, Mr Wardell's boy came here with a Bill for £100 to Mr Jackson for the money but his Son being Abroad had the Keys of his cash so could not come at money.

1755. 15th Decr. Was up Street, Spoke with Chief Jackson, calld in at Mr Jackson's shop where saw Mr Oldfield & Askt him to dine with us on friday next the 19th, which was to be a pay day at Boulby. Mr preston came to my house in the Afternoon with whom conferred about Martin Dunns affaire. Robert Dalton his wife & Brother John came here in the Evening with whom I reckoned & thay discharged John's note to me for 13^{li} he formerly gave me on Said Brother Roberts's Account, when I again discharged him of my House, he, the said Robert, Lives in.

16. came A great Rain last night with the Wind at S° which poweres in every uper Room in all my Houseing and run down into many low roomes in a dismall manner.

17th. went to Boulby with my man John Pearson, called at Grange, from thence to Boulby with said J.p.

18th. went to Steaths with Mr Wardell where we found Neice Jefferson very ill in a breaking out in her thigh which abated in a day or two after.

18. lay at Boulby last night.

19. was a pay at Boulby where Rec^d of William White £15 : 9. also of Thomas Allan for Beef 20 : 1 : 1½, and of all my Tenants for Rent due Mart last.

20. Went from Boulby to Grange where met T.p. with whom went from thence to Gisbro where got about 2.

21. Sunday at home all day.

22^d. Mr Wardell came last night to Cock about Some business with Mr Baker's Tenants at Budford, but he dined at my house. Mr preston came there about Martin Dunn's affair. Mr Wardell went for Boulby. George Sparling came & took Dalton's House at 40/- per Annum.

23. all day at home. nothing Remarkable.

24. at home.

25. Xmis Day at Church forenoon.

26. Mr Jefferson came here from Steaths who paid me £15 : 13/- for a pitt Rope, Stayd all night, went away, 27 in the morning. afternon Same day came Nephew Ra: Jackson.

28. Sunday I was taken ill with pain in my foot like the Gout, took Bateman's drops at going to Bed & was Better.

29th. Ra: Jackson went with me Up Street where met us Wm Corner & Tho: pressick at Wins house & these took an Inventory of moveables & fixtures about the House. about noon came Mr Robert Wilson of Stockton with Mr Maddeson's Letter & A Bond therein from Said Wilson to be executed by him upon my Sending him £100 which I did accordingly, & he executed.

30ᵗʰ. Ra: Jackson went away this morning, about 10 Nateby the Carpenter with Tho: presswick went to porrits Farm where I met them and there viewed the Timber growing upon high freelege⁴¹ Field wherein grows near 30 Trees all which I sold to Said Nateby for nine pounds for which he is to have Six months Creadit.

31. at home in the Evening parson Hubbard came & Sit with me 2 or 3 Hours. Wᵐ Fawcet of Stoddow came there this evening from Kirk Leatham and Stayed here all night, when we Talkt over the matter about my Stoddo Farm he has under me. I let it him at 20ˡⁱ a year under a Lease for 42 years but then he is to build a Dwelling house upon it of my own dementions So as it may be convenient & proper for Such a Farm. I let him Se the Survey of it and he took the number of Acres which is 40ᵃ. 3ʳ. 0ᵖ. he went away for Kirk Leatham again next morning.

1756

1756. January the 1ᵗ. at home all day nothing remarkable.

2ᵈ. at home all day. in the Evening Ó presswick came to reckon with me, when paid me to Ballance £2: 10: 0, as also Edward Thornton his last Martmis Rent 6ˡⁱ: 10ˢ. 0ᵈ Sent in by his Wife.

the 3ᵈ. at home.

4ᵗʰ. at home being Sunday which was most Severe Rain all the forenoon with a high Wind at Sᵒ.

5ᵗʰ. Mr Wardell & John Gallon dined here, the latter offered to pay for an ox he had last Spring for his Ship, but not haveing an Account here he deferrd it till I went for Boulby. I went up Street after thay went away, where Spok with Mr Mathews and Mr preston, also Chief Jackson, went to Mrs Chaloners to Se her Son William, but she was gon to Skelton & he to Mr Husband's at the School house where I went to See him but stayed very little there, took leave of him he being to return next day to his uncle Boweses in order to go with him again for London. after I went to Mr Hides and there was Mr Murgatroid, where I stayed about an Houre, in less than that time the latter left us to go home. fine Weather all day Wind at Nᵒ Wᵗ.

6ᵗʰ. at Home.

7ᵗʰ. at Home.

⁴¹ Freeledge, is the privilege of unlimited access to and benefit from.

8th. I went to Boulby calld at Grange, lay all night at the former.

9th. Rid up to pitt Hill, from thence went to Grange, from thence took Will White with me towards Gisbro but meeting with Tho: priswick, the other returned back I got to Gisbro near one. Wind very high at W^t, met Mr Hide & Mr Lassels near the Ellers.

10. at Home.

11th. munth Sunday John pease Junr & his Bro. W^m came here from Whitby dined & went for Darlington, Mr Wardell's Boy came here dined & returned for Boulby. Ra: Mewburn called & left 40/- for A Year's Interest for £50 due 10th Nov^m last. O.S.

12. up Street carried with me a Bill which left with John Husband for Mr Howlet upon Robert Core, for £103. 2. 6 for which to have the money on mich day next. Spoke M^r preston, also Wm Mewburn, who appointed to call upon me on Wednesday next, to go and Se my oxon at Grang. John porrit came & paid me his last Michaelmas Rent 7^{li} 10^s. Account his Bill £1: 3: 9.

13. All day at Home.

14. I went to Grang Mr Pearson with me. Soon after we got there Wm Mewburn came, viewed the Oxon & Sheep & then we went to Boulby, but Mr Wardell met us at Barn when viewed 4 oxon of his from thence went to Allom House where Mr Mewburn Stayed about 2 hours & went for home.

15th. Mr Wardell & I went and dined at Steaths where John Gallon paid me £12:9:6 for Beef got last Spring, also Richard Andrew for more Beef £11:0:0, when appointed with Mr Jefferson to go with him to Whitby on tuesday next the 20th. lay all night at Boulby.

16. in the morning went to Grange where T.p. came to me with whom came Home about 1. in the Evening Mr Hide calld upon me to know if could Lend Mrs Chaloner £1500, to pay off A Mortgage upon Tockets to whome promist to let him know in a months time, if I could help her with the money.

17th. Sent for Will Green & gave him a letter received last post from Mr Bedson of Scarbro & advised him to go therewith this morning to his Father at Boulby which promist to do, with whom Sent a Letter from Durham that came last post. Same day Richard Lincoln Sent me £4 I lent him the 19th Sep^t last.

18th. at Church forenoon, Mr Wardells Boy came here, dined & returned with Letters in the Evening. Mr Hide, Mr Lasscels & M^r proddy came & Sit the Evening the two former Suppt but the latter came after. all went away about eleaven.

19. Mr Wardell came here in his Way to Ellemore, Stayd and Dined, but I dined at the Cock with Mr Robinson, Mr Skottowe & Mr Beckwith, haveing the Highway Sessions that day, parson Conset his Son & divers others, in all 13 of us, dined. Spoke Mr Skottowe

about his Interest money, also Mr Sugget about his, also Mr Hide about the Mortgage of Tockets.[1] Mr Beckwith paid me for Tiles & Lent Money 16^{li} in all 19^{li} 11:6, also John Husband paid me £103:2:6 for my Bill to Mr Howlet Lent him last monday for that Sum. in the Evening Mr Fox came here to whom gave my Bill on Mr Core desireing him to receive money for the Same at the Excise tomorrow, also Spoke to him about the Sale of Stainton Estate belonging Nephew Spencer in County of Durhome, Glover Knaggs proposeing to buy it.

20th. I went to Steaths Tho: presswick with me, called at Grang & Boulby, but did not light, breakfasted at Steaths from whence went with Mr Jefferson for Whitby, calld at the Warehouse at Sands end & went into the Room. Violent Wind at S.W. but fair Weather.

21. Sundry people paid me more, vide books.

22^d. Set out about 10 in the morn w^{ith} Mr Jefferson. A most Violent Wind at W^t S:W. but fair. calld at Boby and lited but Stayed very little, calld at Grange, where lited, from thence came home about 4 in the Evening.

23. at home all day.

24th. at home all day, John price came here and Stayd all night.

25th. being Sunday I was at Church the forenoon. John price dined & went home.

26th. went up Street. Spoke Mr Jackson about a Bill for £100 odd money who promist to take one, Spoke Mr Mathews about Mr Yowards[2] affair, also M^r preston who came & dined with me. when we Settled a day for meeting Mr Martin Dunn & his Attorny Godard about my takeing the formers Security for £400. when we agreed that M^r preston should give him notice to meet us at Stokesley on Tuesday the 3^d of Feb^r next.

27. Mr Conset came & paid me £54: 7: 6 for 6 months Interest due the 11th Inst for £2900. in the afternoon I Rid out to view my Farm at Long Hull, John Hawman my Tenant went along with me. at my return John Aysley & Alick pulman came, thay being my partners as overseers of the highways this year, when also came Robert Beednel & his Son in Law from Whitby about Danyel Ling of Lofthouse, their Tenant there, who will neither pay any Rent or go off his farm which I have a Mortgage of for £120.

28. at home a most fine day as also was yesterday. Robert Beednel calld here this morning about the Same cause as before & offered to put in my hands their Farm at Lofthouse, which refused,

---

[1] Tocketts, Tockets, Toccotes, a township near Guisborough.

[2] Ralph Yeoward, son of Richard Yeoward, died Oct. 1, 1781; aged 72, buried in St. Mary, Bishophill, York. This is probably the person referred to.

M[r] Hide & two Church wardens came w[ith] A Brief for A great fire[3] to which I gave half A guiney.

29. about 9 in the morning by Appointment I met M[r] Foster, M[r] Bottom, Richard outhard & Richard clark of the Jury John Aysley & Geo: Sparnel with my Self being new officers for the high ways, also John porrit the old officer, when we views the highway to Upsell also Barnaby Lane, Locerons[4] Lane, Wilton Lane, the lane from Dunsdale Beck to Tockets gate, from thence we went to Waterfall and viewed all the Whitby Road to potter Beck that belonged Gisbro Township, noteing down the Want of Scowring & repairs of Causeways. got home about 4 in the Evening, but we went to Diner after viewing Hutton Lane, appointing to meet again at half after one when we begun with Willton Lane & ended at potter Beck.

30. at home all day nothing remarkable, but fine weather.

31[t]. went to Stokesley where met me at Andersons M[r] W[m] Hodshon from Allerton, who brought me the Reverend M[r] Henry Wastell[4a] of Symonburn in Northumberland his Bond for £300 which money I paid him in part £284, & allow[d] £16 more for 1 years Interest for £400, the Said M[r] Hodshon ows me. I dined at Stoxley w[ith] 6 or 8 more, Some of whom I did not know, calld at M[r] prestons & M[r] Howlets, Spoke with them, both left Stockesley near two. on my way home called at pinchingthorp where met me at my little House there W[m] Hobkirk, to whome gave directions for makeing A Conduit throw the Entry. Stayed near an Hour there & came Home, Joh[n] Ager came w[ith] me from Stokesley. Tho. presswick went & came home with me. a fine day.

Feb[r] 1[t]. Sunday at Church forenoon, my Mason Wallis of Lofthouse came here, went to Church, & Home in the Afternoon.

Feb[r] 1756. 2[d]. I was up Street calld at M[r] Jacksons Shop where Spok to him & Son, also Chief Jackson, in the market M[r] Loram, M[r] W[m] Suttons Clark, came to me with whom came Home & he paid me £520 for his Masters note & Interest. A fine day. Wind S.

3[d]. I went to Stokesley, T.p. with me, where at M[r] prestons met M[r] Martin Dunn also M[r] Goddard, an Attorney of Durham, with one M[r] John Sibbald, I guess an other Attorney of Same place, with the two former Executed Mortgage Deeds to me for £400, Lent Said M[r] Dunn, came home after dineing at M[r] prestons, where got about 4. A fine day, Wind but a hard frost & very Cold.

---

[3] A Brief was issued on July 30th, 1755, on account of a fire at Robert Town (Yorks). The fire had caused a loss of £11,890. There was another the same year for a fire at Holberton, Devon, where the loss had been £1,248. (Bewes, *Church Briefs*, 1896, p. 325.)

[4] Locerons Lane, Lowcross.

[4a] Henry Wastell, B.A., 1711; M.A. Peterhouse, 1714; Fellow, 1711-14; Deacon, Ely, 1714; Priest, London, 1715; Rector, Markenhall, Essex, 1718-23; Simonburn, 1723-71. Died at Simonburn 1771, aged 82.

4. hard frost but fine day, Wind S went to Grange, T.p with me. Stayd A little, from thence went to Boulby where they was killing an ox for John Gallon. Sent T.p to Steaths with orders to call upon Mr Jefferson to desire his company the forenoon, where he came & dined Staying till after 5, after he was gon came Mr Wardell from Ellemore, last from Stockton, he has been from Boulby Since the 19th past, 16 days, next morning the 5th we Sent for Mr Jefferson. the ox was Cutt up weighed 89^{stone} 6^{li} in the quarters, Hide 8st 8^{lb}, Tallow 11^{sto} 3^{li}. we dined upon Stakes & after went with Mr Wardell to Grange, where we measured 2 oxon, Rook & Bullet, went to See the feeding Sheep after Set out with T.p. for Gisbro, who met me there. I got home about 5. Frost abated, blowed fresh, Wind at S.W. but fair.

6th. A general Fast, went to Church forenoon which was So Crowded with people as I never See the like before, Fine dry Weather but Wind very high at SW^t. Wardell's boy was here for Letters dined & went back.

7th. at home all day John Aysley came to Reckon with me, but haveing mislaid his bill he will draw an other & come again an other time.

8. Sunday at Church forenoon, fine Weather, Wind S.W.

9. up Street, went with Mr Hide to Mrs Chaloner to Speak to her about £1500 She wants to take upon a Mortgage upon Tockets Estate. She deferrd her Answer till tuesday the 17th Instant that She had the Approbation of her Uncle Bows, Spoke to M^r preston about £1000 he wanted for John Rowntree upon a Mortgage to Whom agreed to give a full Answer Same day fortnight. Mr Lawson came & brought me a Ballance for Weighing gold, for which paid him 5/- also Docktor Bisset came, to whome gave half a guiny for 2 Books he formerly Lent me. John Rigg & his Son, a young man near 20, the latter haveing Bound himselfe to Fra: Easterby of Whitby for the Sea but haveing done it without the knowledge of his parents, was Sorry for what he had done & wanted to be off the Contract. So I writ to M^r pease with them, they intending to go next day to Whitby in order to have him released if possible.

10. I went for Boulby my Servant J.p. with me where was Killing 2 oxon for Mr Jefferson, who was there, also his Nephew Nathaniel Campion where Mr Oldfield came to us & all dined there & Stayed to near 5.

11. Weighed the oxon one was 116^{sto} 6^{li}, the other 100^{sto}, 7^{li}, reserved 3^{sto} 8^{li} for my Self. Captain Campion & his Mate was present at Weighing. Thomas Knaggs came there and Spoke to me about the purchase of Nephew Spencers Estate at little Stainton, who I apopinted to meet me at Gisbro on munday next to Confer further about it. I went With Mr Wardell to pitt hill, from thence to Barn, & he left me soon after, then went to Grange, in my way

found 4 or 5 men beginning a new hedge, to fence out A new lane from Street Houses through Rocliff up to high Rocliff Gate. At Grange I found my Servant John peirson with whome came home. very fine Weather for many days past. Wind mostly at S°. W^t.

12th. I went for Allerton about 10 in the morning, my Servant T.p. With me, got well there about 4 a Clock but did not Stop by the way. Mr Crosfield came & Sit with me till 8.

13. being fair day I went in the morning to the Beast Market, but very few Cattle there, at my return met with M^r peter Conset of Braworth who paid me £34 for a years Interest for £850. about 10 we Set out for home & got well there about 4 in the Afternoon but Stopt nowhere, had been some rain last night with Strong Northerly Wind but none in our passage home.

14th. all day at home. John Rigg came to Speak to me about his Son who had bound himself for 3 years to Sea: as menconed above, but he got him released on paying 5 guinys to Easterby. Also Wm Hobkirk came & Spok to me about his Work.

15. Sunday. I went to Mrs Joanna Consetts funeral at Normanby where I was a Bearer, all the Company dined being Invited to be there. at 12 the Curate of Marton preacht & performed the Office, it was near 5 ere all was done; after I came home with Servant T.p. A most Violent Wind at W.N.W. but not much Rain.

16. Kit Johnson's Wife came here to inform me her Husband had been very good last week & not in the least in Liquer, haveing promist them before his Master O pressick that if he & Johnsons Wife gave him A good report Weekly for 10 week that I would give him 12^d a Week for that time. So She came today to give me an Account of his behaviour the last week which being good I gave her 1/- for the 1^t time. Glover Knaggs & Tho: White of Easington came to Speak to me about the purchase of Little Stainton, thay to call upon Mr Fox on tuesday the 24 Inst. to go along with him to view it. John Martin, with Mr Fox and his foreman King met here about a difference among them. the former haveing the latter for his Tenant gave him notice about 3 weeks ago to leave his House next may day, but that being too Short a time King was not willing to leave it to that notice, which occationed a difference among them, but after much debate they agreed upon termes. Mr Cave & John Hawman came and the former bought the little Hay pike upon Hawmans ground, to give me 50/- for it but if found good to be 55/- Mr Mathews called here and left the Votes[5] and told me Mr yoward would pay me Interest half yearly.

17th. I went & dined at Mrs Chaloner's, and settled with her the 1500^{li} I am to advance upon A mortgage of Tockits, the money to

[5] The published numbers of the votes after parliamentary debates.

be paid about old Lady day[6] next. about 4 I came Home where came John Applebee of Hanthorn hive[7] to Aske my Advice about a Will made by his Wives Bro. Richard Reah, my Tenant of Ayslaby, came here for some quick.[8] Sent for John Martin about the difference betwixt him, Mr Fox & John King, which I thought had been ended yesterday. he promised to do all he can to Settle it.

18th. I went to Grange with Mr Thomson of Shields where showed him my Convenences. from whence went to Boulby. met Mr Wardell at the Barn and viewed his oxon, from thence to Allom house. while we were at Dinner came John Tose of whitby who dined with us where we Stayd 2 or 3 hours. from thence we went to the Barn and viewed 4 oxon for which Toes bid him 14^{li} 10 a peice but thay could not agree. from thence Mr Thomson and my Servant T.p. with my Selfe came for Gisbro where we got about 6 at night. Wind at N.E. blowed hard with Some Snow.

19. John Aysley came here to acquaint me that Mr Turner[9] desired some bad places on the way might be repared, So as he could pass in his Coach from Kirkleatham to Gisbro where he intend to come on munday the 23^{d} Instant to meet the Rest of Justices in order to Settle Watches upon the Coasts agreeable to the King's proclamation.[10] Mr Jackson came and paid me £103 : 6 : 0 for my Bill upon Nephew George Jackson I gave him the 31^{t} past, when he presst me to take £600 of him at Interest. Mr Hide came to Acquaint me of Mr Turner's being there as above & hoped I would dine with him.

20th. at home.

21st. at home. Fine dry Weather with Some frost. Wind N. to N.W.

22. Sunday at Church forenoon. Wind West and dry.

23^{d}. I met Mr Turner & above 20 other Gentlemen at Cock haveing the King's proclamation Read by Mr Spark at Cross attended by A number of Constables & many Gentlemen about 20 of whom dined at Cock. Mr Turner went away about 3 & I left the Company about 4. John Nicholson came and paid me 24^{li} for goods bought

[6] April 5th. The Julian calendar was not accepted in England till Chesterfield's Act (24 Geo. II. c. 23) passed in March 1751. It ordered that in future the first of January should be the beginning of every year in and after 1752, and that in England in 1752 the 2nd of September should be followed by the 14th September. There was much opposition to this latter rule and some people marked their disapproval by making a distinction between Old and New Christmas Day and also between Old and New Lady Day, but the latter distinction was not very long-lived.

[7] Hanthorn. Hanthorn House on Stockdale Moor.

[8] Came for some *quick*, living plants for a hedge, especially hawthorn; compare our "quick-set" hedge.

[9] Mr. Turner. Cholmeley Turner of Kirkleatham, died May 9th, 1767. It was he who erected the mausoleum there in memory of his son, Marwood Turner, who died in 1739.

[10] The Seven Years War had begun.

of me. Mr Wardell was here today also Geor. Mewburn, John Hawman and said Nickleson appointed to meet me at Grang on thursday the 4th</sup> of March to buy my sheep. Mrs Chaloner's Gardner came to ask my Advice About buying proper Seeds for Field Sowing. John Aysley came also to consult about Highways.

24thI went above 11 a Clock to Grange with T.p. where I handled my Fatt sheep & ordered a Wether & Ewe to go for Boulby to be killed next morning which was done Accordingly.

25th. Mr Jefferson & his Nephew Campion came & dined at Boulby & Stayed till evening.

26. the sheep was cut up, the wether weighed near 8 stone in the quarters and the Ewe near 7 Stone. Sent a quarter of the Wether to Mr More, and the same to Mr pease. brought a fore quarter Home & cut the shoulder of the other forequarter and gave it to Mr Wardell, and the rest sent to Mr Jefferson at Steaths, ordered the Ewe and all the fatt to be sold the Workmen, the former at 3^d A pound & the latter at 4^d. After Went up to the pitt Hill with Mr Wardell, from thence to Grange alone, where met me Tho: Pr: with whom came home.

27th. John price's Wife came here in her way to Steaths & dined, also Mr Wardell's Boy who stayed all night in order to drive 10 sheep that was brought here 2 or 3 days ago for his Master. Fine dry Weather, having been no rain for a month or 5 Weeks. Wind in different quarters, the Roads good as ever was known, the Season of the year Considered.

28. at home all day.

29. Sunday, at Church forenoon.

March 1^t. up Street. Spok with Mr Jackson, Mr Preston who dined with me. Maddeson & his Brother calld at my Door who I appointed to meet at Mrs Chaloners to Settle matters about my advancing £1500 upon a Mortgage of Tockets, so am to make the money ready about old Lady day. Mr Wardel calld here, who dined at Cock with Mr More & Mr Sutton, who met there about the Allom affaire to little purpose, he went for Boulby about 4 in the Evening. Wm Mewburn and his Brother James called here in their way to Grange to See my Oxon. Mr Cass paid me for Westland Hay 2 : 12. 6 which Cost me 4^{li} the price I took it at from Westland.

2^d. all day at home, writ to M^r preston that would advance £1000 to his Clyant John Rowntree upon a Mortgage 4 P.Ct, the money to be paid at May day next to the Excise & Received £100 for my Bill on Robert Core. Stayed till after 9.

3^d. at home till near 3, when went with Alick pulman to View yarm lane there being 4 Workmen by Windhill makeing hills to defend the Horse Causeways, gave them 8^d for each A pint of ale. Went to near Belts and came home. Exceeding fine Weather Wind at W^t & Seemingly Settled.

4. I went to Grange where met me Wm Toes and another Butcher from Whitby also Jn° Nickelson with Geo Newburn & John Hawmand to buy my fatt Sheep, but we could not agree on price, thay only bid me 45/- for the parcel. So we dined and parted, I went to lay at Boulby that night.

5th. the *Darling* came and lay on to take in Allom. Capt Nath. Campion came to Boulby to See the Ship Loaded. Mr Wardell went down the hill about 10, when I came from thence called at pitt hill in my way to Grange where Stayd an houre, from thence came home in my way In Skining Bank the Este Side met Tho: presswick going down Brotton hill Mr More overtook me in going a Shooting, we parted at Millam beck he going in at Brotton Gate, from thence came home about 2. fine Weather Wind at W.

6. at home till 6 in the Evening when went up to Cock where I met Mr Hide, Mr Jackson, Mr Foster, & Mr Bottom. after Some time Richard Walker came to us on whose Account we met, he haveing Some difference with his Sister Walker & her ten Children, we talkt the Affair over & Stayd till after 10, but could not agree them.

7th. Sunday at Church forenoon, toward Evening Wm Brotton the Mason & A. pulman came here, the former about comeing to work which he promist to do in a fortnight, and the latter about highways.

8. up Street. Spoke Mr Jackson, who promist to furnish me with £600 at May day next to Assist me in Lending John Rowntree £1000. at Said May day, called in at M^r prestons but he was not in Town, though his Son was there, with whom was M^r peirse, where stayed ½ an hour, from thence the latter & I went to the Cock, where met with Mr Murgatroid & Mr Hide. Soon after Came Mr Turner, With whome 12 or 14 of us dined. he Shewd us a Letter he Received per Express from Ld Rockingham Custos Rottolorum about procureing recrutes for Some new raised Regiments, the press[11] is very Hott at Whitby & Geo Newburn & John Hawman came here at night. after much wrangling Sold them 40 Sheep at Grange for 37/6 a peice, to meet there the 11th to Chuse them out.

9th. I went to Boulby with T.p calld at Grange where T.p. left me & returned home. I went to Boulby, where I lay that night. next morning, the 10th Jn° Longstaff brought £100 & desired I would give it M^r preston on Munday next about 10. Mr Wardell & I went to Lofthouse by Easington, in our way met Mr Sugget who promist to pay me a years Interest for £1000, at Lady day next, the same being due 23^d Dec^m last. went to Mr Mores with whome Rid about his Ground at South Lofthouse to See his Husbandry, which I did not Like. After the Ride we came back to his House and there dined, where we Stayd till after 5, and went to Grang in our way

[11] The activity of the press gangs.

to Boulby, but Will: White, being gon to Kirby Moorside that morning to buy Seed otes, was not returned.

11. Mr Wardell & I went up hill, we parted at Barn he went to Danby about Some Eller wood he bought there, & I went to Grang where met me Geo Mewburn, John Hawman, John Nickleson, Robert Errington & Thomas Sayer, to the 3 former I sold 40 Sheep on Munday last at 37/6 a piece which thay Chused out of 55 & divided among those 3 and took 10 home. after they were gon I sold the other 15 to Errington and Sayer at 28/- Apiece which thay divided, & thay took 4 away, we all dined at Grang upon meat. John peirson back from Gisbro. after I Set out with my Servant & came home.

12. at home al day, gave a poor man Hansel of Gisbro towards buying him a Horse 2/-.

13th. Went to Kirk Leatham along w^{ith} Mr Hide about 10, where we dined with Mr Turner & Mr Davinson of Stokesley, their two Ladys, with Mr Murgatroid & Mr Nelson, I went to Se the Gardens Temple & Green House with many Curiositys also. A fine Large Ox the fattest I ever saw before, which I think will Weigh 120 Stone. we came away about 5 and got home after 6, hard frosty morning but quite a fine day.

14. at home all day, being month Sunday, fine open Weather. Wind E.

15. Mr Errington paid me £15 I lent him the 13th . . . last, also Robert Applebe came and paid me his last Mart Rent £37, out of which Allow his Bill 7^{li}: 3^s: 4½^d. up Street where I paid Mr Preston £100, sent him by John Langstaff, who gave me the same at Boulby the 10th to bring Mr preston. up Street I spoke parson Beckwith,[11a] Mr Murgatroid and Mr Hide, Mr Foster with divers others.

16. at home all day Save rideing up to the quarry where Nicholas patten and Labourers was working. Cold foggy weather. Wind & with Some drisling Rain. John Hawman paid me for 3 Tryal Sheep from Grange 4^{li}: 5^s: 0^d.

17. at home all day.

18. went to Grang. T.p. with me. Stayd there till 1 a clock & came Home. A great Shower of Rain & 2 Claps of Thunder. Wind S^o, but came to W^t in our passage, continued drisling rain till night.

19. went to Stokesley. Set up my Horses at Mr Prestons', but he was not at home. At Mr Howlets' but he was abroad. Went to Bovils where was Mr Skottow & Mr Hurstler. Presently came Mr Turner from Busby In his Coach & 6. Mr Sutton, Mr Beckwith, Chiefe Jackson, Mr Davinson, & Mr Hill of Stainton & A Stranger all dined together at Bovils, the Constables of Cleaveland, all

---

[11a] Roger Beckwith, son of Roger Beckwith of Handale Abbey. B.A. Sidney, 1748-9. Buried at Lofthouse 1757.

appeard there, the meteing was pasuant to an order of Council for all Constables to bring In What Idle Stroleing people to be met with in each Constablere but very few was brought in. I came out before 5 when the Company broke up & Mr Turner Returned for Busby. very Cold. Wind N but not high.

20th. at home all day Sent T.p to Stokesley to buy some of Mr Turners Ox beef of which he bought about 25^{li} at 5^d per li.

21^t. Sunday at home & not at Church. A great Shour Snow in the forenoon Frosty morning wind N.W.

22. up Street where Spoke with Sundry people. M^r preston dined with me. Lent Ric^d Lincoln, on his note to pay at Mid Sumer next, 2^{li}.

23^d. at noon I went to Grange T.P. set me to Skinnington Bridge & returned home, I lay that night at Boulby but before I got there the Wind at NE. I met with great Hazard and difficulty the Storm being Excessive which continued all night, next morning Something abated. I paid Mr Wardell £50.

24. Mr Wardell came with me to Grang, where was come T.p to meet me. Will White went this morning for Scalby^{12} to lend the Kelp men money. I came home about 3.

25. at home.

26. at home.

27. at home. Sent T. pressick to Boulby, returned about 3. very Severe frost and much snow, paid Thomas presswick to House keeping £20.

28th. Sunday at Church forenoon.

29. up Street, Spoke with Sundrys. Sent Mr Jackson A Bill on Nephew Geo: Jackson of the Navy Office for £108, for which he sent his note without money. I was informed that a meeting of the Justices was to be at Gisbro the 12th of April I went to Grang after dineing with John patten at my House, who intends to view Little Stainton in order to by it of Tho: Spencer. Servant John P set me to Skinnington Bridge & returned, lay that night at Boulby.

30th. about 9 Mr Wardell & John Nickolson Set out with me for Gisbro, the former in his way to Bishoprick, the latter to See Some Sheep at Marton, we all dined at my House & thay went away for Marton, it rained all the day & night before. Wind N.W.

31. I went about 9 in the morning for Stockton T.p with me. dined there at Mr^s Dowthwaits called at Mr Maddesons, where I Se his new Wife, he paid me Interest for Sundrys, called at Bells the Stationers and paid him his Bill. 2^{li} 5^s 10^d where Mr Baker came to me with whom went to Black Lyon where came to us Mr Sutton, Mr Sleigh, Mr Brown & Mr Maddeson being Cordially met Togeather, but there was notice brought that 2 men which was taken up for the King's Service that day, haveing made their Escape from the

^{12} Scalby, close to Scarborough.

Bailif who had them under his care, but he & his under . . .[13] by which the 2 men got away, but the under Bayliff entered himselfe for Sea into the Kings Service and promist bring in 20 more & Soon after brought one A likely young fellow who entered for Sea but there happened some difference to Arise among the Gentlemen on Account of the escape which came to high words betwixt M[r] Baker and M[r] Sutton, which lasted some hours, but at last Subsided. we parted about 1 in the morning.

Aprill the 1[t]. I went for yarm about 6 in the morning, where Received money from Sundrys, came from thence about 3, in Company of M[r] Fox, M[r] Cass & Servant T.p, got home about 6. fine day but much snow the night before. Wind N.

2[d]. at home all day.

3. at home. M[r] Skottow & Servant came here about 4 in the Afternoon & paid me in part of Interest due 26 Oct[o] last, £140. went away about 6, fair but Close & Cloudy all day.

4th. Sunday at home, at Church fore noon, frequent Rain.

5th. up Street but did little business, fine day, M[r] Lawson calld upon me to See the faculty[14] I have for Lofthouse Gallery in the Church to make out a titely[15] to M[r] Murgatroid & John Smith to the Middle pew.

6th. at home, fair most of day but much Snow at night & thick fogg with very Cold wind at N.W.

7th. at home.

8th. at home, this night died Morice Linkoln the Sope Boyler. M[r] Wardell came out of Bishobrig & went to Boulby.

9. about noon I went to Grange, where met me M[r] Sugget, with whom I Settled to meet M[r] preston at Gisbro on munday the 26 Inst about the Sale of Some of Said Suggets Estates in Danby, which I have in mortgage for £1000. lay that night at Boulby, where met M[r] Jefferson who I had not seen of 14 or 16 days, he haveing been at Whitby fitting out his Ship for Riga, he Stayed with us at Boulby till 6 or 7 at night.

10th. I went to pitt hill along with M[r] Wardell, wee then went to Barn to see his Bull Calf, from thence I went to Grang where met me John p. my Servant with whom came home where got about 3.

11. month Sunday, at home all day. Snow and Rain every day for many days past with Wind in different quarters.

12th. there was meeting of the Justices viz[t] M[r] Turner, M[r] Robinson, M[r] Skottow, M[r] Hurstler & M[r] Beckwith when thay took off the Watch which have been kept for Some time in all the

[13] line shaved off from the text.
[14] In such cases as that here mentioned, a faculty is a permission issued by an ecclesiastical authority for alterations in the Church fabric or additions to its fixtures.
[15] Title.

Townships in Cleaveland, all the Cunstables appearing for the East
Division, Mr Murgatroid, Mr Smith, Mr Sanderson & Mr Scurfield
of Stockton dined with us. I came home about 4, where met one
Wm Willis from peake. Wm Yeoman of Gisbro came & paid me in
part of £4 I lent him the 12th March 1753. 5/- for the first time,
he being to pay me 5/- a month till the 4^{li} is paid.

13. At home till near 7, when I went up to Mr Hides, where Stayd
near an Hour, from thence to meet Collector of Excise at Cock, of
whem I received 150^{li}. for my Bill upon Robert Core. Stayed to
near 10 & came home.

14. I rid on to Cross fields at Tokets to meet Mr Jefferson and
Mr Wardell there, to view the Farm the former haveing lately purchased the Same of his Brother: Mr Tho: Spencer. After we had
done we came to my House where thay and Mr Fra: Fox dined,
and about 4 thay went for Boulby & Steaths.

^{16} April 14th 1756.   about 12 at night I was taken very ill with
purging & vomiting which obliged me to call the family up, when I
took A vomit of Camamile Floers. being better I went to bed
again, & mended.

15. M^r proddy came & took from my Right Arm about 24^{ozs}
Blood. Mr Foster, John Hamon & John porrit came to Consult me
about A Writ the former had received at the Sute of one Grayham
of York against the 2 latter for 10^{li} as Executors to late Mrs Chamber
of Said York upon which I writ to M^r Ra: yoward to go with
Hammond or porrit, wherein desired M^r yoward to make enquiry
into the Grounds the said Grayham had for takeing out Said Writ
& to let me know.

16. Wm Hobkirk calld here to acquaint me of A Job of paveing
he has taken of Mr Cholmley for paveing Whitby market place.
at home all day. Rain most of the day Wind at S.E. Wm White,
my Servant, came here about 9 in the morning to whom I paid
10 ginnys to buy Cattle at Durham to-morrow & Darlington on
munday next, he went away before ten.

17. at home all day.

18th. Esther Sunday, rain most of the day. I did not go to
Church. O proddy came to Se me & Stayed near an Hour.

19th. fine Weather, most of the day at home. Will. White came
here with 10 Steers he bought at Durham & 4 at Darlington, he
come when all was in bedd, & not knowing where to call So laid
among the Hay in Stable all night, his Steers costin all with Cha(rges)
£70. 10. 0.

20th. about noon T.p Set me to Skinnington Bridge, went & lay
at Boulby that night, Mr Wardell being abroad did not come in
till near 10.

21. I paid Mr Wardell in Silver £36 for which he is to pay me

^{16} This entry is on a separate slip of paper.

again in gold. wee went to Steaths about 10 & dined there, where was Ra: Jackson, we came back to Boulby, where I did not Stay but went alone to Grang, there met me Wm Mewburn to Se my Oxon, but agreed for none he being to meet me at Gisbro on friday next to treat about them. I got home about 6 in the Evening along w^ith Tho: pressick who met me at Grange. Same night Mrs Chaloner Sent to desire a London Bill for £72, but I could not promise one till I acquaint Mr Wardell therewith, So sent Tho: presswick next morning to Boulby with my Leter to Mr Wardell for that purpose.

22^d. at home.

23. Mr Foster came here to whome gave my bill upon Robt Core, payable at 30 days to Mrs Chaloner for £72, which he paid me for, Mr John Jefferson came & paid me to Ballance £55. 16. 4. Stayed all night. Wm Mewburn came with whom I agreed for 3 oxon 2 of them to 30 ginys. each, the 3^d, he referred the price to my Self.

24th April. at home all day, Sent T.p to Stockesley Fair who brought me £4 from Robert Burdon for a years Interest per £100 due 5th september last.

25th. Sunday at Church forenoon Moderate Weather Wind N.

26th. at home.

27th. A Faire at Gisbro, up Street in the beast market, at Mr Hides ½ an hour. Spok M^r peirse. with Mrs Chaloner about a letter I received from Mr Maddeson concerning £1500 I am to lend her. M^r preston & John Rowntree dined w^ith me, the latter paid me £4 for 1 years Interest for £100 due the 8th Inst, also Wm Rogers dined and paid his last Mar^t Rent 7^li: 10^s Mr Sugget & A Chap to buy a piece of his land in Danby came to speak M^r preston And gave orders to draw Writeings for it. Robt Errington of Mask paid me for 8 Sheep £9: 16. W^m young also his last Martinmas Rent £1: 0: 6.

28. at Home.

29. Mr Conset and Wm Mewburn came here, with whom I went to Grang to Se my Oxon where met us Mr Wardill, we dined there & Stayde till about 5 it being very Rainy. Wind S, but when we parted the Wind came to N^o and blowed a Storm. I lay that night at Boulby. Tho: Sayer paid me at Grang for 8 sheep £11. 4.

29th. Stayd & dined at Boulby with Mr Wardell & Mr Jefferson, and came to Grang about 2. where met me J.p with whome I came Home. A fine day John porrit paid me his last Lady day Rent £7: 10.

30th. much Snow. Wind at N.E. and frost at Home. Mary the Wife of John Wilkinson Died aged 83.

May 1^t. She was buried in the Evening. I went to Church with her. Mary Havelock Paid me 60^li 8^s for her note & 2 months

Interest, frosty morning & Rain in the afternoon. Wind N° W^t, at Home.

2^d. Sunday, at home. Snowed most of the day. Wind varyable but mostly at N° & N°E.

3^d. Houses & Hills Covered with Snow. A meeting of the Justices, Mr Robinson, Mr Skottow & Mr Beckwith & Self took the Oaths to act as Commissioners of the Land Tax. when we Signed Land tax Bills & Window Bills for 1756. Land Tax 4/- in the pound, Mr Murgatroid, Mr Proddy, Mr Smith Mr Mat. Conset & Mr Lawson dined with us. Mr Robinson paid me £12. for 1 Years Interest for £300 due 22^d Ins^t, also M^r preston paid me £16 for Dr Wanlas £400, due 3^d April last. Mr Longbottom desired to Borrow £100 but I did not promis to lend it him, but assured him to do it if possible. I gave Mr Mat: Conset a Bill payable to Sight upon Ra: Jackson my Nephew at Newcastle, the same being for Ra: Cooks composition but Mr Conset did not pay me money for it, but to do it a fortnight hence. 4 young Ladys with Wm Mewburn & his Brother Came to See an Ox I had came to day from Grang by Will White, he was the least of 3. I had there. I went this Evening to See John Wilkinson.

May 4th. Mrs Chaloner Sent for Coles being in want of which sent 31 bushels which is to answer for that quantity I am to Send in this Sumer according to my Lease. many of the Neighbours Wanting Hay I Consented to Let them have Some, but not to anyone above 30 stone, they willing paid 3^{d17} a Stone for it, there was Delivered out above 200 Stone to day.

5th. Dolle Boulby came here today and Dined with two Servants from Stockton (where She has been) in her way to Steaths & Whitby, much more Hay went off to-day, great Showers of Snow this morning, the Hills & Houses was coverd with it. Wind at N° W^t.

6th. at home Still bad Weather &˙great clamering for Hay the Whole Country wanting very much. Wind N.

7th. I went to Boulby in the afternoon calld at Grang & Set out A fould garth & a Hogsty. Mr Wardells Boy came here for 10 Sheep left here for him 2 or 3 days ago, lay at Boulby the night. about 10 the 8th I went to Grang, from thence I took Will White with me to Brotton & there left my Saddle Horse at Wm Childs & Rid home on Graytale, the former being ill on A Cold & grease^{18} fair day Jn° pearson met me at Brotton^{19} & returned with me about 5.

9th. month Sunday.

10th. Ric^d Stevenson came & Reckond with me. I pd hime 15/-

^{17} This looks a badly written three, but judging from the price, (10½d.), further down the page, probably 9d. is intended.

^{18} The grease is a complaint in which the animal has a very swollen leg together with an oily discharge from it, in a bad case the hoof may be concealed by the swelling.

^{19} Brotton, a little to the north-east of Skelton.

to Ballance, but I still ow him for Some Users.[19a] Up Street Spoke
Mr Jackson, Mr Nelson, Mr Mathews, Mr Lawson, Chief Jackson,
Richard Stevenson & John patton dined w^{it} me Rec^d of Mewburn,
Hawman & Nickolson for 40 Sheep 74^{li}. Lent Mr Wm Longbotham,
On his Bond at 4 p. Ct, £100, Tho: Allans Brother came here &
Stayd all night.

11. at home. Rec^d of Mr Richard Foster 12. 7. 3 for my Bill on
Robert Core also of Fra: Fox for Jo: Danbys' Rent £1: 5. and of
Thomas preswick for 160½ Stone of hay & Some bad £7: 2:0. W^m
Cornfurth and his mother came over about a Deed betwixt them,
M^r price came here.

12. at home Jane Whitby Sent her present May day Rent 8/-.
John Aysley came here and made me A present of A pair brass
Stirrups. A Shoure or two of Rain & Sleet otherwise A fine day.
Wind in different quarters.

13. at home. all day John price came here in the Evening &
lay here all night to whome paid his Bill 17^{li}: 1^s: 11^d & gave him
in his note for £10. lent him 29th Mar: 1755. p^d him 7^{li}: 1^s: 11^d in
full of said Bill.

14. about noon went for Grang T preswick set me to Skinington
Bridge Will White paid me 6^{li}: 6^s. the remainder of 21^{li} I gave him
to buy Beasts at Egton he haveing bought 2 Steers 3 y^r olds of John
Hartas for which paid him £14: 14.

15. laying at Boulby last night I set out the morning with M^r
Wardell and his Boy on his Way to Sedgefield, we got to Gisbro at 9.
where we dined & he Set out with his boy a little after 10. Fine
warm day, as was yesterday, the Wind S but day at N.W.

16. Sunday at Church forenoon, fine day.

May 17th 1756. last night about 6 John pearson went to Grang
for the fat ox Rook, & Set out thence about 8 and got here about
4 in the morning, many people came to See him among the rest 4
Gentleman owners of Maske with parson Langstaff,[20] Mr Smith,
Robert Corney, he was the Admiration of them All for Size & fatness.
Mr Sugget haveing Sold a peice of Land in Danby Dale I had in
mortgage with other Lands the Said peice being Sold to one Ra:
Rudd I met them at M^r prestons Chamber where I Received £150
the whole price the land was Sold for, & a Deed was executed, the
partys executeing was Mr Sugget, my Self, Ra: Rudd & Mr Duck
of Danby as a Trustee. Mr Mathews paid me 12^{li} for 1 year Interest
for £300 due the 10th March last. Mr Hide and Willm Mewburn dined
with me. In the Evening I went up t o the Cock and Stayed with
the 4 Gentlemen till near 11.

[19a] Users, used of animals, i.e. useful animals. A cow is called a good
user if it produces much milk.
[20] Thomas Longstaff, B.A., Trin Coll., Cambridge, 1739; Deacon, 1739,
Lincoln; Priest, 1740, Chester; Rector of Normanby.

18th. Mr Wardell's boy came out of Bishoprick with 6 Steers & bated here in his way to Boulby. Mewburns Servant came here in order to take away the Black ox Rooke for Sunderland. Set out hence with him about 8 in the Evening.

19th. John Wilkinson came over to bid farewell intending to go next morning for Ormsby to live there with his Son & Daughter Mewburn. about 6 in the Evening I rid about my Ground to view the pasture but the grass in it is very poor as the like I never See before at this time of year the Season haveing been so bad Scarce A night without frost in Some degre for Some months past. the Wind now at East and Cold.

20. all day at home, young Mr Jackson came here about noon & paid me £600. lent me by his Father I went up at 7 in the Evening and gave Mr Jackson my note for the Same payable at 6 months 4 P.Ct. Mr Jackson of Lackinby being there I Sitt with them till near 10.

21. at home all day. John Rigg came here & removed the Clock in Old Stare Case to left hand passage to little dineing Room. I sent Thomas p. with a printed Declaration of War against France published the 18th Inst, which I received this days post, to Mr Turner who kept it but returned it next day.

22. Sent T. presswick to Stocksley, my Self all day at home.

23d. Sunday at Church forenoon, dined at Mrs Chaloners where was Mr Hide, Miss Maddeson, Miss Thompson & 2 Children. I came home after diner. Will: White came here from Grange in the morning & went to Church twice with whom John pearson went to Grange about 6 to bring here the Read Ox Looby in order to go for newcastle to be there Slaughtered by Henry Mewburn of Sunderland.

24. the above ox came here about 3 in the morning, Old parson Conset & Wm Mewburn dined here, was up Street, Spok Mr preston & Mr Mathews, gave Mr Lawson Clerk the faculty I had for Lofthouse Gallery, to draw a Title I am to give Mr Murgatroid & Jno Smith for the middle pew, the former to 3 Seats therein, & the latter the Rest of the pew. the North pew or part I retain for my Self & the South pew is for Said Smith, many people came to Se the Ox, among the Rest Mrs Challoner, Miss Maddeson & Mr Hide, thay came in to the House to See the pictures I lately had from London & had a Glass of Wine.

25th. at Home. in the Evening I went to the Sitting of Excise and Recd £100. for my Bill on Robert Core. This Day begun painting the Spouts & Windows.

26. I went to Grang. Willm postgate along with me at 7 in the morning. when there I sent for Mr Sugget with whom came two Balifs he being under an Arrest at the Sute of Ra: Franklain my Tenant for £50. I then Sent for Franklain but he was gon to

Whitby, but his Wife came who & Sugget were both very obstinate but after some debate thay agreed before me & the Balifs that Franklain Should pay all the Charges which came to about 3 gunies & Mr Sugget was to Answer & repay them again at Martinmis next. So the Baliffs Rec^d 2 g^{ins} for their Charges & Mr Hancock the Attorney in the Cause is to have the other ginny paid him for his Charges. Mr Sugget Lent Franklain Wife 6/- to pay the Baliffs. I then went to Boulby where Saw Mr Wardell, with whom Stayed 1½ hour & came to Grange but did not light, from thence came home with W^m postgate where we got about 5. he Stayd & Supp^t & went home.

27th. I went to yarm where Rec^d of Mr T. peirce 1 year's Interest for £200 due from his Nephew Wm Hodshon the 16 of last may, 8^{li}. about 2 in the Afternoon I went to Ayslaby along with Richard Corker & Richard Reah with John price where viewd the Hall & Gardens also Richard Corker's farm but could not Settle the Outstand for Wm Armstrongs Farm for want of the plan & Survey, when went to Richard Reah's and viewd his Barn in order to build him a new one, then also gave orders for puling down the pidgin Coat, from thence went to Stockton where met Mr Maddeson about the Mortgage of Tockets. Stayd there all night & Set out the 28th for Gisbro, about 7 in the morning, called at Marton to See Wm Walker's Stoned Horse[21] got home about 10. parson Conset came here & paid me 31^{li}: 10^s: 11^d for my Bill given his Nephew Mr Mathew Conset upon Ra: Jackson of Newcastle. in the Evening came Cozen pease from Whitby & lay here all night.

29th. his Son W^m & Daughter came here from Darlington all three, with Mr Fox, dined, & near 2 the 3 former went for Whitby, Cozen pease paid me as a Ballance of an Account 15^{li}: 16^s: 8½^d.

30. at home went to Church forenoon.

31. up Street at Mr Hides, M^r preston dined with me. Tho: Allan Came here from Boulby to buy meat. paid me for G Theakers Beef 1^{li}. 11^s. 8^d and Heads & Hearts 4/-.

June 1^t. I went to Caldgate fleet[22] with Mr Baldock, Mr Cass & O: preswick where bought O preswick ½c Deals to be 10 gins & ¼c to be 2^{li}: 5^s. 0^d, got home with Same Company about 7. in the evening.

2^d. about 9 this morning I went with Mr Hide my Servant T.p. with us to S^{ir} Wm Foulses[23] at Ingolby Manner, where dined Mr Howlet, Capt Scottowe, Dr Rain, Sir W^m, his Lady & eldest Daught^r with Master Foulis. came out about 4 and got Home about 6, fine

[21] Stallion.
[22] Cargo Fleet near Middlesbrough.
[23] Sir William Foulis of Ingleby Manor, bart., married in 1721 Mildred, eldest daughter of Henry Dawnay, Viscount Downe. Sir William died in 1756 and was buried at Ingleby. His widow died 1780, also buried at Ingleby. Master Foulis became Sir William on the death of his father. The eldest daughter, Mildred, died unmarried.

Weather Mr Jackson Sent me £121 : 4 : 0 for Mr Halls year Interest due in Jan^r Apl^e & May last.

3.   I went to the highways, where we had 8 or ten Carts leading Stones & Gravel where we put in a Gantree or Bridge against Cooks ground in yarm Lane where I attended the Whole day till near 6 without meat or Drink Save a little water.   the work was done to my Satisfaction.

4th.   Sent Mr Hide at Mr Maddeson's Request 31^{li} 4^s. 6^d also paid M^r W Jackson at Said Request 31 ^{li}. 10^s. 0^d which Mr Maddeson is to pay me again being in all £62 : 14 : 6.   Mr Boulby came here with his Daughter Ette & both dined when he paid me £52 for 8 years proffit of his Ship *Lyon* Including 1755.   at home all day, fine warm Weather with some drops of rain.

5.   Rid out the forenoon to View Some Highways in yarm lain, calld at John Wilsons, A pulman & Wm Hobkirk with one Smith of Upsel drank 4 pints of Ale for which left 1/-.   got home about noon, rest of the day at home but not well haveing not had a Stool since the 2^d Ins^t in the morning.

6.   Whitson Sunday was taken very ill for want of Going to Stool with being deprived of makeing water by all which I became very bad & in a most dangerous way, makeing often attempts for A Stool but could not effect it.   Sent for M^r proddy who administered a Clister but without much effect, but a little after had a large Stool making Water and got ease & had a pretty good night.   Sent John peirson for Sister Jackson to Richmond about 6 in the evening.

7th.   I was this morning much better, after noon Mr Wardel calld here in his Way to Stockton, he paid me £26. 5 the same Sum I paid Wm Walker on his Account.   Sister Jackson and her Daughter Dorothy came about 5 this afternoon in a Shase from Richmond, bated at yarm 2 hours.

8.   Neice Jackson Went away & left her Mother here intending to go & remain at yarm Some days.   where the Shase was to be discharged.   Mr Readhead and Wm Armstrong dined here today being Whitson fair day.   parson Conset came to See me and Stayed at least an Hour.

9th.   at home all day frequent Showers of Rain.   Wind in all quarters 2 Carts and Wood Carriag went for Timber & deals to Caldgate Fleet.   I went to Mrs Chaloners about Tockets affair.

10.   I went to Stockesley to meet the Commissioners about the Devision of Marsk, where we all 7 met at Bovils & heared read over the Award in a foul draught and Settled divers matter about the Affare.   I set out about 6 & left the Rest of Commissioners very busie, which would keep them at least an Hour longer I got home near 8.   T.p. along with me.   Mr Scarth overtook me in going about a mile from Gisbro he being one of the Commissioners went along with me rest of the way.

June 11th. I went with Mr Foster to Stockton, got there about 8 where met us one Mr Thomas Benson from Carlisle and another Gentleman along with him, the former haveing A mortgage upon Toketts from late Edward Chaloner Esqr for £1500, and it being agreed to pay the Same off, I was requested to advance money for that end which I carry^d with me & paid the Same to Mr Benson, who Executed an Assignment of said Mortgage. Mr Wm Maddison, Mr Foster & the other Gentleman present Set out about 6 & got home near 9, much rain both going & returning.

12. at home all day. sent 60 half deals to grange.

13. month Sunday. at home, much rain, in the Afternoon Mr Raisebeck the Attorney and his Son called here in their way to Hinderwell (as he Said) on Account of the difference betwixt Mr Beckwith & his Bro: Marshal, but he did not light.

14. at home, dined at Mrs Chaloners with none but the family but Mr Hide & Mr Murgatroyd came after. I Settled with her about the Mortgage of Tockets when Mr Foster paid me £9 : 10 : 9 for the Interest from 5th Aprill 1756 to the 2^d June after the Deeds bearing date of that day. I returned him 10/9 as a gratuty. after noon John price came here.

15th. John price went with me to Grange where Stayd Some time, from thence went to Boulby when he went to Steaths and Stayd all night as I did at Boulby, but he came up the next morning—16 in order to value some thing I left there, but Mr Wardell haveing the *Darling* on at Steaths with Kelp from London he could not attend the valluation, So price went for Whitby to get a Certifficate from thence for Ayslaby & I came to Grang when Settled with Will White about 6 months Wages for my people ther ending the last of may last, from thence I came for Gisbro. Wm White Set me to Millam beck and returned. I got home about 2.

17. John price came here & Stayed till after 3 and went home but did not bring a Certifficate but had one promised. A Shower of Rain about 2. I paid Tho: pressick 10^{li} for one years Interest for £250 due the 7th Mar: last, also 15^{li} for his years Wage due this next midsum^r. Duke Blenco paid me his last Lady day Rent for 1756.

18. I went out by 4 in the morning to Boulby with T.p, where was made a pay for 6 months ending the last of may, then Rec^d for said may day rents 14^{li} 6. 0. Mr Oldfield dined with us, Mr Sugget came there about his own affairs. Robert Campions Scoot^{23a} laid on with Coals.

19. in the morning I was to Grang where Left with Will White £31 and Mr Suggett came there again with whome Settled that he & Mr Wardell Should go on thirsday next the 24th Ins^t to Danby

^{23a} Scoot, a flat-bottomed boat.

& view Said Sugget's Estate in order to advise the former in the disposeal of it, I got home about 1, fine Weather with frequent Shours of Rain.

20th. Sunday, at Church forenoon. W[m] white came here in the morning went to Church. about 3 Went for Darlington with whom sent 26[li]. 5[s] to buy Stock.

21. about 7 in the morning Jn[o] Daltons Chimney took fire & burnt out at top but was Soon got under without doing much harm. drew of 16 gall[ns] of Gin & 3 gallons of Green Usquebagh[24] but these wanted 2 quarts of the former & near one of the latter. W[m] White came from Darlington but bought nothing but went for Grange. up Street went into the Cock & Stayd above an Hour with M[r] Hancock the Attorney, from thence to M[r] Hides with Whome Stayd an Hour, went to View Dalton House & came Home.

22[d]. I went about 6 in the morning to Chapel bridge to Se people. Set to work at the high Ways. from thence went with John Aysley to Upsell[25] in our way met W[m] Hobkirk to whome gave directions about repairing the broken Causeways. From Upsel John A. & I came again to Chapel Bridge & Stay'd Some time there with the work people, from thence home, after dinner M[r] Cass came & paid me 1[li]. 4[s] for 12 months Interest for £30 due the 4th Inst. About 2 I went to meet M[r] Foster at Spring wood of whome bought a lott of Small wood to be 8/-, there being about a dozen ends from thence Again to Chapel Bridge & then Home.

23. at Home all day, fine Wether.

24. John pease Jun[r] came here in the morning from Stockton paid me £16 for a years Interest for £400 due 23[d] Ap[l] last also £11. 10 from A. Dunn for his last Martinmas Rent. Paid M[r] pease his Bill £3: 11: 4. Same day Rec[d] of Richard Clark £40 the principle upon his Bond & 16/- for 6 month Interest. also of Thomas Nateby £9 for freelidge Wood Sold him. Rob[t] Thomas was with me about business.

25th. at home much reain great lightning & Some claps of Thunder last night with a Strong Shower of rain this morning.

26. at home.

27. Sunday at Church forenoon. John pease & his Bro W[m] came here for Whitby the former brought me £8: 8 from his Father as the Ballance of a Small Account.

28. James Mewburn & Brother W[m] came & paid me 80 ginnys for 3 oxon returned them 3 gins again. Tho: Warton came & paid his last May day Rent £22, Includeing allowances. Lent John Rowntree of Hemlington & his Son £1000 on their note but am to have a mortgage executed for the Same in a few days. begun throwing out the foundation for a new Stable at low end the Great

[24] Whisky.
[25] Upsell, Upsall, near Ormesby.

Garden. The Taylors got done in hanging the Rooms, that is the little new Dineing Room & old parlor.

29. At Home & much among the Workmen.

30. at Home.

July the 1th. Cozen Martha Reed came here on Horseback with one of Tho: Lyth Sons. Set up the new Stable door Case.

2^d. Sister Jackson & Cozen Reed Set out for yarm on the former's Return home. A pulman carryd her on Horse back I gave her 10 ginnys & 5 or 6 Silk Scarves. about 4 I Rid out with John Aysley to view Waterfall High, was returned at 6. very fine day.

3^d. at home, fine Wether.

4th. Sunday forenoon at Church much reain in many places but not So here.

5. up Street where Spok with M^r preston Mr Smith Mr Jackson and many others. Sent Mr Lawson the original Faculty I had for build a Gallary in Lofthouse Church to take a Copy of it and return the originall again. I allso received a Copy from him of the Deed I executed to day which I made to Mr Murgatroid & John Smith of the midle pew in the said Gallary.

6. at Home. A fine day & very Hot weather.

7th. S^{ir} Wm Foulis Stept out of his Coach and called to See me & after walkt on foot to Mrs Chaloners where he and his Family was to dine I am to meet his Son tomorrow at Boulby.

8th. I went to Boulby, took T.p with me to Skinington Bridge called at Grange, at Boulby Mr Fowlis came there over the Moors about 10 with 2 Servants, after viewing the Ginn then at Work & Allom House we dined & Stayed till near 4, from thence Mr Wardell went with us to Grang, after viewing the place we went In & drank 2 Bottles goosberry Wine & Stayed till 5, calld at Grang gate & drank 2 pints of Ale, from thence Mr Wardell returnd. the rest came with me to Gisbro where Mr Foulis lited & we drank Some Madera Wine & Water, he set out about 8 for Ingolby.

9. At Home all day most fine Weather Wind in different quarters.

10th. I took A: pulman with me to Grange before 6. in the morning, from thence to Boulby but Mr Wardell being abroad Wee Stayd very little, went up to Rock & Viewed the Works,²⁶ met with Will White at Barn, who went with us to grange gate but I did not go down but came to Skelton where I calld to see Mr Hall who got Home the day before from Bath, London & other parts of the South, haveing been out since the 17th November last, which is near 8 months I did not lite at Skelton but got home about 2.

11th. month Sunday, at Home.

12th. up Street, Spoke Mr Jackson, M^r proddy, Mr Spark, Mr Foster, with young M^r preston & Mr Mathews, he came & dined with me, three Mowers begun to Cut down my Grase, in the Evening I

²⁶ Alum Works.

walkt down to Se them & gave them a Shilling to drink. Mr Mathew Conset Sent me by his Steward Maddeson £54 : 7 : 6 for 6 months Interest due the 11th Ins^t. James Jackson paid me his last Lady day Rent 3^{li} : 10^s. 0^d.

13th. the quarter Sessions was held here this day where was upon the Bench Mr Cholmley Mr Robinson, Mr Skottowe & Mr Beckwith with M^r preston Clerk of pease. Little business was at the Court. I dined at Cock with them.

14. I went to Speak with Mr Tho: Cooper, Collector of Excise, but I rec^d no money for my Bills, Spoke to him about the Duty upon Silver plate of which he Said they had Instructions about it, all plate to be entered 40 days after the 5th of this month, to pay 5/- for every 100 oz : but nothing for any under that quantity.

July the 15th. I Rid to Se the paviers at work on the highways on this Side Upsel where Stayed with them near an Hour & returned. Sent my own Cart & another for Tyles to Caldgate Fleet the Same came from Mrs Dowthwate.

16. all day at home. had 3 Carts went for Tyles So that there is comd in all this day & yesterday 1500. I walkt down to the Hay field from there to Factory to Speak Mr Fox about Mr Jeffersons affair. Sent A. pulman to Grange with a basket of Garden Stuff for Mr Wardel to be Sent him from thence.

17th. at home very fine day got all low middow mown.

18. Sunday at Church forenoon. Mr Wardells boy came here, much Thunder and rain in the night & next morning.

19. Thick fogg most of the day, Lent Mr peirse on Bond £100, also Mr Anthony Wild of Munck Hesledon In C^o Durham on Mortgage £200. which paid to Mr Maddeson on his note til the Deed was got ready M^r preston gave me the old Deeds belonging John Rowntree as did Mr Maddeson those of Mr Wilds.

20. John Husband came here & weighd all my Silver plate of which for keeping was 297 ^{oz} : & for disposeing of by Mr Howlet 101½^{oz} which John took home with him Thomas Collings of Darlington & Robert Allan came here in order to go to Grang to Se my Wool. Robert Allan after thay John Husband & my Self Dined, he went alone to Boulby and Mr Colling Stays here all night to go with me to Grange tomorrow morning.

21. Mr Colling Set out with me about 6 in the morning for Grange, Servant John peirson with us where Mr Colling viewed the Wool and bargained for the Same at 10/- p Stone, 18^{li} to the Stone, to pay at Chrismis next, Robt Allan came to us there & thay went for Darlington about 10. I went to Mr Mores at Lofthouse where after Some Stay we Sent for Wm Johnson & Jno Smith, overseers of the high ways, w.th whome & Mr More wee went to view the highway through Rosscroft ground belonging Mr More who urged that the said highways belonged to N^o Lofthouse to repair but we could not

agree thereto as that Estate was purchased formerly from Handel Abby,[27] it was a part of S° Lofthouse & belonged to that Mannor whereof the High ways through the said Rosscrofts belonged him alone, or S° Lofthouse. after we returned went to View the Church, north ile of which being greatly out of repair in the Roof it was agreed to take it off, which being covered with Lead to Sell the Same & put a new Roof thereon and cover it with Grey Tiles. I after went & dined with Mr More. Stayed till near 8 at night & went from thence to Boulby & lay there all night.

22d. about 5 this morning came on a most Severe Rain which Continued most of the day, about 11 John peirson came to me at Boulby and about one a Clock I set out from thence, calld at Grang, from thence came home where got about 3. Rained all the Way. Wind at N.E, but very Warm Evening and fair. John pease came here yesterday with his Wife from Whitby, lay all night & about 5 this morning thay went for Darlington, but I did not Se them.

23d. At home till about 4 in the Afternoon, I went with Mr Hide Mr Jackson Doctor Wain & Mr proddy to view the place where the Bridge is about Building betwixt Tockets & Skelton Ellers, John Benneson the Mason being the undertaker, we all stayed about an Hour & Benneson was there when was fixed upon the place for Building it but the foundation was partly begun with ere we got there. Close day but fair.

24th. at home all day very fogge Weather & drisling rain all day Wind at N.

25. Sunday, at Church forenoon. Close day but fair till afternoon then fine Weather but rain in the night following.

26. up Street; Spok Mr Mathews, Mr Lawson & Mr preston, the latter dined with me, paid John Husband his Cyder Bill 1li: 16s: 4d also duty for my plate 200 ozs 10/- Recd of John Rowntree for odd Interest 1li: 1s: 0d.

27. Mr Botham paid me A years Interest for £100 due 12th June last also Mr John Clark the Same for d° Sum due 23d D° month. Soft hayweather.

28. fine hayday had 2 Carts leading hay, Mr Skottowe came here about 11 desireing me to lend him £500 upon a new mortgage I promised him £100 in a month's time and the Rest about 2 months after, he did but Stay to drink a glass of wine. & Returned. Wm Brotton the mason came to work haveing been absent not well about 16 days, got all hay ledd out the low ground.

29. begun Mowing in Calvert Close 4 mowers got done. A fine day.

30th. begun a pike of hay but about 10 came on Rain but only drisling which put the worke people off but about 2 thay begun

---

[27] Handale Abbey, also called Grendale. Founded 1133. A small house of Benedictine nuns.

again, and at 4 more Rain but soon over when they went to work again. Wind W, and got done A fine evening.

31. Rainy day, at home.

Aug. 1st 1756. Mr Wardell & Wm White came here about 10 in the morning the former Stayd about an Hour & went for Ellemore, the Latter went for yarm about 4 in the afternoon for the fair next day, this being Sunday, at Church forenoon.

2. I went about 5 in the morning for yarm fair, Servant T.p with me. where Received about £200 for Rents & about 2 I went to Ayslaby, haveing a Barn there in building for Richard Reah when Settled with his Brother Corker, & laid all night at Richard Reahs.

3^d. About 11 I went for Stockton where dined at Miss Skafe's Sent for Mr Maddeson to Speake him about Mrs Chaloner's affair relateing to Tockets Mortgage also about Mr Wilds Mortgage. Set out about 3 for home where got about 6.

4th. A fine Hayday about 4 in the Afternon I Rid out to See the Workmen now in building Skelton Ellers Bridge next Tockets, gave them 1/- to drink thay being Fixing the Center.

5th. at home. Wind N.E. not a hopeful hay day but opened the pike & lead the hay out Calvert Close & layd most of it upon her.

6. at home only went to the paviours near upsel about 4 in the Afternoon & came home. A fine day.

7. Mr Wardell came here out bishobrig where he has been Since the 1st Inst. he dined here & I went with him to Skelton where we Stayd at the Alehouse & drank 2 potts of Boumbo when he went for Boulby & I came home Staying a little at the new bridge in building at Skelton Ellers. Set off with John Benneson in his way home, he being the undertaker, parted at Tocketts lyth gate, he going for Kirkleatham. Thomas pressick went this morning for Grange & Boulby with whom Sent 20 ginnys for Wm White but he brought it back, as it was to buy Sheep at Hambleton he had money enough without it. Rec^d of John Thomas 1 years Interest for £30 due 10th past £1 : 4 : 0.

8. month Sunday at home Jno Gallans Wife came here & dined with me, her Husband being at Shields with his Ship loaden & ready to Sale. 5 of his prentice Ladds left him & came home to Gisbro & other places in the neighbourhood. I sent for 3 or 4 of their parents who agreed to carry them back to Shields She giving 10/6 towards there Charges, but after thay went away next morning a Letter came from the Master that he had got hands & Sailed comeing the lenths of Steaths this day & Sent the letter on Shore. So the parents & ladds went a Wast Journey.

9. I went to speak M^r preston & gave him minutes of a Lease betwixt Wm Fawcet & me for his Farm at Stoddo for 21 years from

May day last John Wilkinson & his Daughter Mewburn, with Jos^h
Ager came & dined w^{ith} me. Tho: Day Sent me a year's Rent for
Dew Sike field due Martinmas last 4^{li}: 5^s. also 12 months Interest
for £20 due 7th may last & 16/-. Gregory Rowland paid me 1 years
do for £20 due the 4th Ins^t.

10. at home Spok Mr Foster about Sending the people of Tockets
to fill up the new Bridge end at Skelton Ellers.

11. about 2 Mr Boulby called here in his way to Whitby out
Bishoprick where left his 2 Daughters but did not light. about 4
I Rid out to Se the paviours in Barna²⁹ lane but Hobkirk was then
working for upsel. N: patton, A pulman, & John Weatheril was at
Work.

12. Sent Thomas p. to Stockton & to go to Ayslaby with £10
for John price now in building a Barn for Richard Reah. about 4
a Clock I went to the highway and Spok Wm Hobkirk who promised
to come the day following to Tile the new Stable. in my coming
home much rain fell & I took Shelter at Robert Rigg Barn & Stayed
with him near an hour, when the rain abated and I took Horse &
came home, but the rain came on again & continued all way
home.

13th. a very Thick fog & rain most of the day.

14th. A very fine day. Wm Hobkirk came about 5 in the morning and begun with Tyleing the Stable & got all covered in about
7 at night, haveing great help and my Self frequently among them
all day.

15. Sunday, at Church forenoon. Mr Wardell's Boy here. A
very fine day. Wind S.

16. paid Tho presswick to House Keeping £20.

17th. in the afternoon Mr Cha: Turner³⁰ Mr Cholmeley³¹ one
Mr Willoby & the Revd Mr Hugill of Smeeton³² came to my House
& told me thay intended to go to See the Grang Farm. thay Stayed
very little but drank each a dram of usquebah & desired I would go
& Sit the Evening with them which I did & Stayed till near one in
the morn. Mr Hide & M^r proddy was with us till that time.

18th. about 7 in the morning I went to meet Mr Michael Smith at
Skelton Ellers Bridges where we met with John Benneson the Mason
& Settled Some matters about the Bridges. I returned about 9 and

²⁹ ?Barnaby.
³⁰ Turner (a) Cholmeley Turner, married in 1709 Jane, daughter and
heiress of George Marwood of Busby. His will is dated 1752. (b) William
Turner, brother of Cholmeley, married Jane Bathurst, daughter of Charles
Bathurst of York. His only son (c) Charles Turner of Kirkleatham was
made a baronet in 1782, was M.P. for York, and died 1783.
³¹ Francis Cholmeley of Brandsby was born 1706, and married Mary,
daughter of Edward Ferrers of Baddesley Clinton, Warwickshire. He had
one son, Francis (born 1750), who succeeded him.
³² This is the Smeaton near Richmond, Yorks.

P

went up to Excise of whom Received £100 for my Bill upon Core
& the Gentlemen above not being gon. I went into their Room to
see them but stayed very little & returned home. 3 of them told
me they intended to go with me to Grang the next day. much rain
in the morning and a great Shower in the Afternoon near 6. Wind,
S.E.

19. about 9 in the morning I called upon Mr Cha: Turner, Rev^d
Mr Hugill & Mr Hen: Cholmeley, who went with me to Grang where
after viewing the place, went for Boulby, but Mr Cholmeley left us
at Barn & went for Whitby, after viewing the Sheep fold park &c
went to Allom House Stayd an Hour or more when about 6 M^r
Turner & Mr Hugill went for Gisbro with their Servants and my
man John pearson, but I lay at Boulby that night.

20. Mr Wardell went with me to pitt Hill, from thence to see Some
of his oxon to view my Stock in the park, from thence to Grang
where viewd 20 Hamleton Weathers[33] new bought In, also went
down to view the Breamires & low ground, afterwards went into
the Granary & drank some Wine left the day before, when Set out
for Gisbro with my Servant J.p where got about 4.

21. the masons begun dressing Stones for building the old Barn
end, ready to fall, thay haveing put a new door into the orchard over
against the new Stable the day before. about 2 I Rid down to Robert
Harrisons at Fellbrigs to see a pair of Steres in order to buy them
but did not Agree for them.

22^d. At Church forenoon. Mr Wardell Boy came here.

23^d. Wm Hobkirk came here & paved the new Stable, Same day
M^r preston came here who gave me Cozen peases will to be Sent
him first optunity, very few day for a fortnits past but what has
been rain with the Wind in every quarter, much hay down in a Sad
condition & a great deal to mow.

24th. at home much rain towards night.

25th. Some Rain in the morning but fine Weather in the midle
of it, about 11 I went for Tho: Weatherills' near Stockesley to See
Some Steers and Sheep but he was not at home.

25th. Continued, & had parted with his Steers, but I See the
Sheep in my way home. I called at Mr Skottows about the affair
of his new Mortgage, who I spoke with & Settled his comeing here
for £100 to be lent him on munday the 6th of September but did
not light. I also called at Mr Lees & paid for a load of old Slates
got this Spring. I Stayed about an hour when they Shewed me
their House which is greatly above what I expected. in comeing
home it fell abundance of Rain & I was Sore wett, my Horse loosing
a Shew made me longer in geting home. at night much more rain,
all hay that is out and Corn is in a dismal condition, the Wind
moderate but very variable.

[33] Hambleton wethers.

26th. much rain last night & part this morning, the first Lady day fair,³⁴ at home all day.

27. the 2^d fair day. Mr Wardel came here this morning with whom I walkt into the Beast Market, was at Mr Jacksons & Mr Hides. M^r preston Wm Mewburn, & Mr Wardell dined with me, the latter returned to Boulby Same Evening.

28th. at home Save going to view the Bridges at Skelton Ellers which I found near done in the mason work.

29. Sunday at Church forenoon. A fine day.

30. a very fine day brisk Wind at N.W. I went to Grang about 3 in the Afternoon, from thence to Boulby where lay the night.

31. in the morning I went up St & met Tho: Hill of Barnby and John Nicholson at the park, to whom I sold 6 Steers at ten pounds a peice 10^{li} to take them away before Michaelmas next, T.p met me at Grang with whom got home about 3 A very fine day, Wind N° W^t.

Septemb^r 1st. at Home all day, Wm White & Tho: Jackson brought from Grang 5 packs of Wooll in a Waggon with 4 oxon & 2 Horses to be Sent to Darlington for Tho: Colling, there being 90 Stone of it, Sold him at 10/6 p. Stone, thay returned about one. fine day.

2^d. a very fine day, got the low Barn finisht in building the Gavel³⁵ end & part of each Side Wall they being ready to fall.

3^d. Rid out to Upsel to Se the highways where was Working Wm Hobkirk Alick pulman, N. patton & Some Datale men³⁶ A fine day.

4. At home all day, fine Weather but some light rain.

5. Sunday at Church forenoon, John price came here last night on his return from Steaths, went to Church forenoon, dined &c went home to Ayslaby, Mr Wardel Servant was here. Soft Weather, but not much rain. Wm Willas from peake came here afternoon, Stayd an hour or more & went away.

6th. Thomas Weatheril Sent In five large Wether Sheep. Mr Skottow came here with M^r preston & Dined here, to the former I lent £100 on his note which with £52: 10, lent him also on his note the 23^d of Augt last. being in all £152: 10: 0, it is agreed that I am to make up the said Sum £500, for which is to give me a new Mortgage to be dated the 26th of October next & that £160 is to be

³⁴ The autumn fairs at Gisborough were: August 26, the first Lady Day Fair, 11 days after Assumption (for linen & cattle), August 27, September 19 and 20; first Monday after Nov 11 (for horned cattle). The feasts of the Blessed Virgin were the Assumption (August 15) and the Nativity (September 8).
³⁵ Gable end.
³⁶ Daytale or datale men were paid by the day and not by the piece. The modern dataller has to keep the pit and its roads in it in order. The eighteenth-century datale men were paid sixpence a day and the name was not confined to miners.

allowed me out of the said £500 for 6 months Interest for £800, due the 26th of April last past. Thick fogg in the morning, with frequent driseling Rain, but fine afternoon.

7th. A very fine day, but a frost in the morning, at home all day.

8th. Mr Hide came down this morning to Shew me Some State Cards from Mr Turner. A frost last night but fine day. My people at Grang begun Sheering Wheat to-day.

9th. I went for Grang about 1. Thomas pr Set me to Skinnington Bridge, lay that night at Boulby fine day.

10. Set out in the morning for Grang but it rained which made Stay at Barn half an hour till it was pretty fair, Stayd at Grang till 11, it raining most part of the time but then broke up & fine Weather the remaining part of the day, got home about 1.

11. Mr Hide came here with Whom agreed to go to Skelton which we did about 2, where we dined with Mr Hall, his Lady, M^{rs} proddy, one Mr Gibert,[38] parson Waugh, Capt Lassels, his Bro: parson Lasscells, Mr Thos proddy, Mr Hide, & my Self, we returned about Six at night.

12. month Sunday, Mr Jefferson's maid servant calld here in the Afternoon at home all day fine Weather.

13. Mr Mathews came to me about Mr Youars[39] affairs and Dined with me, M^r preston came after diner & p^d me £8 for a years Interest due for £200 from Lyonel Vane Esq[40] 18th July last, & Mr Isaac Scarth came, to whome I paid £4: 15: 0 on Thos Weatheril Account, built a Butteris in the Back lain against the fold garth Wall by Brotton & patton. A very fine day. Wind S°, John Aysley with one of Stango[41] came about putting up boundry Stones in the Highways in Whitby Road, also did Robert Thwaites about the Same at Hutton &c. Sent 4 packs of Wool to Thos Colling at Darlington With Lime & Coal Carts.

14th. at home all day, fine Weather.

15th. went in the morning to the highways near Chapel Bridge and Set out a Causway about 16 yards long & 3 yards Broad, to be paved by Wm Hobkirk. about 11 went with Mr Jackson to Se Mr Tully at Kilton,[42] in our Way met Capt Lasscels going for Stockton Races, and after met Mr Hall and Mr Gilbert going to take the Aire on Barnaby Moor, we dined with Mr Tully & came home about or near 6. Stayed at Skelton to view a Barn in repaireing, met Mr Hall & Mr Gilbert again, on foot got home after 7.

16. I dined at Cock with the Justices, Mr Robinson, Mr Skottowe

---

[38] Gilbert.
[39] Yeoward.
[40] Lionel Vane, of Long Newton, in the County of Durham, son of George Vane (who died July 21, 1750) and Anne, his wife. Lionel was the eldest of his four sons.
[41] Stanghow.
[42] Kilton, near Lofthouse.

& Mr Beckwith, also Mr Smith Mr Sanderson & a Stranger, the Brewster Sessions was that day Stayd till 3: fine Weather. Sent another pack of Wool by John pearson in going to lime.

17 Sep^t. A very thick Fogge morning but Calm, and no rain. in the Afternoon I went to view the paviours in the highway opposet Cook well, where Stayd an hour & returned.

18th. Some Rain. wind at N°E, very unhopeful Weather.

19. Sunday at Church forenoon Mr Hide being abroad Mr Waugh the Dean of Worsters Son did the Service & preach^t. Small rain most of the day. Wind N°E.

20th. Fair day here A great Concourse of people at it. Mr Hurstler Sent a year's Interest for £828 due the 12th Ins^t 33^{li}: 2^s: 4^d: M^r preston, M^r peirse, Mr Wardell Wm Mewburn & Wm Marshal dined with me, of the latter I Rec^d £4 for a years Interest for £100 due Same day, & to the former I paid his Bill in Dents affair £30, was in the beast Market, Spok with Sundrys, Mr Mathews came to me about M^r youards affair, & many other people upon Sundry Occasions. A fine day tho a thick morning. Wind E.

21^t. I went in the forenoon to Se the Workmen in repairing the Brick Arch bridge near Riggs Barn, in the Evening I went to the Excise & rec^d £100 for my Bill on Robert Core on Works Account A man brought here 22 Sheep for Mr Wardel out Bishoprick, Stayd all night & went himself to Boulby but left the Sheep here to Rest a day. Same Evening came Mr Jefferson & his Wife in there way from London, last from Allerton In a post Shase, but to York in the Stage. Niece Manly came with them to Wentbridg in going to live with an old Gentleman near that place, one Mr Bradshaw.

22. at home with M^r & Mrs Jefferson after noon thay went up to Visit Mrs Hide, he being abroad.

23. Mr Jefferson took a walk with me to See my Oxon, he then went to the factory & brought up Fra: Fox to diner, thay after went again to the Factory. Mr Tully & Doctor Waugh Came to See me & Stayd near an Houre & drank two or 3 glasses of Wine. Mrs Jefferson went to see Mrs Challoner where was two of Dr Waughs Sisters & Miss Maddeson (she returnd in the Evening).

24. Thick Hazy Weather & Small rain all the forenoon.

25. very thick Weather with drisling Rain. Mr Jefferson & his Wife went for Steaths at 9 or 10.

26. Sunday at Church forenoon.

27. Mr Mathews came & paid me for old Silver plate Sent Mr Howlet about 101½ oz^s £25: 15: 3. Spoke with Mr Bottom about laying on a highway Sess, Rec^d of Thos. King 1 years Rent p^r Commondale Mill due Martinmas 1755. 12/-.

28th. I went for Boulby, T.p. Set me to Grang where they were Sheering Barly in far Roger Close, night following abundance of Rain. I met with Mr Baker at Boulby & Mr Jefferson, the former haveing been there 2 or 3 days where we all dined with Josep Thornhill Wm Marshal, & I lay there that night.

29. I dined again at Boulby, after Diner Mr Baker & I Rid up to the pitt hill and from thence went to Grange, Stayd there an Hour, from thence Will. White set me to Mellam Beck, but parted with Mr Baker at Grange Gate.

Sep^t 30. thick rainey morning in the Afternoon I Rid out to view the Highways but there was none at Work. fine afternoon.

Octo. the 1^t. Wm Willis came here with whom I reckoned about his Kelp and paid him £9. 14: 0 to Ballance against lent money & his Rent Mr Hall calld here on Horseback but did not light. Mr Baker and Mr Wardell came here yesterday about noon and dined, after thay both went for Stockton, the latter purposeing to Stay in Bishoprick about 14 days. Mr Mathews keeping Court today at Gisbro calld here to whom gave Gylbys Bill on M^r yowards Account for £80. and am to have money for it tomorrow.

2^d. Bro: Jackson came here. T.p. Went to Stockesley with Mr Mathews' note for Gylbys' Bill to Receive money for it but brought it back which will be paid on munday the 11th Ins^t.

3^d. Sunday, forenoon at Church Wind high and at W^t.

4th. Wind very great at W^t with Rain in the night before. was up Street, Spok Sundry people, bought of Wm Rogers 4 bushels Wheat for Seed to be 6/- per bus to come on munday next. Mr Masterman dined here M^r preston & Wm Mewburn came to us after dinner. Will Rogers dined, he Walkt down the Ground with Brother Jackson to See my oxon. Will peacock came to Borrow money but I lent him none.

5. Brother Jackson & I went to Grang Set out with T.p, about 6 in the morning, Ordered T.p from there to Steaths to let them Know at Mr Jeffersons that we would be there at 12, to dine with them, accordingly we went but he was at Whitby going there the day before with Mr Boulby, but we dined with his Wife & Miss pease & Stayd till ½ after one & went by Dale House to Grang without calling at the Allom House Mr Suget was to have to met me at Grang but did not come. So we came from thence & Got home about 6. I Rid from Grange upon Brother Jackson's Black Horse & he Rid mine.

6th. Tho: Allan, to whom Lent 2 ginnis, came here about 6 in the morning in his way to See his Mother at Sadbirge in Bishoprick went from hence after 7 & Bro: Jackson Set out Soon after for home. A fine morning. wind W^t, afternoon very thick but no rain till after Sun Set, when the wind began to blow and became excessive So as in the night to blow down trees & unrooft Houses also hovels of Rape seed to the great loss of the Owners, it began at W^t or S°W^t & came Northerly in the morning.

7th. Clear Skie, Wind N°, but excessive high, the like haveing

Scarce been ever known, it blowed down a Barn at Boulby (I formerly Built) quite to the Ground wherein Mr Wardell had much Corn, the Corn uncut in the Fields of which there was a great deal & even that in Sheaf out o' Doors was torn to pieces, & much of it Shaken lost, & distroyed, the height of the Wind was much in the night & early in the morning about 7 the excess abated & a fine Suny day ensued.

8th. John price came here from Ayslaby yesterday after noon and was here till this morning, his business was to Inform me of the damage done to my Houses there, haveing blown down Ric^d Cocker's Stables with other mischief among the Houses. Mr Wardell Servant came here in his way to Ellemore to Inform his Master of the Barn at Boulby being Blown down with other damage done there by the great Wind on Wednesday night last.

9th. Thomas Allan returned from Sening^{43} his Mother who he left very ill, dined & went for Boulby. Soon after Mr Wardell Servant came here from Ellemore dined & went for Boulby. fine Weather Since the great Wind.

10th. month Sunday, Mr More's Clark came here about his Uncle Suggets Affairs, the former haveing large demands upon the Latter. Sent John pearson this afternoon to Grang about Wm White coming here to morrow with Straw, very fine day Wind W^t.

11. up Street to look after Seed Wheat bought of Wm Rigg of Ureby, 8 bushels at 6/2 delivered 2, & paid him, the other 6 is to be delivered at Saltburn on fryday next 3 o'clock. Wm Rogers delivered other 4 at 6/- paid him £1: 4 & is to Deliver other 16 next munday. I signed at M^r prestons office a request for the Commissioners of Mask Devision to meet there on friday the 29th Inst to put a final end to that affair.

12th. got done with Masons & Carpenters in building for this year, was at Chapel Brige to Se the pavers and to See the old House on Duke Blenco Farm and gave directions for Staying it to Tho. Nateby. A cold angry day but not much rain. Wind S.W or more Westerly, at home.

13. at home John Dale Brought Some Cheeses for Cozen pease & me & dined here upon a Hare, Mr More Sent me yesterday. frequent Showers of Rain but not Considerable.

14. afteroon went to Chapel bridge to See the pavers at Work where came to me Mr Wardell in his way from Ellemore. I came home with him where he Stayed an Hour & went for Boulby, he has been abroad 14 days, pretty much Rain at Night.

15th. at home all day.

16. about 2 in the afternoon. Hawmon & Halleday came to Se a fatt cow & a lame Ox, the latter being in the low ground and not very able to Walk so far, ordered the Gray tale Horse to be

^{43} Seeing.

saddled to Ride down, but when I got upon his back he begun to plung & Threw me down at Stable door & falling upon my left Arm Hurt the Elbow very much, So that I had a bad night with it.

17. Sunday all day at Home very thick & foggy Weather Wind E.

18ᵗʰ. After diner I went for Stockton, T.p. with me. he cald at Mʳ Hursleys to get a Moidor⁴⁴ Changed, which was paid in his last Interest, but not good, at Stockton, went to Mʳ Maddesons who paid me £8 : 12. for 6 months Interest from Mʳ Marshal also £4 for Mʳ Jordesons 6 months due in March, where Mʳ Geo : Crow paid me £36 for 12 months Interest due 28ᵗʰ Insᵗ. in the Evening Mʳ Brown & Mʳ Maddeson came & Sit with me till 11, where was in an other Room 3 Gentlemen & 6 Ladys, two of which was Miss Dowthwate & Miss Bowlby, my Niece. I went & Sitt down in that Company A little, but after drinking a glass of punch retired to the two Gentlemen.

19ᵗʰ. about 6 in the morning I went to yarm being faire day where Will White met me who bought for me 3 Steers with a tup & 7 weathers I did business with many people receiving Sums of money from Sundrys. I set out about one in my way home, Mʳ Wardell Servant Jack overtook me with a led Horse, a Servant being behind with 10 Sheep, Jack lay here all night & went to Boulby with Wᵐ White next morning with the 3 Steers & 8 Sheep.

20ᵗʰ. near noon Mʳ Wardells other Servant & the 10 Sheep came here & Stayd all night. Wᵐ Hobkirk begun pointing the new Stable yesterday morning.

21. At home all day. nothing materil, thick hazy Weather, much Corn to get in.

22ᵈ. I Set out about 11 with T.p for Boulby, went to Lofthouse, calld at Mʳ Mores but he was not at Home, called at Mʳ Sugget but he was abroad, from thence went to Grange where they were Sowing Wheat with 3 plows, from thence after passing Some firs and Horse chestnuts in the Watergarth I set out for Boulby where lay all night, gave Some papers to Mʳ Wardel about the Works.

23ᵈ. Set out about 10, called at Grange where Mʳ Sugget met me about his affair but little to my Satisfaction, about one T.p. met me there with whome came home, drisling Rain. Wind E. much corn out.

24. at Church forenoon, thick hazy Weather. Wind at E. Mʳ Wardell Boy here.

25ᵗʰ. up Street, called at Mʳ prestons but he was keeping Court that day at Wilton, So could not Speak to him about Mʳ Skottows affair, this day a meeting was appointed but none appeared, gave Mʳ Mathews a Bill upon Nephew Geo : Jackson for £100, payable at

⁴⁴ The moidore, now obsolete in England, was worth 27 shillings. Though Portuguese it was then legal tender in England.

30 days but he did not pay me money for it, only his note, till paid, which I desired might be paid 14 days hence. Wm Mewburn dined with me. with whom appointed to go to Eston to See 4 Steers he had lately Bought of Mr Hurstler.

26. in the morning I went with T.p. to Normanby, calld at Mr Consetts but did not light, from thence went to Wm Mewburn's at Eston where viewd his Steers, which is very good ones but in too high Condition for Wintering. So did not buy them. wee went from his House to Normanby. I light at parson Consetts & went to See him he haveing lately had a Severe fitt of the Gravell but was then quite well & Chearful after voiding a large Stone. I dined at his Nephew Consetts as did the parson, Wm Mewburn, an old Lady, Mr Consett, his Wife & her Sister. I Stayed till 3 and came away but in my passage home this Side of Chapel Bridge my Horse made a great Stumble & was very near falling, which So greatly Shockt me that I Strained again my left Arme of which I became very lame, it not being yet well for the hurt I got of it from the fall my Horse gave me the 15th of this month as menconed before. I also Strained the Wrist of my Right Arme & it brought on the Gout pains in my Right foot. I went to the Excise & Rec^d £100 for my Bill on Robert Core payable at 28 days for Works Account, fine Weather Wind at E.

27th. begun puling up the old pavement betwixt the old Stable & the new one, by Hobkirk Balmer & the Gardner, but Hobkirk & Balmer went away early in the forenoon, but to come again tomorrow. fine day Wind at E.

28th. begun paveing by the old Stable Door & little House end, M^r preston calld at Door in his way to Marsk & Spok to me about Mr Skottows' affair, in the Afternoon Mr Skottowe himself came here to speak to me about renuing his Mortgage and to Borrow £1000 more, but I could not determine with him anything about it till Some time after this. fine day.

29. Wm Armstrong calld here on Horse back but I did not See him, he was in his Way to Boulby. at home all day.

30th. at home most fine Weather, got paved to South end of new Stable.

31. Sunday at Church forenoon. Mr Wardell Boy here for Letters. very fogge morning but broke up A very fine day.

Novemb^r 1. fine morning & the day So ended. Wind N^o. up Street forenoon, Spok with M^r preston where I Signed at his office the Award for the Division of Marsk & Ridcar field also an other payper about Commissioners Wages. Mr Michael Smith was there, was at Mr Hides about John Benneson the mason for Building the 2 bridges at Skelton Ellers, & appointed a meeting on munday next the 8th Instant peter fishburn brought me a Wild Duck & Mallard for which gave him 1/6. M^r preston alone dined with me before we parted. Mr Hall & Mr Spark, the Attorney, came to us to whom I Shewed the Security given me for £1400, wherein his two Brothers[44a] might be released, but the two attorneys did not think it proper to be done. So left the thing as it was. had the Liqueris taken up to day Tho: Knaggs the Tanner came to Speak to me about my Stable at Sandsend for the new officer of Excise at the place.

2^d. N. patton was Setting two Course of parsnips at the East end of the miding Stead, the Gardner Dungd two places in the Orchard for planting liqueris[45] upon next Spring, about 2 came Ra: Jackson & his two Sisters, Rachel & Dolle, from Richmond, but last from yarm where thay lay last night, Mr Hide came & Sett with us at least 2 hours.

3^d. rainy forenoon, but fine Weather after till night. Wind N° & N° W.

5th. fair morning but not hopefull to continue. Nephew Ra: Jackson with his two Sisters Rachel & Dole went from hence about 10 in the morning intending for yarm to lay there at night.

5th. about 2 in the Afternoon I went for Boulby T.p. with me, who returned at Skining bank where came to me Mr Mack Donald, with whome parted the other side Skinnington Bridge went alone to Grange where thay were paveing the new fold garth from whence went to Boulby where lay all night.

6th. Mr Jefferson came to us in the morning about 9, he & Mr Wardel went to View the Farme he lately Bought of his Brother Ric^d Spencer at Liverton & I went along with T.p (who came there about 8) to Grang, where met Will White who came with 3 Fatt oxon from Gisbro I Stayd about 2 hours and got home about 2 where found Will Hobkirk plastering the new Stable, paid Alik pulman and John Walker for repairing 3 Rainges & a Lock 1^{li}: 15^s: 0^d.

7th. Sunday. at Church forenoon, fine day but Cold, Wind N.

8th. frosty morning. Wind N° but came to Fine afternoon. A very fine day. John Bowcer came & paid me 4^{li}. 1 years Interest for £100 due the 6th Inst gave Mr Mathews my Bill for £200 upon Robert Core, payable Mr Samuel Howlet at 30 day, but gave me his note only without money. So that he owes me for this Bill & that I menconed before in all £300. was up Street, Spoke Mr Hide & Wm Watson about the Bridges, who told me thayd paid John Benneson £95 odd money towards them, called at Mr Jacksons to acquaint him that I intended to pay him in the £600 I borrowed of him on my note the 20th May last, I proposed paying in the money the 22^d of this month, but if he could Spare it should keep it a month

---

[44a] George and Thomas are engaged, Mr. Hall desired his two brothers might be released.
[45] Liquorice.

longer, he prest me to continue it further but I refused to do so. Hawman & Hollyday paid me for a lame ox, including 16/5 for Beef I took of him £12 : 12 : 5 out of which I gave them 20/- for Killing & Selling him.

Novemb^r 9th. at home. Mr Wardell Sent a boy for Letters who brought Mr Core's october Account which returnd, there was a Ship on to day to take 60 Tons of Allom. fine day. Wind at S°.

10. Wm Hobkirk came to pave at mid day end, Servant Tho: Jackson came with 2 Horses from Grange to carry from Gisbro a pair Broad Wheels made per T. Nateby.

11th. at home. fine Weather.

12th. I went out about 8 in the morning with T.p. to Mr Skottows at Ayton where met me M^r preston & his Son with a new Mortgage on my Advance £800, of which I paid him on two notes before £152 : 10 & today £287 : 10 & he allowed me £160 for 6 months Interest due Aprill 26 last & I gave him my note payable on demand with Interest, also from Said 26 October last, which made in all £800, he signed the Mortgage and a Bond, M^r preston & his Son Witnesses to the both as also to my note. I got home betwixt 4 & 5.

13th. at home Duke Fogge in the Evening brought me his last May day Rent £22 : 14 : o, allowed him 14/8½ for 2 years Land tax at 2/- due Lady Day last.

14th. month Sunday, at home, thick cloudy Weather but fair Wind So.

15. fare day at Gisbro bought a Cow & Calf from Coatham. She gon 3 & the Calf 10 days old. Cost 6^{li} : 1^s : 6^d. up Street in the Beast market calld at Mr Jacksons Shop. Wm White came here & Paid me £40 from Thomas Addamson in part for Wheat and he bought 4 Steers 2 of them gone 3, & 2 gon 2 years old. Cost in all 28^{li} : 5^s : o^d. Tho: Hill of Barnby paid me for 6 oxon bought last Summer £60. Mr Mathews paid me £100 for my Bill on Geo: Jackson given him the 24th of last month M^r peirse came & dined here as did Thomas Hay and many others in the Kitching. Mr Wardell's Boy was here for Letters.

16. an other boy here with letters but did not Stay till post came. I Received from Wm Yeoman pr. T.p 1^{li} : 15^s in part of £4 he ows me. Rec^d Some time before 5/-, remainder 2^{li}. Thick foge day, not much rain, Wind S°, at night came on much Rain.

17th. Waters very great in the morning. Wind N° & raind much which occationed the greatest flood here that has been known for Some years.

18th. A Snowe morning as it had been most of the night. Wind N°. paid Tho: p. to House Keeping £20. frost in the afternoon, A Clear Sky.

19th. Severe frost all day, Wind N in the Afternoon entered 9 Children into the School and Six went out. Mr Harly of Stockton came here in Evening & Sit an Houre, gave him 2/6 & he went to lye at Oliver presswicks.

20th. Frost very Strong in the morning, clear Sky, but about 10 it began to Snow excesively & continued many Hours, but brok up about 2 & became more frost like. Wind at N, the Hills & ground Covered thick with Snow.

21. Severe frost but Clear Sky. Wm White came here in the morning in order to go for Darlington to buy Cattle & Set out from here near 10, with whom sent 30 ginnys. being Sunday I was at Church forenoon. Wm Anderson came here in the Evening to Ask my Advice about a Letter he had Received from A Cousin at Skarbro, giveing him an Account of £50 a piece being left him and two Sisters Tate & Ripley, the latter of Steaths. I gave him 2/6 to help him on his Way to Scarbro.

22^d. went up Street, was at Mr Jacksons Shop, at Mr Hides. Mr Mathews came down with me & paid me £200. for my Bill on Robert Core. the 8th Ins^t. Mr Hide, Mr Nelson & Mr Mathews dined with me. after diner Mr Richardson & M^r preston came In, the later Paid me £100 from M^r peirse for his Bond drawn 19th July last, & I paid Mr Nelson £5 : 14 : 0 for half of a Lottery Ticket begun drawing this day. James Jackson Paid me his last Michaelmis Rent 3 : 10 : 0, Mr Sugget calld here in his way to Stockton, fine day but a frost and Cold, near Night Some Snow.

23^d. frosty morning Wind N^o E. about 11 one of Stockton came here and Soon after one John Mewburn, both Sent here by Mr Wm Turner & his Brother Mr Wm Sleigh, with their Joynt Bond for £500, which Sum I paid John Mewburn and Received the Said Bond, who with the other man dined here and togeather went for home after one for Stockton. Wm White brought 2 Steers he'd bought at Darlington. after dinner he went with them & other two from hence for Grange, about 3 came on much snow. Mr Sugget calld here in his Way from Stockton.

24th. paid Mr Jackson his Bill for shop goods 11^{li}. 6^s. 2^d A very Cold day & Strong frost but fair.

25th. Mr Jefferson & Mr Wardell came here and Sent for Emmit the Tenant of Tocketts farme, who came and after Some debate Settled the method of his leaveing it at May day next. after about noon Wm Armstrong came being sent for to meet the 2 former but the thing was over before he came, he Mr Jefferson & Mr Wardell dined with me, the former went away after dinner & the two latter before 3. A frosty day but faire. Wind N^o.

26. A gentle Thaw till about noon & then came Rain & the ground mostly bare. Wind W & very like rain, at night pretty much.

27th. John price came last night, & this morning we had a reconing and it appeared after all Workemens & Tradesmens bills

is paid I was then in his Debt £34: 0: 4, which Sum I paid him
& he went away in the Afternoon. fine day but frost. Wind N°.

28th. A very Severe frost but not much, Wind at N°. M[r] Wardell
Boy here at Church forenoon.

29th. up Street, Saw M[r] Nelson, M[r] Hide, Chief Jackson, M[r]
Spark, the latter Showed A letter he had to the Justices & Commissioners for puting in execution the Act for Impressing men for
Mariens & Land Service. parson Consett and M[r] preston dined
with me, the latter brought me M[r] Skottows last Mortgage Deed
from the Register Office, M[r] Boulby calld at the Door but did not
light for I was up Street, he being in his way from Stockton, no
frost today but good weather.

30. fine day & no frost. Tho: Hudson & Walker brought me 4
Cross Bows new Strings & mending the Locks 5/- in all 13/-

1 Dece[m]. about 10 I Set out for Boulby called at Grang. Stay
there 2 or 3 hours viewd all the Oxon of which was 7 feeders & 17
for Work also, the feeding of which is about 57[li]. went to Boulby
where lay all night, next morning, 2[d], went with M[r] Wardell to
Steaths where dined with M[r] Jefferson and his Wife & Miss Boulby,
after diner two of parson Todds[46] Sisters came & drank Tea. Sent
for one Ripley that marryed a Daughter of Doctor Anderson. Ripley
& his Wife came, She haveing a Son & only Child now with M[rs]
Danby at Gisbro, but he is a Child to a former Husband she having
none to this, but Ripley being a poor Drinking man and she not
much better & much in Debt my business was to try at the Request
of M[rs] Danby, at the Instance of M[r] Hide, if any thing could be
got out of £50 Leggacy left by a Relation at London, but Ripley
& his Wife being So very poor that there is little hope, lay all night
at Boulby.

3[d]. Rid up to pitt hill from thence to Grange with M[r] Wardell
where Stayd an Hour, then we went to Lofthouse, called upon M[r]
Suggit, then went to M[r] Mores about 10. but he was in bed, who came
not to us of more than an Hour. We had great debates about Rosscroft high way &c. but to no purpose, after brakfast we parted & I
came Home, M[r] Wardell went to Dine with M[r] Oldfield, met M[r] Hall
on foot & little before his youngest Son on Horse back.

4th. M[r] Hide came to tell me Sir W[m] Foulis died this morning
about 5 O Clock, no other occurences, fair Wether Wind S°.

5th. Sunday at Church forenoon, came a Sargeant & Shewed me
a letter that he was come here to beat up for Vonnters to morrow.

6th. the Captain & Sargeant came down but did not stay, thay
beat up this forenoon. I was up Street & Spoke with the Captain
again when was a dispute about one of the pressmens men, that had
Inlisted the day before which M[r] Foster was very warm in the Cause

[46] Abraham Todd, M.A. Peterhouse, Cambridge; Deacon, London, 1721;
Priest, York, 1723; Rector of Welbury, 1730.

as not fairly done, but to little purpose for the Captain determined to have him before a Justice of the peace next day. Ra: Franklain of Upton came here about Mr Suggets affair & was with M^r preston. Fine weather but some Snow.

7th. Wm Hobkirk came & Set the fore Room barrs and altered the Gun Closet grate. Fine Weather, went to the Excise and rec^d £150 for my Bill on Mr Core.

8th. favourable weather at home all day.

9th. A Servant came with a letter from Ingolby Manner Inviteing me as a bearer to Sr Wm Foules Funerall to be the 11th Instant at 11 in the morning. John peirson went from hence before 5 in the Morning for Grange, Boulby & Staths, he carryed from me £150 for Mr Wardell, the money I Rec^d last from the Excise. a very fine day.

10. A very hard frost Clear & Calm.

11th. about 7 in the morning Set out for Sir Wm Foulis Furneal calld at Mr Skottows at Ayton, Stayd about an Hour in which time came the Recruteing Captain. Mr Scottow my Self and two Servants Set out for Ingolby where wee got about 11. Soon after came all the bearers who were Mr Maulever, Mr Skottow, Mr Robinson, Mr Hall, Mr Conset Mr Hoar, Mr Davinson and my Self, we Had a Cold Dinner, none but the bears Sitt down & parson Hazel,[47] the Corpes was brought about 2. and the bearers Rid in Coaches to the Church, and the Corpes was Carryed in a Hearse, after the Servis done we went back to the manner House Save Mr Hall who went away, we Stayed but little, Mr Skottow Mr Robinson Mr Conset and my Self came to Ayton where parted and I lay at Mr Skottows that night.

12th. being Month Sunday, I came Home in forenoon fine Weather but frost.

13th. at Home all day and not up Street. Wille pease and an other boy came here in their way to Whitby thay just bated and went away about 1, fine day Wind S.W.

14. at Home all day.

15th. at Home fine Weather.

16. I went for Boulby calld at Grange, from thence to Boulby where came to me Mr Jefferson and Stayd till 7.

17. this was pay day when Mr Jefferson, Nath. Campion & John Gallan came up and dined with us at pay. I Rec^d Sundry Rents as also from Jn° Gallan for Thos: Presswick 2 years proffitt for his Ship £16: 5: o.

18th. Tho: presswick met me at Grange but calld at pitthill, and came Home but had a badd night.

19. was Sunday but I was not at Church being not Well.

20. Was up Street. A meeting of the Justices was today about

⁴⁷ Samuel Hassell, Deacon, York, 1716; Priest, 1718; B.A., St. John's, Cambridge, 1716; Curate of Ingleby Greenhow, 1719.

Enlisting Soldiers, thay got only one. Robert Appleby of pate Hall came here to attend the Justices haveing a Warrant Served on him by yarm people for not Working at the High Way in that Township he liveing in Worsel liberty. M͏ʳ Skottow desired £20 in part of £200 for my note I gave him the 26ᵗʰ of october last.

21. at Home.

22. M͏ʳ Foster came and paid me 6 months Interest for £1500 due the 2ᵈ Inst, John pearson went to Grange with 2 Horses to bring Barly, but other 4 Horses returnd with which brought in all 36 bushels.

23ᵈ. gave a Doale about the Town and other givfts about £10 in all. Tho: pressick Recᵈ from M͏ʳ Lasscels 5ˡⁱ and paid it to John Benneson about Bridges.

25ᵗʰ. Xmis day. at Church forenoon, the Weather has been very fine for the Season which has Continued above a month. Wind mostly in that time at S° or off Land.

26ᵗʰ. Sunday at Church forenoon. M͏ʳ Wardells Boy was here for Letters.

27ᵗʰ. W͏ᵐ White & Thomas Jackson brought here from Grange about 30 bushels Barly to make out a Steeping 60, for Malt delivered at Oliver pressicks Killn. I paid Will White 10ˡⁱ: 10: to Clear with the Work people at Grange. Ra: Jackson came Here to live with me.

28ᵗʰ. Tho: Weatheril came here about 2 & Settled an Account with me about 5 Sheep Sent me last Summer I paid him 1ˡⁱ 10ˢ Ballance & gave him 11/6 besides.

29ᵗʰ. Duke Blenco paid his last Michaelmis Rent 2: 15: 0. Thomas Allans Brother of Darnton the Cooper Calld here & dined in his way from Boulby.

30. Settled Thomas pressick Books for the year 1756 when paid him to Books 18/9¼ and then also £20 to Housekeeping.

31. Nicholas patton of Eston called here to Speak to me about M͏ʳ Sugget.

END OF 1756.

ADDITIONAL NOTES

Page 51. May 1. "Blue stones under."

Dr. J. E. Hemingway, of the Geological Department of the University of Leeds, has written the following note:

As far as I understand it, millstones must be of coarse texture and porous. The first prevents too close a contact between the stones and with the second factor prevents the meal from becoming heated. A millstone further must be tough, so that fragments are not broken off and mixed with the meal.

These requirements have been satisfied by the Millstone Grit, a coarse sandstone which forms the moorlands of the Pennines. Many of the so-called "Derbystone" stones, i.e. millstones of which Professor Whiting speaks, were quarried in Yorkshire. As he says these are fawn or buff in colour, but only after long exposure to the weather at or near the ground level. If these sandstones are really fresh they are off-white to grey-blue. Although one would expect the Millstone Grit to be used in the Dewsbury district for millstones from time immemorial, I cannot, on consideration, think that they would be called "Bluestones" by the layman. I reluctantly dismiss it.

A rock known as "Bluestones" occurs over a limited area to the south-west of Keighley where it gives its name to one of the innumerable Melstone Grit quarries—Bluestone Delph. Although very tough, this rock is exceedingly fine-grained and only little porous. Further, it occurs in only small fragments. It would be quite unsuited to milling, and I mention it only because of its name.

A final possibility is the Niedermendig lava from Andernach in the Eifel. This has been used for milling from Roman times, when the *lower* stone of the quern was made from millstone grit and the upper from imported Neidermendig lava. During the nineteenth century N. Lava was used extensively by millers and it was, and may be yet, a common sight to see a discarded N. millstone outside a mill. There was one at Leathley, another near Shadwell, and others at Ripley and Goldsborough. But this rock is black, though it may have looked blue under a dusting of flour.

I feel this third possibility is the most likely, though it doesn't completely satisfy.

Page 53. July 31.

The riots seem to have occurred from the 20th April to November. For instance, 200 persons riotously assembled and made an assault on a mill at Crigglestone. On April 27 rioters to a considerable number made an attack on the mill of John Greenwood of Dewsbury, in which attack a female rioter, Martha Autey, seems to have taken a leading part. On 6th May, William Nursey, blacksmith, with about a hundred others, broke into a mill at Thornhill, and on the 20th June, 1740, Mug mill was the object of an assault. (The York Assizes Papers are now in the Record Office.)

Page 172. Sept. 1.

Spayed heifers were those which had been surgically operated upon to prevent any future calving. The operation is very little in use at the present day.

INDEX

Names which are found on every page in either of the diaries are here omitted.

Rudd, Ralph, 200
Rufford, 82
Ryecroft, 93
Ryley, 76

Sadberge, 214
Saddleworth, 21, 65, 110, 111
Sager, Mr., 130, 134; Robt., 130
Salkeld, Mr., 20, 24; Mrs., 23
Saltburn, 175, 215
Sandal, 30, 88
Sanderson, Benj., 89; Joshua, 43;
  Mr., 145, 156, 163, 196, 213;
  Nicholas, 5
Sandsend, 150, 186, 218
Sardinia, King of, 128
Saunderson, Dr., 45
Savile, Sir George, 82
Sawforth (Stockport), 109
Sayer, Sayers, John, 142, 143; Thos.,
  193, 197
Scalby, 194
Scar, 120
Scarborough, 185, 220
Scarth, Isaac, 153, 202, 212
Scholes, 7, 8, 30, 46, 56, 64, 68, 69,
  71, 75, 80, 87, 90, 95-7, 102, 103,
  109, 110, 125, 126, 128, 129, 131
Scholey, 66
Scholihull, 54
Scott, Mr., 67, 73, 90, 117, 119
Scugdale, 142
Scurfield, Mr., 196
Seaford, Lord, 129; Lady, 129
Sedgefield, 199
Sedgewick, Mr., 161
Senior, James, 91; John, 23
Shackleton, Mr., 19, 87; Wm., 51,
  61, 66, 67, 70, 72, 74, 83, 87, 90,
  92, 98, 100, 112, 113, 116
Shaftesbury, Lord, 44
Shaley, 97
Sharp, Daniel, 15
Shaw, Christopher, 130; John, 100;
  Jonathan, 104; Mr., 73, 75, 76,
  78-81, 83, 88, 90, 91, 93, 94,
  98-101, 103, 105, 106, 107, 109,
  117, 119, 126, 129, 133, 134;
  Thos., 21, 72
Shaw-head, 37, 73, 97, 129, 130
Sheafhouse, 100
Sheerness, 112
Sheffield, 5, 22, 30
Shelley (Shaley), 11, 72, 121, 126
Sheriff-moor, 120
Shields, 149, 190, 208

Shipley (Shepley), 6, 11, 60, 62, 68,
  73, 79, 90, 95, 101, 124, 126
Shire Hall, 77, 93
Shirt, Timothy, 31
Sibbald, John, 187
Sidebottom, 152
Sillaburn, John, 146
Sinderhills, 85, 101, 115
Simonburn, 187
Skafe, Miss, 208
Skarth, Isaac, 174
Skelmanthorp, 33
Skelton, 140, 141, 143, 147, 149,
  156, 162, 166, 168, 170, 171, 177,
  184, 205, 208, 212
Skelton Ellers, 140, 146, 148, 152,
  153, 158, 159, 161, 162, 167-9,
  171, 174, 207-9, 217
Skinnington, 168; Bank, 140, 164,
  192, 218; Bridge, 170, 176, 194,
  196, 199, 205, 212, 218
Skipton, 45
Skirhall, 93
Skottowe (Scottow), 139, 154, 173;
  Capt., 201; Mr., 145, 147, 152,
  154, 155, 158, 162, 166, 167, 181,
  185, 193, 195, 198, 206, 207,
  210-12, 216, 217, 219, 221, 222
Skye, 125
Sleigh, Mr., 153, 155, 167, 171, 177,
  194; Wm., 151, 160, 177, 220
Small-shaw, Smawshaw, 39, 105,
  106
Smeaton, 209
Smith, 107, 202; Isaac, 16; Joe, 72;
  John, 3, 46, 47, 103, 131, 195, 200,
  205, 206; Joshua, 68, 71; Michael,
  147, 209, 217; Mr., 4, 5, 6, 7, 33,
  39, 40, 78, 148, 153, 172, 177,
  178, 196, 198, 199, 205, 213;
  Robert, 60; Thos., 58
Smithy Place, 22, 60, 63, 77, 79
Smocks Moor, 128
Snowdon, Geo., 147, 160, 162;
  Moor's clerk, 168
Snowgatehead, 63
Sofley, 21, 64, 71, 89, 102, 103,
  106, 112, 135
Sowerby, 36, 74, 81
Spark, Mr., 156, 163, 169, 174, 205,
  218, 221
Sparling, Geo., 183
Sparnel, John, 187
Spencer, Eate, 155; John, 36;
  Madam, 36; Nephew, 139, 175,
  186, 188; Richd., 143, 218; Thos.,

94; Mr., 155, 167, 169; Robert, 183, 184
Wilton, 165, 187, 216
Win, Sir Rowland, 29
Windhill, 191
Windsor, 80
Winterbottom, 87, 122, 125
Wintringham, Dr., 5
Witten, Mr., 80
Wordsworth, John, 135
Wood, Abrm., 75; Geo., 100; John, 89, 107; Jonathan, 100, 115; Joseph, 75; Mr., 78, 100
Woodhead, 12, 13, 67, 83, 97, 109, 111, 115
Woodhead, Abrm., 57, 59, 65, 66, 70, 135; Benj., 63; John, 94, 135; Joseph, 5, 13, 54, 86, 88, 106; Joshua, 37, 43, 47, 68, 131; Miss, 103; Sarah, 86; Thos., 106
Wood-nook, 66
Woodsome, 90, 119, 128
Woofenden, Joseph, 89; Joshua, 41, 61, 68, 71, 78, 84; Mrs., 106; Thos., 106
Woolston, 14
Wooldale, 5, 12, 20, 25, 33, 39, 50, 56, 59, 61, 63, 64, 66, 71, 72, 73, 75, 79, 80, 84, 88, 101, 102, 109, 110, 119, 126, 130

Woolraw, 99
Wordsworth, John, 135; Mr., 18
Workhouse, 91
Worman Hole, 158
Worsel, 167, 223
Worthy, John, 124
Wortley, Jos., 6; Mr., 66

Yarm, 141, 146, 149, 152, 155, 156, 159, 166, 169, 174, 177, 195, 201, 202, 205, 208, 216, 218, 223
Yates, Geo., 45
Yatom, Yatholm, 17, 71, 88, 90, 95, 134
Yeoman, Miss, 178; Mr., 156; Wm., 196, 219
Yewtree, 98
Yeoward, Mr., 139, 159, 162, 163, 165-7, 170, 172, 181, 186, 189, 196, 213, 214
York, 4, 5, 10, 27, 44, 61, 69, 70, 71, 76, 90, 104, 108, 125, 131, 139, 175, 196, 213; Archbishop of, 144; Duke of, 111
Youar, Mr., 212
Young, John, 180; T., 144; Wm., 197

Zouch, Chas., 30

For EU product safety concerns, contact us at Calle de José Abascal, 56–1°, 28003 Madrid, Spain or eugpsr@cambridge.org.

 www.ingramcontent.com/pod-product-compliance
Ingram Content Group UK Ltd.
Pitfield, Milton Keynes, MK11 3LW, UK
UKHW010340140625
459647UK00010B/731